Memory, Narrative, Identity

D1585634

TENDENCIES: IDENTITIES,

Series Editor: Peter Brooker

Other titles in the series are:

Narratives for a New Belonging: Diasporic Cultural Fictions
Roger Bromley

Deconstructing Ireland: Identity, Theory, Culture
Colin Graham

Cruising Culture: Promiscuity, Desire and American Gay Literature
Ben Gove

Race and Urban Space in Contemporary American Culture
Liam Kennedy

Fundamentalism in America:
Millennialism, Identity and Militant Religion
Philip Melling

Memory, Narrative, Identity

Remembering the Self

Nicola King

Edinburgh University Press

© Nicola King, 2000

Edinburgh University Press Ltd
22 George Square, Edinburgh

Transferred to Digital print 2003

Typeset in Melior
by Pioneer Associates, Perthshire, and
printed and bound in Great Britain by
Marston Lindsay Ross International Ltd,
Oxfordshire

A CIP Record for this book is available from the British Library

ISBN 0 7486 1115 0 (paperback)

The right of Nicola King
to be identified as author of this work
has been asserted in accordance with
the Copyright, Designs and Patents Act 1988.

Contents

Acknowledgements

I would like to thank the following: Peter Middleton for getting me started, and for providing intellectual stimulus from the early stages of this project; Peter Brooker for his editorial support; Trudi Tate for invaluable advice about the process of writing; Daniel Wolpert and Sarah Bunker for technical help and advice; Kate Fullbrook for reading and commenting on part of the manuscript; Bernard Tucker and the English Department of the former LSU College of Higher Education, Southampton, and members of the English School of the University of the West of England, Bristol, for their support; Jo Croft, Angela Dewar, Susan Gladstone, Sally Gutierrez, Maggie Miller (another Barbara Vine enthusiast), David Murray, Johanna Renouf and other friends and members of my family who have joined in conversations about memory over the years.

The author and publisher would like to thank the following for permission to reproduce copyright material: the author, Bloomsbury Publishing, McClelland Stewart (Canada) and Doubleday, a division of Random House, for quotations taken from Margaret Atwood, *Cat's Eye*, published by Bloomsbury Publishing 1989, © 1988 by O. W. Toad, Ltd; Verso Books London/New York for quotations from Ronald Fraser, *In Search of a Past*; Sterling Lord Literistic Inc. and LittleBrown & Co. Publishers for quotations from *My Father's House: A Memoir of Incest and Healing*, © 1989 by Sylvia Fraser; Bloomsbury Publishing and McClelland Stewart (Canada) for quotations from *Fugitive Pieces* by Anne Michaels published by Bloomsbury Publishing, 1997; International Creative Management for quotations from *Beloved* by Toni Morrison © 1987; The Harvill Press for quotations from Georges Perec, *W or The Memory of Childhood*, Editions Denoël, 1975, English translation Harvill and David Godine, 1988; LittleBrown & Co. for quotations from *Landscape for a Good Woman* by Carolyn Steedman; Penguin Books UK and the

Peters Fraser and Dunlop Group for quotations from *Asta's Book* ©
Kingsmarkham Enterprises 1993 by Barbara Vine and *A Dark Adapted
Eye* © Kingsmarkham Enterprises 1986 by Barbara Vine.

This book is dedicated to the memory of my mother, Paula (Dewar)
Brown, to my father, and to Jim.

Series Editor's Introduction

Contemporary history continues to witness a series of momentous changes, altering what was only recently familiar ideological, political and economic terrain. These changes have prompted a new awareness of subjective, sexual, ethnic, racial, religious and cultural identities and of the ways these are constructed in metropolitan centres, regions and nations at a time when these spheres are themselves undergoing a period of critical transition. Recent theory has simultaneously encouraged a scepticism towards the supposed authenticity of personal or common histories, making identity the site of textualised narrative constructions and reconstructions rather than of transparent record. In addition, new developments in communication and information technology appear to be altering our fundamental perceptions of knowledge, of time and space, of relations between the real and the virtual, and of the local and the global.

The varied discourses of literature and media culture have sought to explore these changes, presenting life as it is negotiated on the borderlines of new, hybridised, performative, migrant and marginalised identities, with all the mixed potential and tensions these involve. What emerges are new, sometimes contradictory perceptions of subjectivity or of relations between individuals, social groups, ideologies and nations, as the inner and public life are rewritten in a cultural environment caught up in religious and political conflict and the networks of global consumption, control and communication.

The series *Tendencies: Identities, Texts, Cultures* follows these debates and shows how the formations of identity are being articulated in contemporary literary and cultural texts, often as significantly in their hybridised language and modes as in their manifest content.

Volumes in the series concentrate upon tendencies in contemporary writing and cultural forms, principally in the work of writers, artists and cultural producers over the last two decades. Throughout, its consistent interest lies in the making and unmaking of individual, social and national identities. Each volume draws on relevant theory and critical debate in its discussion *inter alia* of questions of gender and sexuality, race and ethnicity, class, creed and nation, in the structuring of contemporary subjectivities.

The kinds of text selected for study vary from volume to volume, but most often comprise written or visual texts available in English or widely distributed in English translation. Since identities are most often confirmed or redefined within the structures of story and narrative, the series is especially interested in the use of narrative forms, including fiction, autobiography, travel and historical writing, journalism, film and television.

Authors are encouraged to pursue intertextual relations between these forms, to examine the relations between cultural texts and relevant theoretical or political discourse, and to consider cross-generic and intermedia forms where these too bear upon the main concerns of the series.

Peter Brooker
University College, Northampton

'But we didn't know that then'

Leon Greenman is a British Jew who survived Auschwitz; in 1994 I heard him give a talk at an anti-Nazi League meeting in Winchester, where he made connections between the persecution and murder of the Jews by the Nazis and the racism of the present. He narrated his story with precise attention to facts and details, including the ironic chain of circumstances that led him to Auschwitz. He was married to a Dutch woman and happened to be in Holland when it was occupied by the Nazis. Initially imprisoned in a transit camp, procedures to free him were set in motion but the camp commander did not open his mail and read the letter authorising Greenman's release until after the train taking him and his wife towards the East had left. Greenman describes the moment when, after arriving at Auschwitz, he saw his wife being taken away on a truck – to the gas chambers, although, as he said, he 'didn't know that then'. This phrase haunted his narrative, repeated several times: it marked the moments when emotion broke through what was otherwise a rather detached, dead-pan delivery. His memory of that moment seems to have been deeply affected by what he didn't know at the time of the event: what he also has to remember is the painful fact of his own ignorance, as if not knowing was in some way culpable, as if it deprived him of a degree of moral responsibility, or of human agency. His memory has been forced to assimilate later knowledge which now also belongs to the wider realm of 'history': what he can never recover is the 'innocence' of the time when he 'didn't know'.

Greenman's account raises key issues about the function of memory and the ways in which it is reconstructed in narrative and implicated in notions of self-identity – an identity which, for Greenman and others, is rehearsed again and again in a narrative which attempts to recover the self who existed 'before'. His experience is an acute example of the fact that much human experience or action takes

place under the mark of 'what wasn't known then': what we remember
are events which took place in a kind of innocence. This paradoxical
'knowing' and 'not knowing' is the position of any autobiographical
narrator, who, in the present moment of the narration, possesses the
knowledge that she did not have 'then', in the moment of the experience. All narrative accounts of life stories, whether they be the
ongoing stories which we tell ourselves and each other as part of the
construction of identity, or the more shaped and literary narratives of
autobiography or first-person fictions, are made possible by memory;
they also reconstruct memory according to certain assumptions
about the way it functions and the kind of access it gives to the past.
There are moments when memory seems to return us to a past
unchanged by the passing of time; such memories tend to be suffused
with a sense of loss, the nostalgia out of which they may be at least
in part created. We long for a time when we didn't know what was
going to happen next – or, conversely, to relive the past with the
foreknowledge we then lacked. But memory can only be reconstructed
in time, and time, as Carolyn Steedman puts it, 'catches together
what we know and what we do not yet know' (Steedman 1986: 141).

   This book explores the complex relationships between memory,
identity and narrative: the articulation of this relation is a function of
assumptions about the nature of memory itself. As long ago as 1690
John Locke wondered:

suppose I wholly lose the memory of some parts of my Life, beyond a possibility of retrieving them, so that perhaps I shall never be conscious of
them again; yet am I not the same Person, that did those actions, had those
Thoughts, that I was once conscious of, though I have now forgot them?
(1975: 342)

Consistency of consciousness and a sense of continuity between the
actions and events of the past, and the experience of the present,
would appear to be integral to a sense of personal identity. Linda
Grant writes about how her mother, suffering from dementia and
loss of short-term memory, is engaged in the task of 'continuously
inventing for *herself* (and the rest of the world) a coherent identity
and daily history' (Grant 1998: 156). It is commonly accepted that
identity, or a sense of self, is constructed by and through narrative:
the stories we all tell ourselves and each other about our lives.
However, it is not only the *content* of memories, experiences and
stories which construct a sense of identity: the concept of the self
which is constructed in these narratives is also dependent upon
assumptions about the function and process of memory and the kind

of access it gives us to the past. Hayden White (1973) has analysed how historical narratives tend to be organised according to one of the tropes of tragedy, comedy, romance or irony, and clearly the subject may construct a narrative – or a series of mini-narratives – of his or her life in the mode of any one of these at any time, not to mention the conscious and unconscious embroiderings and elaborations which make these stories more interesting. In everyday social discourse, and in much conventional autobiography, these narratives tend to elide memory as a *process*: the content is presented as if it were uniformly and objectively available to the remembering subject, as if the narrating 'I' and the subject of the narration were identical. Part of Locke's answer to his question about continuity of identity was: 'To which I answer, that we must here take notice what the word *I* is applied to' (1975: 342). The split between the two voices or identities – what Christa Wolf describes as 'the memory of ourselves . . . and . . . the voice that assumes the task of telling it' (1976: 4) – has now been clearly identified within narrative theory, and further emphasised and developed within Lacanian psychoanalysis.[1] Greenman's experience is an extreme example of this split: his narrative makes clear the radical break between the self who did not know what was about to happen to his wife, and the self who, belatedly, did know.

It is this complex and shifting relationship between past and present selves in first-person fictional and autobiographical narratives that I explore in this book. For most of us, perhaps, no radical break or trauma disrupts the sense of flow from past to present: we may feel quite different from our childhood or teenage selves, and events such as the birth of a child or the death of a parent do constitute marked 'stages' which may divide the pattern of our lives into a 'before' and 'after'. But experiences such as war, migration, abuse, assault or serious accident may make the relationship between the self 'before' and the self 'after' much more problematic. When I say 'I went to the cinema yesterday', the connection between the 'I' who makes this statement and the 'I' who watched the film is obvious. When Pip, on the first page of Dickens' *Great Expectations*, says: 'So I called myself Pip, and came to be called Pip. I give Pirrip as my father's family name', a complex relationship between 'Pip' and the first and second 'I' is clearly in play. When a Holocaust survivor says, 'You're just walking, but you're dead now. Because I was sure I am dead now,' the confusion of persons and tenses reflects the problem of narrating in the present events which seem unfinished but which also seem to have happened to someone else: 'where the rhythms of chronology disintegrate together with the anticipation of survival. Another persona emerges to echo in the present . . . a voice that normally would have receded with time' (Langer 1991: 190).

The complex nature of the relationship between past and present selves is also acknowledged within the process of psychoanalysis. Here the mechanisms of forgetting, fantasy, screen-memory and 'afterwardsness' are deployed in the construction of a (possibly) much more provisional sense of identity than that which common sense might demand. The paradox here is that the human subject whose identity and sense of life-continuity have been profoundly disrupted by trauma might be in need of the restoration of the kind of 'wholeness' which (particularly) Lacanian psychoanalysis calls into question. If, as Amos Funkenstein has suggested, 'the systematic destruction of self-identity of inmates in concentration camps was also an attempt to destroy their narrative of themselves' (in Friedlander 1992: 77), then the task of the psychoanalyst might be the restoration of that narrative. Dori Laub suggests that the psychoanalytic encounter might be the place where the traumatic event is 'given birth to', or experienced as if for the first time (Felman and Laub 1992: 57).

The debate over 'false' or 'recovered' memory of childhood sexual abuse also brings into particularly sharp focus the question of the relationship between what is apparently remembered and the subject's present sense of self.[2] This debate has highlighted two quite different assumptions or theories about the process of memory, both of which can be found in Freud and which persist in his writings in a rather uncomfortable tension with each other. One model, illustrated by Freud by means of an analogy with archaeological excavation, assumes that the past still exists 'somewhere', waiting to be rediscovered by the remembering subject, uncontaminated by subsequent experience and time's attrition. The other imagines the process of memory as one of continuous revision or 'retranslation', reworking memory-traces in the light of later knowledge and experience. Memory, suggests Walter Benjamin, 'is really the capacity for endless interpolations into what has been' (1979: 321). Post-Freudian psychoanalytic (and literary) theorists have developed the notion of 'afterwardsness' (Laplanche's term) from Freud's scattered references to *Nachträglichkeit*[3] in order to challenge commonsense notions about the nature of time and experience, and also to develop a model for the writing and reading of narrative. This theory suggests that, following a potentially traumatic but 'unregistered' original event, 'only the occurrence of a second scene can endow the first one with a pathogenic force' (Laplanche and Pontalis 1973: 113). These models of memory are explained and explored in the first chapter of this book.

Both the models outlined above have cultural resonance: assumptions

– often untheorised and taken for granted – about the functioning of memory underpin the ways in which a culture positions itself in relation to the past. It is not only a question of how and what individuals remember and how they represent their memories, but also what might be termed a cultural struggle over the construction and meanings of memory within culture, the ways in which we construct the very means and possibility of remembering. Whilst I would want to resist the notion that what might be termed collective or national memory works in exactly the same way as individual memory, nevertheless, the first model of memory – as recovery of the 'pure' past – seems to be at work in nationalist movements which appeal to an idealised organic past, as in Nazi Germany, or to traumatic events of the past which maintain a victimised identity and assert a right to compensatory and exclusive possession, as in Serbian memory of the fourteenth-century battle of Kosovo.[4] Hence I explore articulations of memory as nostalgia within cultural and historiographical discourse: nostalgia expresses itself not only as a mode of remembering the past as lost, but also as a regret for the passing of a 'true', 'spontaneous' or 'organic' form of memory.[5] The pervasiveness of such notions in popular culture is well illustrated by an Italian tourist brochure for the Lake Trasimeno district: 'Each one of us bears inside, even unwittingly, the memory of a very remote era, of things experienced by former generations, of lost sounds and rhythms.' Modern life 'produces in our ego a sense of tenuous and penetrating absence'.[6] Such nostalgias are often (and often unconsciously) informed by 'memory' of the imaginary plenitude of the pre-Oedipal, the lost 'oceanic' unity of mother and infant – what Laura Mulvey has described as 'the pre-Oedipal as Golden Age' (1987: 11). We see this 'memory' at work in narratives as diverse as *Beloved*, Toni Morrison's 'rememory' of slavery, and Barbara Vine's popular psychological thriller, *A Dark Adapted Eye*.

Using the concept of *Nachträglichkeit*, on the other hand, Lyotard suggests that 'the search for lost time can only be interminable': the 'immemorial' is 'always "present" but never here-now, always torn apart in the time of consciousness, of chronology, between a too-early and a too-late' (Lyotard 1988: 20). The 'too-late' here suggests the moment of Greenman's narrative reconstruction of the 'too-early' moment when, deprived of foresight, he saw his wife being taken away at Auschwitz. Andrew Benjamin has developed this idea of time into a way of analysing narrative as a 'ternary temporal structure articulating repetition' (in Fletcher and Stanton 1992: 149). In my analyses of the autobiographies I discuss in the following chapters, I suggest a threefold model of narrative as 1) the event; 2) the memory of the event; and 3) the writing of (the memory of) the event. It is the third stage of this process that constructs the only version of the first to which we have access, and memory is the means by which the relationship between the event and its reconstruction is negotiated. Our reading of certain texts – particularly those of Barbara Vine – also employs the memory of the *reader* in the deciphering of clues and the reconstruction of events: we read in 'anticipation of retrospection'; 'what remains to be read will restructure the meanings of the already read' (Brooks 1984: 23).

In Barbara Vine's novel, *The Chimney Sweeper's Boy* (1998), Hope, daughter of a famous novelist, Gerald Candless, is asked to write a memoir of her father by his editor. He tells her of 'the recent popularity of a certain kind of memoir. I mean the child's memoir of a parent, usually but not invariably a father'; a memoir which would include 'his origins, his background, his family, what he came out of' (35–6). After Hope's refusal, he goes on to think of *And When Did You Last See Your Father?* (Blake Morrison 1993) and 'that Germaine Greer book he had admired with all the detective work in it' (*Daddy, We Hardly Knew You*, 1989). He could have added to the list Margaret Forster's *Hidden Lives* (1995) and now Linda Grant's *Remind Me Who I Am, Again* (1998) and Lisa Appignanesi's *Losing the Dead* (1999). In the last few years there has been a proliferation of family or parental memoirs in which the writer attempts to recover or reconstruct the lives of his or her own parents whilst also exploring the ways in which their lives and experiences might have helped to form the writer's own sense of self – sometimes also as an act of denial or resistance. Appignanesi writes that members of her generation – born just after the Second World War – 'are suddenly interested in our parents' pasts which we feel are linked with our own buried ones' (81), and Grant that: 'It is my fate now, in the middle age we never believed was coming, . . . to scramble among the ruins of my mother's memory in search of my past, of who all of us are' (28).

The autobiographical texts of Carolyn Steedman and Ronald Fraser, published in the 1980s, are more self-conscious and theoretically informed versions of this genre, with the memory and identity of the writer more central to the reconstruction. Autobiographical texts which are not ostensibly about the writer's parents are often also marked by their actions or absence – Sylvia Fraser's sexually abusive father, Georges Perec's mother, killed at Auschwitz when he was six – and problematise the memory and identity of the subject. Fraser's narrative traces a clear cause for her distress; for others, genealogy, the tracing of family trees, seems to be a crucial way of establishing a history and finding a point of origin which will, of course, always recede before our grasp. In one way or another, these texts demonstrate the subjects' complex process of negotiation – of resistance, identification or over-identification, hostility or idealisation – with parental figures who may be unknown, mysterious, absent or all-too-present. Steedman writes of 'the way in which my mother re-asserted, reversed and restructured her own [life] within mine' (8), and how she grew up 'believing that my identification was entirely with her, that whilst hating her, I was her, and that there was no escape' (55). This mutually destructive identification is explored in extreme form in the final chapters of Morrison's *Beloved*.

As Vine suggests, reconstructions of the lives of our parents are often also necessarily acts of detection and the excavation of secrets – the 'wilfully obscured and venomous secret' (4) of Appignanesi's Jewish father's wartime experiences, Forster's grandmother's illegitimate daughter, Steedman's illegitimacy, Sylvia Fraser's prolonged abuse by her father, the true identities of Vine's protagonists. But even as she openly appeals to the narrative gratification of the successful act of detection, Vine also acknowledges (in *A Dark Adapted Eye*) the 'doubt at the heart of things'. In several of these narratives the failure of memory or the habit of deception makes the truth inaccessible: their very titles suggest the impossibility of ever fully 'knowing' who the parent 'really was'. Appignanesi says that 'it can hardly be coincidental that I want to remember, to uncover, to know, at the moment when my last gateway to family memory – my mother – is losing hers' (1999: 7). Her parents survived the war in Poland – her mother by passing as an Aryan – and then emigrated to Canada, even there 'finding it expedient to keep up the habit of double identity . . . Identities, in my family, seem always to have been there for the making' (28–9). In many of these narratives of the self we are witness not to lives and identities as fixed and given, but improvised, constructed, negotiated in conditions of danger or shame, class or family conflict. 'Identities are not discovered, but rather actively constructed by individuals' (James 1994: 72): reading and writing are constitutive of this process, which also always takes place within a particular social formation.

The texts analysed here highlight quite clearly the ways in which particular assumptions of the process of memory are embedded in narrative, and the kind of 'self' which constructs and is constructed by this double process of remembering and representing. All might be described as narratives of the self, but none are straightforwardly autobiographical, three are entirely fictional, and two are novels that take a historical event – slavery and an infanticide in *Beloved*, the

Nazi murder of Jews in Poland in Anne Michaels' *Fugitive Pieces* – as their starting point. What is foregrounded by this juxtaposition is the nature of narrative 'truth', the role of memory in the construction and reading of narratives of the self, and the ways in which narrators and writers position themselves in relation to the personal and historical past. In Chapter 2 I discuss two autobiographical texts – Ronald Fraser's *In Search of a Past* and Carolyn Steedman's *Landscape for a Good Woman* – which suggest that it is impossible to recover the past 'as it really was', demonstrating memory as subject to a continuous process of retranslation. In Chapter 3 I analyse a memoir and a novel which assume a very different model of memory: Sylvia Fraser's autobiography *My Father's House* uses the 'techniques of the novelist' to re-create a traumatic past – her experience of sexual abuse by her father – according to the trope of repression and recovery, the rediscovery of the buried past. Margaret Atwood's novel *Cat's Eye*, whose 'form is that of an autobiography' although 'it is not one', uses a similar structure to enable its subject-narrator, who has also 'forgotten' a traumatic childhood, to 'see [her] life entire'. The novels of Barbara Vine discussed in Chapter 4 are acts of detection, attempts to discover the truth of the origin of their protagonists who have also been marked by childhood separations and by class antagonisms. They demonstrate Steedman's observation that family secrets 'produce myths of origin that serve both to reveal and conceal what is actually hidden from view' (66), and the centrality of memory to our experience of plots and lives – our own and those of others, real or imagined.

The autobiographical texts of Ronald Fraser, Carolyn Steedman and Georges Perec are oblique and decentred, approaching their subjects indirectly: through oral social history in Fraser's *In Search of a Past*; other texts and lives in Steedman's *Landscape for a Good Woman*; and narratives of fantasy and adventure in Perec's *W or The Memory of Childhood*. All three deal with painful childhoods marked by loss and lack which cannot be compensated for in memory: Fraser's in the upper-class country house of England between the wars; Steedman's on the shaky borderline between working- and lower middle-class south London in the 1950s; Perec's in France under German occupation in the 1940s. Perec's fragmented, decentred 'autobiography' is the main focus of Chapter 5. Fraser, Steedman and Perec also articulate the relationship between individual and cultural memory, the psyche and the social, as do Anne Michaels and (especially) Toni Morrison. The Holocaust and the enslavement of African peoples stand within Western culture as the two most extreme and traumatic assaults on individual human identity and on historical memory; Perec bears witness to their destruction, Morrison and Michaels to their (partial) reconstruction. In *Fugitive Pieces* the pain of individual memory (the murder of the protagonist's family by the Nazis) is both assuaged and intensified by the idea that the earth itself partakes of his longing: 'We long for place, but place itself longs. Human memory is encoded in air currents and river sediment' (Michaels 1997: 53). In Chapter 5 I also interrogate Michaels' metaphorical and metaphysical tropes of memory. Toni Morrison's purpose is to 'make some memorial, somewhere where these things' – the unspoken and unspeakable history of the Middle Passage – 'can be thought'.[7] Here the author restores an interior life to people who were either presumed not to have one, or whose subjectivity had never been fully represented. In my sixth and final chapter, I explore this novel's coinage of the term 'rememory', which draws together some of the central concerns of this book: the representation of traumatic memory, both personal and historical; the notion of memory as a continuous process of 'retranslation'; and the appeal and danger of memory as nostalgia for the imaginary plenitude of the pre-Oedipal mother–infant relation.

We remember in different ways at different times: the same memories can be recalled voluntarily, and resurface involuntarily. Moments of the past can be invoked by words, smells, tastes, and sounds: we represent these moments to ourselves in visual images, in stories, in conversations. When people try to articulate the *ways* in which they remember, metaphor seems inevitable: one person will talk in terms of photographs, or of videotape; another will describe a 'black box' inside her containing traces of all the events she has ever experienced; another might remember the past as what Woolf calls 'a long ribbon of scenes' (1976: 77). Freud's archaeological site; psychology's filing cabinets and information retrieval systems, neuroscience's engrams and 'neural networks', Derrida's textual metaphors of footnotes and supplements: all these metaphorical accounts of memory indicate that it cannot be thought or represented except in terms of something that already determines how we conceive of it. For Jonathan Morse, 'Memory's problem' is 'the inability ever to say, through time, in changing words, what we have seen, and having seen, know as such, for ever. As we speak, our words only footnote other words, deferring meaning, margin by margin' (1990: 158). It is the relationship between memory, temporality, writing and identity that I explore in this book: it is in and through writing that memory constructs itself as inevitably 'belated', but it is through writing that its 'immediacy' is also re-created.

Notes

1. See Gerard Genette (1980), *Narrative Discourse*, trans. J. E. Lewin, and Jacques Lacan (1981), *Speech and Language in Psychoanalysis*, trans. Anthony Wilden.
2. See Frederick Crews, *The Memory Wars: Freud's Legacy in Dispute* (1995) for a discussion of this controversy.
3. Translated by Strachey in the *Standard Edition* to the works of Freud as 'deferred action'.
4. I am writing this in May 1999, during the NATO bombing of Serbia, in response to the ethnic cleansing of Albanians from the disputed province of Kosovo.
5. Terms used by Pierre Nora (1989) in 'Between Memory and History: *Les Lieux de Mémoire*', *Representations* 26: 7–25.
6. *Azienda di Promozione Turistica di Trasimeno* (1995), 'Discover the Hundred Faces of the Trasimeno'.
7. *The South Bank Show* (1987), 'Toni Morrison', ITV, 11 October.

$$=== 1 ===$$

Memory in Theory

INTRODUCTION

Memory can create the illusion of a momentary return to a lost past; its operations also articulate the complex relationship between past, present and future in human consciousness. Ian Hacking has suggested that the intense focus on memory in a wide range of disciplines towards the end of the nineteenth century was 'part of the secular drive to replace the soul with something of which we have knowledge' (1995: 251), and it was in the field of psychoanalysis that this new focus found its most interesting mode of expression. The late twentieth century has also seen an increased focus on questions of memory as the generations which experienced the atrocities of the two world wars die out, and as new or revived national movements base their demands on memories of oppression or trauma. The 1990s were marked by a particularly intense and painful dispute over the question of whether it is possible to recover long-buried memories of infantile sexual abuse. The recent insistence on the role of memory might also mark a renewed desire to secure a sense of self in the wake of postmodern theories of the decentred human subject.

I begin by analysing two contrasting models of memory within psychoanalytic theory which inform the different ways in which the processes of memory are reconstructed in narrative, and the construction of the self who does the remembering. The first is suggested by Freud's frequent use of the analogy between the recovery of the buried past and the excavation of an archaeological site; the second by his reference to the 'retranscription' of memories and the structural principle of *Nachträglichkeit*.[1] *Nachträglichkeit* (and its adverbial form *nachträglich*) is a term used frequently by Freud but never developed by him into a consistent theory: it has been translated by Jean Laplanche as 'afterwardsness' (in Fletcher and Stanton 1992).

This concept makes explicit the fact that memory, operating as it does in the present, must inevitably incorporate the awareness of 'what wasn't known then': it has been developed by Andrew Benjamin and Peter Nicholls into a tool for the analysis of narrative and our relation to the past. Nicholls suggests that : 'To remember is . . . not simply to restore a forgotten link or moment of experience, nor is it unproblematically to "repossess" or re-enact what has been lost' (1996: 53). The concept of *Nachträglichkeit* unsettles the belief that we can recover the past as it was and unproblematically reunite our past and present selves, although the assumption that memory can give us direct access to the preserved or buried past retains a powerful hold on our culture: as Frederick Crews suggests, 'the very idea of repression and its unravelling is an embryonic romance about a hidden mystery, an arduous journey, and a gratifyingly neat denoument that can ascribe our otherwise drab shortcomings and pains to deep necessity' (1995: 166).

Freud was, of course, particularly concerned with memories of trauma – real or imaginary – which disrupt the 'normal' functioning of memory and produce hysterical or other pathological symptoms, and the models of archaeological excavation and of *Nachträglichkeit* were both developed to address the phenomenon of repressed or traumatic memory. Much work on memory has also focused on trauma as producing 'a history of the modern subject as a history of implication. This subject is recognised by its inextricable ties to what cannot be experienced or subjectivised fully'.[2] But Freud also explored the ordinary or non-pathological processes of screen-memory, fantasy, forgetting and remembering in ways which acknowledge the complex unconscious processes by which we remember and forget, and which problematise the idea of any simple chronological relation between past and present in human experience. Christopher Bollas has suggested that the '*passing* of time . . . is intrinsically traumatic' (1995: 119), and that it is within the 'ordinary' processes of memory that the self is continuously created and destroyed.

MEMORY AS ARCHAEOLOGICAL EXCAVATION

The archaeological analogy appears in Freud's writings of the 1890s and, although modified during the course of his work, is never entirely abandoned, emerging finally in 'Constructions in Analysis' in 1937. In *Studies on Hysteria* Freud describes his 'first full-length analysis of a hysteria': 'This procedure was one of clearing away the pathogenic psychical material layer by layer, and we liked to compare it with the technique of excavating a buried city' (Freud and Breuer

1893–5: 206). In 'The Aetiology of Hysteria' he says that 'the fact that the scenes are uncovered in a reversed chronological order . . . justifies our comparison of the work with the excavation of a stratified ruined site' (1896: 198). Here the site is described as *ruined*, but in the 'Rat Man' case history of 1909, burial of memory entails its *preservation*. Freud told his patient that

everything conscious was subject to a process of wearing away, while what was unconscious was relatively unchangeable; and I illustrated my remarks by pointing to the antiques standing about in my room. They were, in fact, I said, only objects found in a tomb, and their burial had been their preserva- tion: the destruction of Pompeii was only beginning now that it had been dug up . . . The unconscious, I explained, *was* the infantile; it was that part of the self which had become separated off from it in infancy, which had not shared the later stages of its development, and which had in consequence become *repressed*. (1909: 57–8)

Here several important controversies raised by psychoanalytic theories of memory are signalled: the timelessness of the unconscious; the splitting of the ego; the implied identification of the 'infantile' with earlier stages of human civilisation; the theory of repression; and the idea that the past still exists, 'somewhere', to be rediscovered by the remembering subject. 'Repression' here suggests an apparently complete forgetting, the burial of aspects of the past in the uncon- scious, as if behind closed doors: it is a model upon which Sylvia Fraser very clearly depends in her account of memory recovery. In 1907 Freud claimed that there was 'no better analogy for repression, by which something in the mind is at once inaccessible and pre- served, than burial of the sort to which Pompeii fell a victim and from which it could emerge once more through the work of spades' (1907: 65).

In 'The Aetiology of Hysteria' Freud implicitly acknowledges that interpretation must come into play to complement the 'work of spades', and that memory is textual as well as spatial: 'the numerous inscriptions, which, by good luck, may be bilingual, reveal an alphabet and a language, and, when they have been deciphered and translated, yield undreamed-of information about the events of the remote past' (1896: 198). Walter Benjamin develops Freud's digging metaphor, whilst also insisting that language is

the medium of past experience, as the ground is the medium in which dead cities lie interred. He who seeks to approach his own buried past must conduct himself like a man digging . . . He must not be afraid to return again and again to the same matter; to scatter it as one scatters earth, to turn it over as one turns over soil. For the matter itself is only a deposit, a stratum, which yields only to the most meticulous examination what constitutes the real treasure hidden within the earth: the images . . . that stand – like precious fragments or torsos in a collector's gallery – in the prosaic rooms of our later understanding. (1979: 314)

Benjamin here suggests that the 'real treasure' hidden within memory consists of 'images' which can only be uncovered by a long process of excavation; they can only be reconstructed within the language that is always inevitably a translation or interpretation. In the case of Dora, Freud uses the archaeological analogy, but adds: 'like a conscientious archaeologist, I have not omitted to mention in each case where the authentic parts end and my constructions begin' (1905a: 41). In fact, in the case histories Freud does not always distinguish the material presented to him by his patients from his own summaries, which inevitably involve the act of interpretation. To use the terms employed by Peter Brooks in his analysis of the 'Wolf Man' case history (1984: 272), *fabula* (the story, or events) and *szujet* (the plot, or narrative representation of the events) are conflated, and the *szujet* 'is formed out of material that is supplied by récits' (or *fabula*) in a 'complex agreement of narrations' (Gardner 1990: 91). This is the process we see at work in Sylvia Fraser's autobiographical reconstruction.

According to Freud, the analyst is in a much better position than the archaeologist because in the unconscious of the patient 'all the essentials are preserved; even things that seem completely forgotten are present somehow and somewhere, and have merely been buried and made inaccessible to the subject' (1937: 260). Marie Cardinal reconstructs the process of her analysis in *The Words To Say It*: she became convinced that 'the mind picks up everything, files it, classifies it, and keeps it all . . . Every event, . . . no matter how ordinary, . . . is catalogued, labelled, and locked away in oblivion, but marked in consciousness by a signal which is often microscopic.' Her analysis, she says, gave her a means of access to this past: 'first of all I understood the system of signals, then I found the secret for opening most of the doors, and, finally, I discovered the doors which I thought were impossible to open, and in front of which I stood, desperately marking time' (1983: 125–6). The process involved here recalls Benjamin's insistence upon repeatedly 'digging over' the same ground and the acts of detection in which Vine's and Atwood's narrators, and Sylvia Fraser, are engaged. The belief that all the events of one's life are 'recorded' and potentially available for recovery persists in spite of research which suggests that memory does not work like a video-recorder: 'it isn't a place, a store-house or a machine for recording events', but 'an intricate and ever shifting net of firing neurons . . . the twistings and turnings of which rearrange themselves completely each time something is recalled' (Grant 1998: 289).[3] As for Fraser, Cardinal's 'discovery' that nothing in the past is lost, that all experience is 'filed away' somewhere, waiting to be rediscovered by the remembering subject, is both painful (when memories are of trauma or loss) and comforting (wholeness and integration are possible).

The metaphors of archaeological excavation and the finding of keys to open the locked doors of memory suggest the act of remembering as the uncovering of a *secret*. As Hacking puts it (in the context of his discussion of multiple personality):

Memoro-politics is above all a politics of the secret, of the forgotten event that can be turned, if only by strange flashbacks, into something monumental. It is a forgotten event that, when it is brought to light, can be memorialised in a narrative of pain. (1995: 214)

The psychoanalysts Nicolas Abraham and Maria Torok have developed the idea – obviously also metaphoric, and connected with the semantic chain of burial and excavation – of the *crypt* as the psychic container of the unspoken secret. Such secrets can cause the kind of 'transgenerational haunting' given dramatic form by the appearance of Beloved in Morrison's novel.[4] In many of the texts I discuss here, the discovery of a secret buried in family history – Sylvia Fraser's abuse; Steedman's illegitimacy; the fate of Perec's mother; the true origin of Vine's protagonists, Jamie and Swanny – is the motivating force of the plot or constructed as a formative moment of the subject's identity. Some 'secrets' are never discovered – the fate of Jakob's sister Bella in Michaels' *Fugitive Pieces*, the identity of Jamie's mother – others are narrated in a way which resists the 'memorialisation' to which Hacking alludes.

For Sylvia Fraser, the detective work of memory is incomplete without the 'memory' of her body: after she has begun to remember her abuse, she re-experiences it physically and involuntarily. As with Freud's hysterical patients whose bodily symptoms revealed that they were 'suffering from reminiscences', the body itself is imagined as an archaeological site which preserves the experiences of the past. But such experiences are inevitably reconstructed in language, and the term '(re)construction' as Lis Møller points out, is 'suspended between different understandings of psychoanalytic interpretation in Freud's work', and, I would add, between different models of memory and its 'recovery'. It suggests the idea of the accurate archaeological reconstruction of the past, but is also 'the mark of the fictionality of the psychoanalytic interpretation' – and of any narrative 'reconstruction' of 'lost time' (1991: xi). In 'Constructions in Analysis' Freud makes it clear that an inevitable part of the analyst's role is, precisely, 'to make out what has been forgotten from the traces which it has left behind or, more correctly, to *construct* it' (1937: 259). Later he adds: 'We do not pretend that an individual construction is anything other than a conjecture which awaits examination, confirmation or rejection' (265). The provisionality of such construction suggests that it will remain open to later *re*construction, not in the sense of the rebuilding of a ruined city, or of restoring the past 'as it really was', but as a continuous process of revision and retranslation.

NACHTRÄGLICHKEIT

As Sebastian Gardner suggests, 'no mental act can be relied upon to relay meaning: interpretation has become necessary in order to establish that there has been a synthesis, and not a rupture, of past and future' (1990: 90). It is this sense of rupture which is foregrounded in recent developments of the notion of *Nachträglichkeit*. The double meaning of 'reconstruction' outlined above suggests that Freud finds it almost impossible to 'preserve' his model of memory as preservation: it is inevitably undercut by another model, that indicated by the term *Nachträglichkeit*. On 6 December 1896 Freud wrote to Wilhelm Fliess:

I am working on the assumption that our psychic mechanism has come into being by a process of stratification: the material present in the form of memory traces being subjected from time to time to a *rearrangement* in accordance with fresh circumstances – to a *retranscription*. Thus what is essentially new about my theory is the thesis that memory is present not once but several times over, that it is laid down in various kinds of indications. (Masson 1985: 207)

This passage is problematic in that it is based upon a physical model of the mind which Freud never entirely abandoned and upon which much of his theory depends. The context suggests that he is here talking about the *physical* reinscription, at three different levels of 'registration', of memory-traces – something close to what neuroscientists have since called 'engrams' – upon the cortex; this discourse of memory is yet to be integrated with the field of psychoanalysis. Laplanche and Pontalis include this quotation from Freud in their entry for 'deferred action' in *The Language of Psychoanalysis*, suggesting that this account can be assimilated to the process of *Nachträglichkeit*. If the 'fresh circumstances' according to which memories are 'retranscribed' are read as the *actual* fresh circumstances of the life of the subject, including those circumstances in which the events of the past are remembered, this becomes a productive model for memory, and one which is close to the structure and effect of narrative itself. It also suggests that the construction of the self is a provisional and continuous process, rather than the 'recovery' of an 'original' identity. Laplanche and Pontalis describe it thus:

[E]xperiences, impressions and memory-traces may be revised at a later date to fit in with fresh circumstances or to fit in with a new stage of development. They may in that event be endowed not only with a new meaning but also with psychical effectiveness ... It is not lived experience in general which undergoes a deferred revision but, specifically, whatever it has been impossible in the first instance to incorporate fully into a meaningful context. The traumatic event is the epitome of all such unassimilated experience ... Human sexuality, with the peculiar unevenness of its temporal development, provides an eminently suitable field for the phenomenon of deferred action. (1973: 111–12)

The clearest example of the ternary temporal structure of *Nachträglichkeit* is the case of Emma, described in Freud's 'Project for a Scientific Psychology' (1950 [1895]). This patient had an acute fear of going into shops alone, apparently caused by an incident at the age of twelve when she went into a shop and was laughed at by two male shop assistants; she thought they were laughing at her clothes. Her phobic response seems out of proportion to the event: in analysis, she remembers an earlier scene, which took place when she was eight. She had gone into a shop to buy some sweets, and had been sexually assaulted by the shopkeeper, who had grinned at her and grabbed her genitals through her clothes. This incident had been 'forgotten' – or not 'registered', according to Lyotard's reading[5] – but the trauma, which had not been experienced as such at the time, was triggered by the second event with which it had certain similarities. The connection between the two scenes was made during the analysis.

In the case of the Wolf Man, Freud explains: 'At the age of one and a half the child receives an impression to which he was unable to react adequately; he is only able to understand it and be moved by it when the impression is revived in him at the age of four: and only 20 years later, during the analysis, is he able to grasp with his own conscious mental processes what was then going on in him' (1913: 278). The first 'impression' was the 'primal scene', the sight of his parents copulating *a tergo*, like animals; the impression was revived at the age of four by a dream of white wolves in the tree outside his bedroom window. In between occurred his 'seduction' by his sister and a threat of castration from his Nanya, and what Freud refers to as his 'sexual researches' which precipitated the phobia apparently caused by the dream. Freud's own later footnotes, or supplements – *Nachträg* also means 'supplement' – themselves represent his 'reconstructions' of his own constructions: the 'primal scene', he suggests, may have been at least in part a fantasy, constructed out of the child's observation of dogs copulating, or a 'primal phantasy', phylogenetically inherited, or even a construction produced within the analysis, as the patient could produce no clear recollection of the scene.

Here the concept of *Nachträglichkeit* problematises the truth status of the first event, the 'primal scene', although such scenes remain powerful fantasies at both individual and cultural levels. As Linda Williams puts it: 'The child sees or hears *something*, but the material is itself only gradually inserted into a narrative or a coherent picture as it is actively reworked in memory – a reinterpretation and reinscription of the scene, taking place over time in the development of the subject' (1995: 16). Of the writers under discussion in this book, it is Carolyn Steedman and Georges Perec who show most clearly this process of 'active reworking' and 'retranscription' of an early, partly understood event, but the formative experiences of their childhoods are not themselves brought into question. Emma is assumed to have suffered – at the age of eight – the assault she later remembered, although Freud and Lyotard assume that she did not experience it as traumatic at its first occurrence. In the case of infantile experience, it is well known that Freud changed his belief that many of his female patients had suffered actual sexual abuse in infancy, replacing this with the idea that they were fantasising these events; this loss of faith (according to Jeffery Masson) underpins the more recent controversy over 'false' or 'recovered' memory of early sexual abuse.[6] Defining the 'primal scene' as 'an ontologically undecidable textual event' (Lukacher 1986: 24) risks denial of the real 'primal scenes' of abuse suffered by some children. In this book I am not arguing that such events do not occur: rather I am concerned to explore the processes by which they are reconstructed and represented. Roberta Culbertson's account – discussed in Chapter 3 – of the way in which the child experiences and represents such events is instructive here. The word 'infant' derives from 'infans', or 'without speech'; if pre-verbal infants cannot represent their experiences to themselves in words it would seem inevitable that they must be somehow changed or 'retranscribed' when they are articulated later in analysis, narrative or the everyday process of describing memories to others. It is clear in the case of the Wolf Man that the 'primal scene' might well have been produced during analysis or fantasised: in the case of Sylvia Fraser, the memory of a whole series of 'primal scenes', lasting right up to adolescence, is apparently recovered in its 'pure' state, giving access to the hidden 'inner child' who experienced the abuse.

Freud did not limit the application of the process of *Nachträglichkeit* to cases of infantile sexual trauma, or even to individuals: in the case history of the 'Rat Man' he claims that: 'We must above all bear in mind that people's "childhood memories" are only consolidated at a later period . . . and that this involves a complicated process of remodelling, analogous in every way to the process by which a nation constructs legends about its own history' (1909: 87). In *Moses and Monotheism* (1934–8) he describes the foundation of the Jewish religion as a belated response to and later reworking of an original trauma. John Forrester suggests that Freud developed the idea of the deferred or belated nature of trauma from Charcot's work with victims of accidents which were insufficient to account for the degree of neurosis suffered later. In such cases he observed an initial lack of affect, and a period of 'psychical working out': a similar structure was observed after the First World War in sufferers from war neurosis (Forrester 1990: 193–8). Such cases differ from those of infantile sexual trauma in that the element of not *understanding* a sexual meaning is missing; what is involved here is the difference between two kinds of 'not knowing': the sexual ignorance of the child who does not 'know' what he or she is seeing or experiencing, and the 'not knowing' of the subject who 'knows' at the level of mere information what is happening but who is unable to fully experience it at the time.

Dori Laub, a psychoanalyst who works with Holocaust survivors, says that when they narrate their experiences within a therapeutic setting it is as if they are bearing witness to them for the first time: 'the emergence of the narrative which is being listened to . . . is . . . the process and the place wherein the cognizance, the "knowing"' of the event is given birth to'. He describes the monotonous, factual, affect-less narratives of some survivors for whom 'the trauma – as a known event and not simply as an overwhelming shock – has not been truly witnessed yet, not been taken cognisance of (Felman and Laub 1992: 57). Other survivors, such as Charlotte Delbo, describe the effect of trauma in terms of a split between the self who experienced it and the self who 'survives':

I have the feeling . . . that the 'self' who was in the camp isn't me, isn't the person who is here, opposite you. No, it's too unbelievable. And everything that happened to this other 'self', the one from Auschwitz, doesn't touch me now, *me*, doesn't concern me, so distinct are deep memory [*mémoire profonde*] and common memory [*mémoire ordinaire*]. (quoted in Langer 1991: 5)

Here the function of memory itself is described as 'split' between the way in which 'ordinary' events which proceed in 'normal' time are recorded, and the dislocating, achronological nature of the memory of experiences of extremity. Therapists who have worked with survivors of other traumas describe a mode of remembering which retains facts, images and events as a series of photographs which can be looked at briefly but with the emotion to which they might give rise still held at bay. Linda Williams quotes Mrs Oliphant in her analysis of her autobiography: 'All my recollections are like pictures . . . not continuous, only a scene detached and conspicuous here and there'; she describes 'a picture . . . which got itself hung up upon the walls of my mind' (1995: 146). This mode of remembering – or forgetting – is close to that described by Freud in 'Remembering, Repeating and Working Through': in neurosis, 'forgetting is mostly restricted to dissolving thought-connections, failing to draw the right conclusions and isolating memories . . . Forgetting impressions, scenes or experiences nearly always reduces itself to shutting them off. When the patient talks about these "forgotten" things he seldom fails to add: "As a matter of fact I've always known it, only I've never thought of it"' (1914: 148–9). Christopher Bollas has developed the useful concept of the 'unthought known' to describe this mental state: 'the child will know something even if this knowledge has not been elaborated through thought proper' (1987: 111). This idea of 'repression' is quite different from the idea that the subject retains *no* conscious memory of traumatic events: it is closer to the vivid yet dissociated violent images that Sethe (in *Beloved*) cannot prevent her mind from admitting than it is to Sylvia Fraser's total amnesia of years of abuse.

NACHTRÄGLICHKEIT AND NARRATIVE

'If subjects come into being through their relationship with narratives, then narratives are formed in time; but . . . the form of narrative time . . . does not flow in only one direction' (Williams 1995: 126). The 'complex set of psychological operations' at play in the 'work of recollection' (Laplanche and Pontalis 1973: 114) has recently been extended by Laplanche and others into 'a general psychic – and textual – mechanism' which is central to the construction and reading of narratives, particularly those which narrate the life of a fictional or autobiographical subject. For Laplanche

[A]nalytic interpretation consists in undoing an existing, spontaneous and perhaps symptomatic translation, in order to rediscover, anterior to the translation, what it so ardently wished to translate and possibly to permit a 'better' translation; that is to say one that is more complete, more comprehensive and less repressive ... the human being reaches towards a future only because he is auto-theorising and auto-translating: each important circumstance of his life is ... for him the occasion to call into question the *present* translation, to detranslate it by turning towards the past and to attempt a better translation of this past, a more comprehensive translation, with renewed possibilities. The fundamental moments of human temporalisation are those in which this reworking takes place through the afterwards effect (*dans l'après-coup*). (quoted in Fletcher and Stanton 1992: 176)

This process is evident, he says, not only within the psychoanalytic process but 'in the strategies of mourning, of deferral, fantasising or daydreaming' (167) – and in the narrative reconstruction of life stories. Andrew Benjamin has suggested that *Nachträglichkeit* 'can be articulated in relation to the presentation, deferral and subsequent re-presentation of narrative' (in Fletcher and Stanton: 139): what he calls 'the ternary structure of time articulating repetition' (149) can be clearly demonstrated in the case of autobiography, where we have, first, the event; second the memory of the event; and third the writing of (the memory of) the event. Clearly, in some texts the process of 'retranslation' will be more consciously acknowledged than in autobiographies where the the 'I' who speaks is assumed to be one and the same as the 'I' who is spoken of. The texts of Georges Perec, Carolyn Steedman and Ronald Fraser demonstrate what Benjamin describes as the 'present imperfect translation ... ceaselessly ... push[ing] for renewed translation', the 'dynamic of a self-presencing that is always, and of necessity, incomplete' (146). Memory as anamnesis, as a continuous process of re-remembering, is also close to the narrative movement of Morrison's *Beloved*, which dramatises 'rememory' as a cyclical return to an earlier traumatic moment which is re-remembered in the present, in greater detail and with greater affect at each recurrence. The understanding of the reader, as well as the psychic reintegration of the protagonist, Sethe, is developed through this textual strategy.

The narrative reconstruction of a life 'history' provides the opportunity for a rereading of those events which, as described by John Forrester, '*would have been* recognized as a purpose and *would have*

determined the action, had it been anticipated'. 'Analysis' – including the self-analysis which takes place in these texts – 'seeks those
intentions which *would have been* determinate of the good fortune,
or misfortune, of the subject, *had they been recognized as such*'
(1990: 210). Autobiographical narratives reconstruct the events of a
life in the light of 'what wasn't known then', highlighting the events
which are now, with hindsight, seen to be significant. The first-time
reader of a novel reads 'in anticipation of retrospection' (Brooks
1984: 23), building up an understanding of the plot partly through
the continuous action of memory, in a process analogous to the way
in which the subject experiences his or her life for the first time,
without the benefit of hindsight. The reader who rereads a novel
such as Vine's *A Dark Adapted Eye* is in a similar position to the
autobiographical narrator who knows what happened next, how the
plot turned out, and is engaged in a similar process of reconstruction
and interpretation. Paul Ricoeur argues that the reconstruction of a
narrative – in itself the 'retroactive realignment of the past' – in the
act of reading disrupts the common sense notion of time:

As soon as a story is well known to follow the story is not so much to enclose
its surprises or discoveries within our recognition of the meaning attached
to the story, as to apprehend the episodes which are themselves well known
as leading to this end. Finally, the repetition of a story, governed as a whole
by its way of ending, constitutes an alternative to the representation of time
as flowing from the past towards the future, following the well-known
metaphor of the 'arrow of time'. It is as though recollection inverted the
so-called 'natural' order of time. In reading the ending in the beginning and
the beginning in the ending, we also learn to read time itself backwards, as the
recapitulation of the initial conditions of a course of action in its terminal
consequences. (1984: 67)

Martin Amis' *Time's Arrow* (1991) makes this process of retroaction
explicit. In this novel the life of a doctor who worked in the Nazi
extermination camps is narrated backwards, from the moment of his
'death', producing the occasion for the painful evocation of the
reconstruction of Jewish people and communities out of the ashes
into which they were reduced. *Actually* narrating a story backwards
makes it clear that events and the language in which we narrate them
do only work in one direction. But Ricoeur's account does suggest
the process by which Sylvia Fraser and Margaret Atwood's narrator
Elaine read and reconstruct their own life stories, in terms of what
Mark Freeman has called the 'reciprocal determination' of 'endings
and beginnings' (1991: 176): they reconstruct their lives according to
the interpretations they have now placed upon them, whilst also

attempting to maintain the illusion of their earlier ignorance as to the outcome of events. The other autobiographical writers I discuss resist the over-determination which highly reconstructed narratives can produce by deliberately leaving their texts fragmentary and provisional, or by acknowledging memory as Benjamin's 'endless interpolations into what has been'. Barbara Vine also acknowledges that the acts of detection capable of producing a satisfactorily circular solution to a mystery do not always uncover the truth about the past. Dominick LaCapra suggests that narrative 'may be opened to some extent by the attempt to explore alternative possibilities in the past that are themselves suggested by the retrospective or deferred effects of later knowledge' (1983: 18) – the idea that events might have turned out differently, and if interpreted differently, might still be capable of changing the subject's understanding of her life and her self. Several of the narratives I discuss in the later chapters of this book do preserve what Ricoeur calls 'the space of contingency that once belonged to the past when it was present', and avoid 'the retrospective illusion of fatality' (1984: 188). A popular example of this 'space of contingency' is the film *Sliding Doors* (1998), in which two possible stories are played out for the protagonist according to whether or not she catches a train: missing the train means she returns home to find her boyfriend with another woman, thus changing the course of her life. In Vine's *A Dark Adapted Eye* the narrator does trace the 'retrospective' process of 'fatality', but this fails to produce the truth about the origin of the child who is the cause of conflict and tragedy within the plot.

Foucault suggests that 'continuous history is the indispensable correlative of the founding function of the subject' (quoted in Nicholls 1996: 12), and the ability to tell a coherent story of our life – obviously based on our memories of it – seems synonymous with our concept of identity. In *Remind Me Who I Am, Again* Linda Grant describes how her mother, suffering from dementia and memory-loss, was forced to improvise and continuously re-establish a precarious sense of identity. In the context of Freud's account of the case of Dora, Stephen Marcus suggests that we are forced to conclude 'that a coherent story is in some manner connected with mental health . . . On this reading, human life is, ideally, a connected and coherent story, with all the details in explanatory order and with everything . . . accounted for, in its proper causal or other sequence' (1976: 276–7). As Marcus and Steedman show, Freud imposed a logical sequence and interpretation on Dora's symptoms and memories which she resisted and which many have since disputed. However, the telling of a story in which past and present are brought into connection is clearly a necessary and therapeutic process for many, and seems to have been the compelling factor in Sylvia Fraser's reconstruction. This may take place through the psychotherapeutic encounter, or through writing, which, suggests Lyotard, 'is always of some restorative value to the soul because of its unpreparedness, which leaves it an infant' (1990: 33). In Morrison's *Beloved*, Sethe's story becomes bearable when she is able to share it with Paul D – 'to tell, to refine, and tell again' (1987: 99), although here it is the fact of being heard, returning to the same event again and again, that is therapeutic, rather than the construction of a logical story. Narratives such as *Beloved* and Perec's *W* recognise that some events cannot be fully reconstructed or integrated into a coherent story, that something in them will always resist recovery or 'passing on'; Lyotard even casts doubt upon the restorative powers of narrative or of writing, warning that 'there is no salvation, no health, and that time, even the time of work, does not heal anything' (1990: 34).

Lyotard argues for a form of narrative that preserves the disruptive chronological effect of *Nachträglichkeit*: according to this function, the 'second blow' (Emma's visit to the department store at the age of twelve) comes 'before' the first (her assault by a shopkeeper at the age of eight) because it is only on the occasion of the second event that the memory and affect of the first is experienced. Lyotard argues that most narrative is

the setting into diachrony of what takes place in a time that is not diachronic since what happened earlier is given at a later date (in analysis, in writing), and since what is later in the symptom (the second blow) occurs 'before' what happened earlier (the first blow) . . . Narrative organization is constitutive of diachronic time, and the time that it constitutes has the effect of 'neutralizing' an 'initital' violence, of representing a presence without representation, of staging the obscene, . . . and of staging a recollection that must be a reappropriation of the improper, achronological affect. (1990: 16)

Lyotard is here arguing against a kind of narrative which recuperates violence or atrocity into a chronological sequence which negates the disruptive effect of that violence on the nature of time as common sense imagines it. As Peter Nicholls shows, *Beloved* is a text which enacts this disruptive mode of time when the 'ghost' of the murdered baby erupts into the present in the form of a nineteen-year-old girl before the shock of the story of her murder has been narrated. Lyotard argues for a form of writing which 'does not forget that there is the forgotten', which, instead of 'saving the memory', tries to 'preserve the remainder, the unforgettable forgotten' (1990: 26); I argue later that Perec's *W* is a text that enacts this process.

METAPHORS OF MEMORY

It will already have become apparent that it is impossible to imagine or formulate memory and its operations without the use of metaphor. The dominant metaphors employed – often quite unconsciously – within a culture then come to seem part of 'common sense', and to determine the ways in which memory can be thought. The popular idea of memory as a video-recorder or storehouse of experiences is contradicted by recent work on the 'neural networks' which create and destroy memories in a continuous process. Two dominant and distinct ways of imagining memory, which have been implicit in the preceding discussion, are as a series of photographs or visual images, or as a form of language or narrative.

For some, these models are incompatible: according to Donald P. Spence, narrative always involves a kind of 'forgetting' since 'the complex visual scene represented by a dream or an early memory can probably never be completely realised by language' (1982: 28), and '[w]hat is sayable may pre-empt what is really remembered' (92). Claiming that early memories are visual, he says:

> Once expressed in a particular set of sentences, the memory itself has changed, and the patient will probably never again have quite the same vague, nonspecific and unspoiled impression. Thus the very act of talking about the past tends to crystallize it in specific, but somewhat arbitrary language, and thus serves, in turn, to distort the early memory. More precisely, the new description *becomes* the early memory. (280)

Primo Levi suggests that a frequently rehearsed or narrated memory takes on a form which distorts the 'original' memory and then solidifies: 'It is also true that a memory evoked too often, and expressed in the form of a story, tends to become fixed in a stereotype, in a form tested by experience, crystallised, perfect, adorned, which instals itself in the place of raw memory and grows at its expense' (1988: 11–12). In 'A Sketch of the Past' Virginia Woolf writes: 'I find that scene-making is my natural way of marking the past. Always a scene has arranged itself: representative; enduring' (1976: 142). She describes how 'a certain leafless bush; a skeleton tree in the dark of a summer night' embodies the memory of the death of her half-sister Stella: 'The leafless tree and Jack's agony – I always see them as if they were one and the same, when I think of that summer' (141). But she acknowledges the active role of the subject in the 'making' of these scenes, as the painting of Mrs Ramsay which brings together past and present is 'made' by Lily Briscoe in *To the Lighthouse*. For Woolf, a writer, and for most of us, visual memory can only be represented in language. Ian Hacking quotes a passage from Doris Lessing's *The Good Terrorist* which makes particularly clear this transition from visual scene to language in the case of her protagonist Alice:

[W]hen her mind started to dazzle and to puzzle, frantically trying to lay hold of something stable, then she always at once allowed herself . . . to slide back into her childhood, where she dwelt pleasurably on some scene or other that she had smoothed and polished and painted over and over again with fresh colour until it was like walking into a story that began, 'Once upon a time there was a little girl called Alice . . .' (1995: 454)

Here it is clear that even visual memory does not stay 'pure', that it can be painted and polished into a satisfying image which can then produce a story, turning visual memory into narrative. Contradicting the common assumption that early memory is visual or 'eidetic' and later memory somehow always already embodied in language, Hacking suggests that 'memory is in some way compatible with perception, as long as we do not demand images' (251) . . . 'our common conception of remembering, as encoded in grammar, is remembering of scenes, a remembering that is presented, often, by narrating, but is nevertheless a memory of scenes and episodes' (253). Hacking stresses this because he wants to resist the notion that whilst most memory works like a narrative, there are nevertheless especially intense, visual 'flashback' memories that give us immediate access to the truth about the past: all memory, he suggests, begins with scenes and feelings, which are then inevitably transcribed into language.

Walter Benjamin suggests in a passage quoted earlier that the 'images' which constitute the 'real treasure' of memory may only be recovered by a long process of 'digging': he also describes an early memory (of a school leave-taking ceremony) which is already linguistic or textual:

Here, as in several other places, I find in my memory rigidly fixed words, expressions, verses, that, like a malleable mass that has later cooled and hardened, preserve in me the imprint of a collision between a larger collective and myself. Just as a certain kind of significant dream survives awakening in the form of words when all the rest of the dream content has vanished, here isolated words have remained in place as marks of catastrophic encounters. (1979: 303)

Benjamin's metaphor evokes the notion of memory as an almost visual 'engram' or 'trace' physically inscribed on the brain: this idea has its roots in the philosophy of Aristotle and has been developed by Jacques Derrida.[7] In this memory words have almost become objects which continue to embody the affect of the memory; like Woolf's skeleton tree, Benjamin's words and expressions are objects 'endowed with our states of self during our life, mnemic objects that sometimes elicit prior states of being' (Bollas 1993: 33). But these linguistic components of memory are obviously more open to translation and interpretation than non-linguistic images: several of Georges Perec's early memories, analysed in Chapter 5, cluster around letters and words which seem to embody a truth about the past but which he later finds himself 'correcting'.

Edward Casey has described the *body* as a 'memorial container', holding memories of joy or pain which can be relived involuntarily (1987: 173). For Casey the body *is*, precisely, embodied memory, in that it is constitutive of our experience of living in time. Sylvia Fraser describes the process of remembering 'through the body' as she re-enacts the experience of her abuse; Linda Grant describes the case of a man with Alzheimer's who forgot where he parked his car but was able to find his way home by walking, his body remembering the route whilst his mind had forgotten his address (1998: 136). Combining the metaphors of inscription and bodily memory, James Young describes the desire of some Holocaust survivors for their writing to function as a pure 'trace' – and therefore proof – of their experience, without the inevitable mediation of language or the tropes of narrative. Just as their experience is inscribed on their memory, so their desire is to inscribe their experience upon the world. 'Their impossible task is . . . to show somehow that their words are material traces of experiences, that the current existence of their narrative is causal proof that its objects also existed in historical time' (1988: 23).

Woolf wonders whether 'things we have felt with great intensity have an existence independent of our minds' (1978: 77). The belief that sacred places hold the memory of the events enacted there is strong in Native American Indian and Australian Aboriginal cultures. In Morrison's *Beloved*, Sethe believes that traumatic events persist in the places where they occurred, that pictures remain to be 'bumped into': 'If a house burns down, it's gone, but the place – the picture of it – stays, and not just in my rememory, but out there, in the world . . . even if I don't think it, even if I die, the picture . . . is still out there. Right in the place where it happened' (1987: 36–7). She warns her daughter Denver never to go back to where the traumatic event happened, because 'it's going to be always there waiting for you'. Here the 'memory of place' threatens repetition and prevents a moving forward into the present: in Ann Michaels' *Fugitive Pieces* the idea that the 'earth remembers' is a consolation to the child Jakob, who has lost his parents in a Nazi massacre. I argue later that

Michaels' conflation of human memory of real, historical events and the 'memory' of migrating birds and magnetised rock is a mystification of human agency.

Whilst it seems that different *events* are remembered in different ways – some almost immediately represented in narrative, others remaining 'snapshots', others still remembered only 'in the body' – and that different people remember in different ways – some visually, some in language, very young children differently from adults – assumptions about the nature of memory shape not only notions of personal identity but also the relationship of culture to its past, and the nature and structure of the narratives that reconstruct the past.

The Memory of Culture and the Culture of Memory

Ned Lukacher has suggested that the dilemma of the postmodern world is 'to recognize that "mourning is in error" but to be nevertheless condemned to mourn; to be unable to remember the transcendental ground that would once again give meaning to human language and experience but also unable to stop mourning the putative loss of an originary memory and presence that doubtless never existed' (1986: 11). The 'originary memory' is the quest for the memory of a moment of origin, Crews' 'arduous journey' towards the 'hidden mystery' which would reveal the source of our pain: it is also the mythical memory of human origins, the Golden Age of the collective past and the time before loss and separation, described by Laura Mulvey as 'the pre-Oedipal as Golden Age' (1987: 11).[8] Even narratives of the worst kinds of abuse and suffering demonstrate the need to find such a memory 'before' the memory of pain: 'In my earliest memory', writes Sylvia Fraser, 'I am an infant lying on my father's bed, being sexually fondled but blissfully unaware of any deception. Then I was treated with tenderness. That was my Garden of Eden' (1987: 241). This evocation of early bliss and innocence demonstrates the way in which individual psychic and collective cultural myths mutually reinforce each other: they are so powerful because the pre-Oedipal is precisely what we *cannot* remember, but what we *need* to remember as what has been lost. 'Mourning is in error' because this 'transcendental ground' is at least in part a myth, constructed out of the needs of the present.

In his introduction to *Les Lieux de Mémoire*, the French historian Pierre Nora mourns the loss of 'real' memory, 'a memory entwined in the intimacy of a collective heritage' (1989: 8). 'True' memory,

according to the opposition he sets up, is spontaneous, organic,
passed down by unspoken traditions, and thus collective and 'objective': 'false' memory is individual and willed, and ends up in the
archive as a 'gigantic storehouse of a material stock of what it would
be impossible for us to remember, an unlimited repertoire of what
might need to be recalled' (13). *Lieux de mémoire* – archives, libraries,
tape and video recordings, computer files, monuments, even historical
fiction and drama – have become necessary because *milieux de
mémoire* – which consitute 'real' memory – have been lost. Edward
Casey also suggests that '[w]e may already have lost our anamnesic
souls to the collective amnesia embodied in machine memory'...
we may have 'lost touch with the "earth" of memory itself, its dense
loam' (1987: 3–4). Nora argues that although the relationship of
'traditional' cultures to their pasts may have involved the sense of a
break, this was 'not so much a separation experienced as radical
difference as it was a lapse experienced as a filiation to be restored'
(1989: 16).

What is being expressed here is not only a nostalgia for a particular version of the past, but also a nostalgia for a *certain kind of
memory*, one which would enable an unmediated access to the past
and the restoration of lost continuities. This discourse also implicitly
sets up an opposition between a notion of identity as natural, organic
and instinctive and one imagined as mechanical, forced and constructed. Nora is critical of the attempt to recover 'the ephemeral
spectacle of an unrecoverable identity' evident in postmodern culture's
attempts to reconstruct exact replicas of the past, but his argument
is dependent on the idea that earlier epochs *did* have unmediated
access to the past and an unfragmented identity. 'In the history-
memory of old, accurate perceptions of the past were characterized
by the assumption that the past could be retrieved. The past could
always be resuscitated by an effort of rememoration' (17–18). Nora
here makes clear that the myth of full and immediate recovery of the
past is as much a part of social ideology – even in a discourse which
professes to be innocent of ideology – as it is of certain therapeutic
practices.

Such yearnings are also informed by the individual psychic
'memory' of the 'pre-Oedipal as Golden Age'. Ecology and environ-
mental movements; 'New Age' practices such as rebirthing, shamanism
and 'natural' healing; the idealisation of 'traditional' cultures such as
that of the Native American Indians; all are manifestations of this
longing to return to some earlier state of innocence. Such desires
echo Marcuse's challenge to the Freudian theory of repression: in
Eros and Civilization he argues for a rehabilitation of recollection as

liberatory, as a means of access to the memory of the time of 'the dominion of the primal pleasure principle, the *temps perdu* which was the time of gratification and fulfillment' which civilisation teaches us to forget (1969: 185–6). Politically, such longings can be harnessed for liberatory but also for deeply conservative ends: Lewis Lapham has argued for a similarity between 1960s liberation movements and the American New Right, one of the main points of connection being 'romantic arcadianism' (1995: 29), and a return to the community of land and *Volk* was one of the deepest appeals of Nazi ideology.

Lis Møller suggests that 'making the most remote past coefficient to our most intimate depth is a way of refusing loss and separation' (1991: 44): this refusal locates itself in what Mary Jacobus has described and deconstructed as a myth which 'reinterpret[s] the pre-history of the gendered subject in the light of a theory of origins which we are in the habit of calling mother' (1987: 123). The discourse of Casey's and Nora's 'true' memory is (apparently unconsciously) feminine: the 'earth' or 'dense loam' of memory, 'organic', 'bodily', 'instinctive', 'spontaneous', 'non-verbal'; all these terms line up on the feminine side of an undeconstructed opposition. As such, they clearly suggest that it is in the imaginary plenitude of the pre-Oedipal that the socio-political longing for a lost 'unity' or 'community' locates itself. Teresa Brennan locates 'originary memory' even further back: she postulates a 'fleshly memory' of 'inter-uterine communication', of a time when there was no delay between need and satisfaction, as the basis of language: 'the experience of call and answer exists in utero in bodily codes' (1992: 171–2). 'True' memory is here imagined as memory of the body of the mother: in 'The Uncanny' Freud claimed that '[w]henever a man dreams of a place or country and says to himself, while he is still dreaming, "this place is familiar to me, I've been here before", we may interpret the place as being his mother's genitals or her body' (1919: 368). The possibility of 'remembering' the experience of 'inter-uterine communication' is the most extreme version of the belief that memory confirms or produces identity; but the feminist reclamation of the mother's body as the site of plenitude and dyadic union runs the risk of assuming 'postures of infantile dependence in creation myths that both idealize and blame her' (Moglen 1993: 28). As Jacobus points out: 'Division engenders desire', and 'desire engenders a retroactive fiction of unmediated mother-daughter relations whose sign is nostalgia'. She goes on to argue that '[t]here never was a prior time, or an unmediated relation for the subject (whether masculine or feminine) except as the oedipal defined it retroactively. The mother is always/already structured as division by the oedipal; no violent separation can be envisaged, except with an aura of pathos, because separation is inscribed from the start' (1987: 135). Here Jacobus employs the notion of retroaction or 'afterwardsness' in a critique of the nostalgic fiction of pre-Oedipal union. 'Our relation to the past is', as Stuart Hall puts it, 'like the child's relation to the mother, . . . always already "after the break"' (1990: 226).

One way out of the trap of nostalgia based on the imaginary identification of the pre-Oedipal is to argue for a model of memory in terms of intersubjectivity, the mutual recognition of self and other which Jessica Benjamin (1988) argues characterises the mother–infant relation from the start. Casey suggests that '[m]emories are formed from the first *in the image of* the other, primarily the caretaking parent; also *in view of* the other, though not just the literal view. It is a matter of keeping the other in mind' (1987: 244) Although both stress the primacy of the parent/beloved object, what they describe is the process of negotiating *separation* as well as reciprocity. Benjamin argues against the opposition, both in theory and practice, between the 'mother of attachment' and the 'father of separation', suggesting rather that the mother–child relation is, precisely, one of negotiating attachment *and* separation, of learning to recognise the other *as* other. The very word 'identity' suggests the dialectic between identification, modelling oneself *on* the other, and the establishment of the self as distinct, individual, different *from* the other. If the Oedipus complex is imagined as a journey, Laura Mulvey suggests that the doubts and contradictions it throws up are 'stabilized around a resolution in which the temporal process is split into a spatial opposition, structured around the mother/father (a mythic condensation with mother as past and father as future, that suppresses a possible dialectical relationship between the two)' (1987: 9). The desire for a return to the imaginary oceanic unity of the pre-Oedipal is played out and finally shown for the danger it is in Morrison's *Beloved*, where Sethe and Beloved merge their separate identities in a process of mutual identification to the point where Sethe is nearly destroyed. The memory of her (absent) father enables Denver to stop over the threshold of the house which functions as the container of the family's memories, both painful and pleasurable, and seek for help and contact in the outside world. *Beloved* thus enacts the restorative function of narrative in the parallel movements of the re-enactment of the lost mother–infant relation and the trauma of the 'forgotten' history of the Middle Passage; it finally recognises that 'rememory' cannot be the literal repetition that traps us in the past, but a 'retranslation' that allows a movement forward and the recognition of the

past as past. These are recognitions embodied by the narrative structures and provisionality of the two autobiographical texts I discuss in
the next chapter, Carolyn Steedman's *Landscape for a Good Woman*
and Ronald Fraser's *In Search of a Past*. In these texts the complex
identifications between parents and children are also negotiated, and
the self reconstructed in a process of revising and reinterpreting the
past.

Notes

1. My thinking on this question was clarified by Lis Møller's penetrating
   study, *The Freudian Reading: Analytical and Fictional Constructions* (1991).
2. Petar Ramadanovic is here summarising the ideas of Cathy Caruth in his
   review of her *Unclaimed Experience: Trauma, Narrative and History*
   (1996): 'When *"To Die in Freedom"* is Written in English', *diacritics* 28:4
   (1999): 54–67 (55).
3. Grant cites the work of Steven Rose: see his *The Making of Memory: From
   Molecules to Mind* (1993).
4. See Abraham and Torok (1994), *The Shell and the Kernel*, vol. 1, ed.
   Nicholas T. Rand, 158–60.
5. Jean-François Lyotard, *Heidegger and "the jews"*, trans. Andreas Michel and
   Mark Roberts (1988: 11–17). Peter Nicholls (1996) also discusses this
   example in his essay in *Sue Vice, Psychoanalytic Criticism: A Reader*.
   Linda Ruth Williams has a full and helpful discussion of *Nachträglichkeit*
   in Freud's 'Wolf Man' case history in *Critical Desire: Psychoanalysis and
   the Literary Subject* (1995: 125–36). She also employs the concept as a tool
   for the analysis of a wide range of narratives.
6. See Jeffrey Masson, *Freud: The Assault on Truth* (1984) and Frederick
   Crews, *The Memory Wars: Freud's Legacy in Dispute* (1995).
7. See David Farrell Krell, *Of Memory, Reminiscence and Writing: On the
   Verge* (1990) and Jacques Derrida, 'Freud and the Scene of Writing' (1978).
8. The term 'pre-Oedipal' 'may refer to (a) the period of psycho-sexual *development* preceding the Oedipus complex in which the attachment to the
   mother is predominant, or (b) an unconscious psycho-sexual *structure*, in
   which the attachment to and fantasies about the mother are predominant'
   (Elizabeth Wright (ed.), *Feminism and Psychoanalysis: A Critical Dictionary*
   (1992: 345)).

2

Present Imperfect Translation: Ronald Fraser's *In Search of a Past* and Carolyn Steedman's *Landscape for a Good Woman*

INTRODUCTION

Ronald Fraser and Carolyn Steedman map out in their autobiographical texts identities that are in large part constituted by memories of class exclusion and difference: identities that are, however, shown to be tentative, provisional, even fragmentary, based as they are on memories of events that can never be recovered in their 'pure' state, 'as they really happened'. In these texts, and the identities that they construct, the past is not waiting to be rediscovered whole, uncontaminated by the interests of the present: both Fraser and Steedman acknowledge and demonstrate that memory of the past is continuously modified by the experiences of the present and the 'self' who is doing the remembering. Fraser's past is only one of many – individual, not typical or collective – but also one version of his own past, 'a past', not 'the past'; Steedman's title makes explicit the fact that she is constructing a 'landscape', not revisiting the past as 'another country' still to be found, unaltered by the passing of time. 'Memory alone cannot resurrect past time, because it is memory itself that shapes it, long after historical time has passed' (1986: 29).

As Laplanche and Pontalis have suggested in their explanation of the Freudian concept of *Nachträglichkeit*, 'experiences, impressions and memory-traces may be revised at a later date to fit in with fresh circumstances or to fit in with a new stage of development. They may in that event be endowed not only with a new meaning but also with psychical effectiveness' (1973: 111). This is exactly the process we see in operation in the memory-work of Fraser and Steedman, both within and outside the psychoanalytic encounter. Both writers testify to what Laplanche describes as the 'undoing' of an 'existing . . . translation' of the past in order to 'attempt a better translation of this past, a more comprehensive translation, with renewed possibilities' (1992: 176). 'The present imperfect translation . . . ceaselessly . . . pushes for renewed translation': we are witness to 'the dynamic of a self-presencing that is always, and of necessity, incomplete' (Benjamin 1992: 146). Although both writers create a vivid sense of the children they once were and the lives they led, the reader is aware of a gap, or absence, at the heart of each text, as neither writer conveys much of an impression of his or her present life or experience outside of the project in which each is engaged, the painful and provisional reconstruction of the pasts that made them what they are – what they now 'are' is largely left out of the account. Olivia Harris suggests that *In Search of a Past* is in part 'an investigation of its own evasiveness' in its foregrounding of the writer's problem in finding an 'I' with which to speak or write (*History Workshop Journal* 20, 1985: 178), and in his epigraph Fraser quotes Winnicott on the subject's 'urgent need to communicate and the still more urgent need not to be found'. His autobiography, like Perec's *W or The Memory of Childhood*, enacts a double process of revelation and concealment.

Both writers also reinterpret their personal histories in the context of other histories, other lives, as indicated by their subtitles. Fraser's initial project was an oral history of the period of his own childhood from the point of view of the servants who worked for his family: his subtitle, *The Manor House, Amnersfield, 1933–1945*, seems to claim this history as its chief or only subject.[1] Steedman says: 'Before I could write the account found in *Landscape for a Good Woman*, I had to find a history, or rather, I had to find the very stuff of historical practice: a document, a text, some trace of the past, to work on' (1992: 41).[2] She finds this in Kathleen Woodward's *Jipping Steeet*, 'ostensibly a working-class autobiography', and reinterprets her own life story, and reflects upon possible ways of telling it, through the stories of others, including that of her mother, the other 'life' referred to in her subtitle, *A Story of Two Lives*.

Both writers thus attempt to articulate or negotiate the relationship between individual and collective histories, the psyche and the social. Fraser's motives for the series of interviews he conducted in 1967–8 with the former servants of his childhood home already demonstrate the necessary conjunction of the two: he tells his psychoanalyst at their first meeting that he 'set out . . . to discover how the others had lived in the past' because he could not 'find the myth or lie that brings the past into focus' (1984: 6). As such, his recourse to the 'safe' discipline of social history was both an avoidance of the personal – an avoidance he was already quite self-consciously aware of by the time he began analysis – and a recognition that the two are inseparable. He indicates this in an interview with *History Workshop Journal* in 1985. Asked if he was aware of working from a 'script' or a particular set of narrative conventions, he replied:

Class divisions are without doubt what I wanted to explore with the people who had worked at the Manor and who, I felt, could tell me most about them. But of course, I had also lived these experiences intimately as a child. If I had a 'script', I used to think, it was one that came to me not so much from outside but one that I had elaborated from this experience. A myth. So much so, that the underlying purpose of setting out to interview the servants was to destroy this myth once and for all. Feelings of hollowness, passivity, isolation, that the world was made by others, not me . . . would be revealed for what they were: self justificatory fantasies which, in the course of being revealed would, I hoped, be sloughed off like an old skin . . . What happened was the opposite: their testimonies seemed to confirm the myth. (180)

His text is an exploration and an enactment of the interplay between social structures and the structures of the psyche, of the construction and deconstruction of the myths of the self. It also enacts the processes of memory in that much of the text consists of rereadings (and rewritings) – of interviews with the servants and notes made by Fraser on his psychoanalytic sessions – which are themselves interpretations or readings of the past.

Carolyn Steedman sets out more consciously to show how '[t]he past is re-used through the agency of social information, and that interpretation of it can only be made with what people know of a social world and their place within it' (1986: 5). *Landscape for a Good Woman* demonstrates Maurice Halbwachs' notion of remembering as 'a process of reconstruction whereby memories are resituated in the wider context from which their significance may in part derive . . . a remembered incident, image or impression will often disclose an interlocking network of experiences, rooted in particular places and social groups' (quoted in Sheringham 1993: 74). Her text is also a critique of the dominant narratives of working-class autobiography and sociology and of the 'master-narrative' of psychoanalysis, although she acknowledges and uses psychoanalysis as a way of allowing 'the writer to enter the present into the past, allow[ing] the dream, the wish or the fantasy of the past to shape current time' (Steedman 1986: 20–1).

The structure of both texts suggests the temporal process of

Nachträglichkeit in the more generalised sense of the term as a process of revision and retranslation of earlier events in the light of later knowledge, of 'what wasn't known then'. As Andrew Benjamin suggests, because '[m]eaning depends upon narrative time' it is possible to theorise narrative itself as dependent upon, or in itself constituting, the temporal structure of *Nachträglichkeit* as the 'ternary structure of time articulating repetition' (1992: 148–9). Benjamin suggests the 'possibility that *Nachträglichkeit* could harbour – harbour by providing – the temporality of interpretation itself' (149). The 'temporality of interpretation' in autobiography (at least the kind of autobiography which does not efface the remembering and writing subject) is evident within its very structure, which involves three 'stages': (1) the event; (2) the memory of the event; (3) the writing of the (memory of the) event. Both texts under discussion here demonstrate an awareness of the psychic and structural gaps between these three stages, and the fact that they do not necessarily occur in this order (the writing of the memory of one event may prompt the memory of another, for example). The danger for the interpreting reader is the lure or illusion that through a reading of (2) and (3) we can reach the elusive real, the event itself – the event that offers itself unproblematically in conventional autobiography. As Laura Marcus writes of André Gorz's autobiography *The Traitor*, which, Fraser acknowledges, 'started me on this trail (1984: 9), 'there is no sense of a secure standpoint from which the past can be recounted as something already known and complete . . . the beginning, as a structure determining the shape of a life, is given a location, only to be undone as the analysis proceeds and pushed further and further back into the past, to the point where its real existence may even become unsustainable' (Marcus 1994: 276). The point of origin of the past and of the self is always in retreat of our attempts to locate it.

TERNARY TEMPORAL STRUCTURE

As suggested above, Fraser's autobiography demonstrates not just the threefold structure of *Nachträglichkeit* but a continuous, ongoing and necessarily incomplete process of translation and retranslation. To clarify this, I shall number the stages of the temporal process, the order of events, which the book later 'emplots' in a somewhat different sequence:

1. The events of Fraser's childhood between 1933 and 1945, when he lived with his parents, his brother Colin, his nanny Ilse and other servants in the Manor House, Amnersfield, in Berkshire.

2. The interviews which Fraser conducted and recorded between 1967 and 1969 with the servants who worked at Amnersfield during his childhood. He keeps an 'interview diary' and a secretary transcribes the tapes.
3. His rereadings of the transcripts during the summer of 1979, before he begins his psychoanalysis with 'P.'
4. His analysis with P., which begins in September 1979. The last session used in the book is dated May 1983, but the analysis is presumably ongoing. He makes notes after each session. In April 1983 he visits his brother in Rome and records his conversations with him; he also takes his father to a nursing home where he dies.
5. The writing of the book, which involves another rereading of all the material collected in the interviews and the analysis: it is published in 1984.[3]

All the subsequent stages of the autobiographical project are attempts to remember, reconstruct, deconstruct and reinterpret the events of the first, Fraser's childhood at Amnersfield. In stage 4, he begins his analysis with P. by bringing to the first session his interpretation of 2, his interviews with the servants, in the hope that they will provide direct access to, and understanding of, the events of 1. He found himself unable the write the book he had originally been planning (an earlier version of stage 5) because the interviews with the servants functioned neither as an adequate *avoidance* of the personal, nor as an *exorcism* of the past which he was thus hoping to dispose of. On the one hand, Fraser felt that he lacked a *myth* by which to confer meaning on the past – 'I couldn't reach the fundamental understanding which would give meaning to it' (6) – on the other, the interviews only served to reinforce what he had hoped *was* a myth, that of his isolation, hollowness and passivity. Sequentially, the book is organised into three sections, further subdivided into seven, entitled 'We', 'They', 'She/He/She', 'You', 'We', 'Us' and 'I': this suggests a move from the collective to the individual, from the social microcosm of Amnersfield to the psychic structure of the family, from the objectification of others ('They', the servants) and the self ('You', the self as seen by others) to the subjectivity of the 'I'. This should not, however, be taken as indication of a straightforward movement towards the centre, to the heart of the matter or of the subject: '[y]ou want to be the subject of your history instead of the object you felt yourself to be', suggests P. in their last reported session, and Fraser replies: 'The subject, yes, – but also the object' (187), hoping for a synthesis of the two. The structure and mode of narration of the text, I suggest, preserves or presents the subject as still the *object* of his own investigation.

Although the temporal structure of the text and its composition can be clarified by the schema I have outlined above, what is also evaded in the text as we have it is a clear indication of how the writer has selected and ordered his material. We see it 'in the making' in one sense – the interviews, his conversations with P. and his brother about the past – but we do not know how much selection and reorganisation went into the presentation of the interview transcripts and the accounts of the psychoanalytic sessions, how much (and *when*) they were retranslated in the light of later knowledge for the purposes of representation in the book. One example will make this process of elision clear: on pages 25 to 30 Fraser transcribes and comments on an interview with Bert, the gardener at Amnersfield. What we read is a partial transcript of a transcript. The section begins: 'In their fading folders the transcripts continue for three more interviews'. Fraser reconstructs the memory of the visit to Bert, describing the atmosphere of the living room and summarising some of their conversation in a kind of free indirect discourse: 'They had received your letter, hadn't they? Yes, well, as you had tried to explain, it would be a sort of record.' This modulates into Bert's direct speech to his wife: 'Come on, mother, say a word', which Fraser then repeats in italics, indicating direct transcription of the original transcript made by his secretary: '*Come on, mother, say a word* . . . Faithfully transcribed, evidence presumably of your failure to erase them, the words stand meaninglessly at the head of the page. Small matter. Two hundred dusty pages of Bert, preserved in red folders, survive. In the last a series of 8×5 inch cards, each under a different heading, forms an index of his experiences scattered through the transcripts. For once your need for order, clarity, served a useful purpose' (27). Here we are made aware of the ways in which the interviews have already (long before the analysis) been reworked – sorted into folders and organised into cards, commented upon in the 'interview diary'. What is not clear is when the reconstruction as we have it – the words on the page of this book – took place: when he reread the interviews during the summer before his analysis started, or after the analysis, when he was actually writing the book. This may seem an unnecessarily fine point, but it indicates one of the central questions raised by the autobiographical project, that of the position of the speaking (or writing) subject. The elision of the speaking subject and the subject being spoken of further complicates – perhaps inevitably, as we can never be fully present to ourselves – the relation between present and past. Fraser (or Steedman, or Perec, or Sylvia Fraser) could perhaps have provided a meta-narrative of how they selected and constructed their material in order to create the texts we read (and all of these writers do provide some commentary on this process), but this could lead to an infinite regression of meta-texts each commenting on the construction of the one before it, holding out the illusion of direct access to the subject – and to the truth about the past – which always slips away before our eyes.

What Fraser takes to the interviews and his initial psychoanalytic sessions is an explanation of his feeling of hollowness and passivity largely in terms of class: in his second session with P. he says: 'I've been through all the evidence' (the interviews) 'and it confirms what I told you when I first came last month. The house was divided and so was I' (90). His questions to the servants reveal that he was attempting to force on to his subjects and material a construction which would foster the 'myth' of a split founded on class divisions. He asks Carver, the groom, 'Did it never strike you that in a year you didn't earn the price of one of their horses?' (44) but fails to get the right response, as is also the case when he tries to force Bert, the gardener, 'into a corner of total consistency' on his attitude to the gentry. His commentary on these questions makes it clear that he was aware of his attempt to force this pattern on to his material, but not (as indicated above) exactly when this awareness arose. His notes on his second session with P. begin: 'Today I went straight to the heart of the matter: on the one hand, objectively a member of a privileged class I was on the other, unable subjectively to fill the role into which I was born. This split, I said, was foreshadowed in my parents' (91), his father being a member of the English gentry and his mother a younger American. Even as he is speaking he realises that P. feels that all this is somehow irrelevant, or at least too 'theoretical', and the statement could (depending on how long after the session it was written) be read as ironic in the light of Fraser's later understanding of his childhood conflicts. P. helps Fraser to deconstruct (at least in part) this construction and work towards one which is more complete, less defensive, and which necessitates a particular kind of recovery of certain early childhood experiences. Fraser is led towards a re-enactment of a much earlier, more psychic split between his love and hatred for his two 'mothers': his real mother Janey and his nanny Ilse. In these re-enactments within the analytic session we are vividly aware of the remembering subject in the 'present' moment, as we are not in the more distanced, reported sections of the text.

Before I move in closer to Fraser's text to analyse these specific, intensely recalled memories, I want to compare the structural *Nachträglichkeit* or afterwardsness of *In Search of a Past* with that of Steedman's *Landscape for a Good Woman*, which exemplifies its threefold temporal structure in a rather different way. She writes of how 'time catches together what we know and do not know' (1986: 141), and one of her epigraphs is a reflection of John Berger's: 'The present tense of the verb *to be* refers only to the present: but nevertheless with the first person singular in front of it, it absorbs the past which is inseparable from it.' This is another way of indicating the elusive nature of the position of the speaking subject which I suggested earlier: Steedman's narrative foregrounds the way in which the 'I' of the present has been constructed out of, but also continues to rewrite, the 'I' of the past.

One of the most obvious structural features of Steedman's text is the fact that she is telling two life stories, her own and her mother's, which modify and reinterpret each other. Steedman interprets her own sense of difference and exclusion partly in terms of her reading of her mother's life, and shows 'the way in which my mother reasserted, reversed and restructured her own within mine' (8). Her book is about 'how people use the past to tell the stories of their life' (8): it is 'about interpretations, about the places where we rework what has already happened to give current events meaning' (5). She makes frequent use of a term which suggests a process parallel and complementary to that of *Nachträglichkeit*, 'brought forward'. Her dream of a woman wearing a New Look dress – a central memory which will be discussed more fully later – exists as 'an area of feeling ' which is '*brought forward* again and again to shape responses to quite different events' (my italics). She is also aware that the meaning of the dream (and possibly also the details of what is 'remembered', although she does not make this explicit) has developed over time, 'taking on meaning later, from different circumstances' (28). In her reworking of the explanatory 'myth' of psychoanalysis, she is always concerned to situate its processes firmly in the social particularity of the subject: hence '[b]oth my mother and my sister *brought forward* an earlier sense of psychological loss and abandonment – the first exclusion – and interpreted it, still as young children, in the light of social information and exclusion' (118). This is clearly the process Steedman herself is engaged in in her book, in which the Oedipal is rethought in terms of class. As has been suggested, the movement of Fraser's text is the reverse of this process, by which the subject is forced to partly retranslate his earlier class-based constructions in terms of the relation of mother and infant.

Landscape is a complex mixture of personal memory, reconstructions of other lives, principally those of Steedman's parents, theoretical reflection and sociological and psychoanalytic critique. The titles of the main sections – 'Stories', 'Exiles' and 'Interpretations' – suggest that Steedman is engaged in the project of situating and interpreting her own life in the context of other stories, other lives, and other readings; her understanding of her own and her mother's lives has been shaped by the 'interpretative devices' – fairytales, other working-class autobiographies, psychoanalytic case histories – which she explores, reworks and sometimes rejects because they 'don't quite work', however powerful their effect within a culture. Her reconstructions of her own life and those of her parents are also the means by which she critiques dominant cultural myths, so that her story also becomes an 'interpretative device'. Although the third subtitle, 'Interpretations', suggests that interpretation is an activity which occurs after the event (and this section is more theoretical than the others), the first two, 'Stories' and 'Exiles', suggest that the raw material of experience and memory are always already constructed into narratives – 'the compulsions of narrative are almost irresistible' (144) – or interpreted within a cultural matrix. On the first page of 'Stories' she writes: 'We all return to memories and dreams, . . . again and again; the story we tell of our own life is shaped around them. But the point doesn't lie there, back in the lost time at which they happened; the only point lies in interpretation' (5). Similarly, Fraser struggles towards an acceptance of P.'s view that '[w]hat actually happened is less important than what is felt to have happened' (95). But the insistence of certain early memories – of the dream of a woman in a New Look dress, an encounter between her father and a gamekeeper in a bluebell wood, a 'seduction scene' between her father and mother in the basement of their south London house – do suggest the formative and residual power of the event. Steedman would not have become the woman she is without these early experiences, which are presented as if they have remained almost unchanged over time, although their interpretation has developed in the light of later knowledge and experience. Where Fraser re-presents the process of the recovery of early memories within the psychoanalytic encounter – the 'dark joy of the place of finding' occuring towards the end of his 'search' for the 'past' – Steedman uses the model of the psychoanalytic case history in the section 'Exiles' in a more distanced and considered way. The text does not reconstruct the actual moments of remembering: it is as if the subject has always known or remembered these dreams or scenes. This is in spite of the fact that, commenting on the little girls' story she edited in *The Tidy House*, she writes: 'Unknowingly at that time, I interpreted their text in the light of the seduction scene in the cellar . . . that I had not yet recalled to mind' (80). Given that she was three at this time, and that this sexual scene later accumulated so much meaning, the absence of the remembering moment is striking. If early memories can be recovered in later life, the circumstances and context of their recovery must constitute part of their meaning for the subject.

IN SEARCH OF A PAST:
'THE DARK JOY OF THE PLACE OF FINDING'

Walter Benjamin suggests that '[i]t is to cheat oneself of the richest prize to preserve as a record merely the inventory of one's discoveries, and not the dark joy of the place of finding itself' – the moments of remembering which Fraser reconstructs. Using the archaeological metaphor for the process of memory, Benjamin contrasts the 'real treasure hidden within the earth' with 'the prosaic rooms of our later understanding' (1979: 314). In his commentary on Benjamin's auto-biographical fragment Michael Sheringham suggests that 'it is often the memory just discovered or never previously examined which seems to disclose being' (1993: 308). This claim, and Fraser's recovery of early traumatic memory, does of course assume a particular model of memory already outlined in the first chapter – that early experience can be 'recorded' within the psyche, repressed or forgotten and then recovered in its pure or original form – one which has gathered con-troversy around it in the debate over 'false' or 'recovered' memory. I discuss this controversy more fully in my reading of Sylvia Fraser's *My Father's House* in the next chapter. Primo Levi describes how a 'memory evoked too often ... tends to become fixed in a stereo-type ... crystallised, perfected, adorned, which installs itself in the place of the raw memory' (1988: 11–12). Benjamin compares the school he attended as a child which he still passes by every day, and which has ceased through over-familiarity to provide any access to his childhood self, to a newly observed detail of the moulding on the building which does open the way to a new set of associations. In Fraser's text we are witness to both these discourses of memory: those which read like often-recalled and familiar facts or stories which have ceased to bear meaning or which have crystallised into the 'myth' of a split based on class divisions, and the newly 'resurgent' memories where new meanings may be found or 'retranslated'. 'This dark joy of the place of finding' suggests exactly the process under-gone by Fraser during his analysis when two childhood memories resurface in such a way that they are re-experienced within the body of the remembering subject.

These recovered – or reconstructed – memories involve the com-plex relations between the child Ronnie, his mother and his nanny

Ilse, and are prepared for by means of a reconstruction of these relationships within the section devoted to the interviews with the
servants. From these we learn that as a son in an upper-class family
between the wars Ronnie had only intermittent contact with his
parents, a nanny caring for his daily needs. His mother Janey was an
American, thirteen years younger than her husband and only twenty-
one when Ronnie was born: the former servants recall her as apparently 'happy and gay... but there was a remoteness, a distance about
her that I never could bridge' (Ilse, 63); 'Even at the Manor I don't
remember your mother kissing you, there was no physical contact...
In the end I felt she was as much a stranger when she left as when
she arrived' (Mrs Carver, 66). In his analysis, Fraser tells P. that Janey
once said to him: 'I wish we could be more like dogs and children
didn't need us for more than a few months' (92). Ilse also reminds
him of his 'early lack of relationship' with his father, who seemed to
be training him to become a 'little soldier' (72). At this stage, before
and in the early stages of his analysis, Fraser's understanding of these
experiences (and of the fact that some may have been repressed) is
distanced, theoretical: reflecting on what Ilse has been telling him, he
writes, referring to himself in the second person:

Well, all children go through things of that sort, you commented, things
which left scars barely visible to others but which the child never forgot.
More interesting were the things you couldn't remember, had perhaps
repressed, the invisible scars as it were. Blankness – the blankness between
the distance and the closeness of your mother – revealed more important,
forgotten scars, possibly. Because, on the one hand she was like a distant
goddess who could work miracles while, on the other, she was paradoxically
powerless to change those steps that lay, like granite, before you on the
ascent to adulthood. (73)

Some interesting distinctions are made here: between the things
which the child 'never forgot', which 'all children go through', here
associated with his father, and those which he had 'perhaps
repressed', associated with his mother, as well as the child's split
experience of the mother as good and bad, loving and distant.
Perhaps over-subtly, Fraser locates the 'blankness' of memory and
within the self in the gap between the mother's closeness and distance: in the event, the lost memory and the source of his sense of
self-division turns out to be something rather more obvious.
   The split between the child's two 'mothers' is heightened by the
fact that Ilse was German, so that an early psychic split is also echoed
in the realm of the social, and becomes a rupture on the outbreak of

war. Perhaps rather stereotypically, Ilse comes over in her own account and in Fraser's memories as a strict but loving mother-figure who was primarily concerned with keeping her charges clean and toilet-training them. The final extract from the interview transcripts which is used in the section entitled 'You' is Ilse's reply to a question of Fraser's about whether her previous experience of working in an orphanage had proved useful. Having already described the infant Ronnie as a 'quiet, uncomplaining baby', she replies:

In feeding and cleanliness, yes. Perhaps I concentrated more on toilet training than is normal. When you were four months old I had you sitting on a pot in a small chair, tied with a nappy, so that I could clean the room while I talked to you. Later, I tied you on your pot to the end of your bed until you produced . . . I used to tie you to a laundry pole or a tree in the garden if I had something to do close by. It was my way of training you. Many people think it deprives a child of its freedom and they just let it run around. But I don't think it hurts, do you? (85)

Fraser's only comment (he presumably has no independent memory of the experience at this stage) is the ironically defensive and egalitarian 'I wouldn't claim any privilege that an orphan wasn't entitled to.' Ilse's account shocks the reader accustomed to more enlightened child-rearing practices and Fraser's lack of response or affect is so striking that we almost expect a return to this scene. Early on in the analysis P. asks about Ilse, and having described her 'super-cleanliness' and pot-training, Fraser says: 'Despite all that I was happy with her, she gave me a comfort and a security I've never forgotten. When I went to interview her, after a time I fell into a sort of hypnotic trance, like a child finding comfort in her mother's voice . . . As I said it, I realised that I simultaneously longed for and hated the hypnotic passivity I'd recalled' (94). This passivity and powerlessness is reawakened again within the analytic session where the originary experience is remembered – or reconstructed? – for the first time as a result of the process of free association.

Behind closed lids, an unformulated image haunts me; the image of a bundle, curved or bowed, with something or someone next to it on the left. A person: Ilse? is the bundle me, bowed? *Doblegado*. Everything is totally motionless, almost lifeless. Are the indentations in the blanket cords hidden by the material? Ilse watching a silent bundle, intentness mingled with pride in her eyes. Don't move: her pride is my stillness, silence . . . Don't move and everything will be all right. If I retreat into myself, lie absolutely still, she will go away . . . She will go and I'll stay. And when she goes I can move.

'Where to?' P asks, and Fraser replies:

'To my mother . . . I can't go while Ilse is there. She says, "you musn't bother mummy now. Mummy is busy . . . mummy is getting ready to go out". I don't know if it really happened, but it feels like it' . . . Out of the darkness surges a need to hold my mother; a bond, the warmth of an embrace. Since her death I have hardly thought of her. 'I musn't tell Ilse I love my mother for fear I may lose her, Ilse . . . ' In the silence I feel, with a weight I can hardly describe, Ilse's silent, stubborn disapproval of something – clothes, a toy – my mother has bought. Rock-like, immutable, sure of herself, Ilse stands there in silent disapproval. I want my mother, yet I fear to side with her lest I anger Ilse. (96)

This reconstruction re-enacts the child's experience of the split caused by his allegiance to two mothers and the ambivalence within both relationships, and also that between 'wanting, needing to be bound' and '[n]eeding, wanting to be free' (98). As Fraser and P. discuss the scene, the image changes:

A tightness like a band of iron encloses my head and with it the bundle image returns – but now without the stillness. Ilse seems to have gone. I can move, one of the cords is undone; but instead of moving I am overwhelmed with panic. Ilse will think I've undone the bond deliberately. I am even less able to move than when tied. (98)

His frustration and anger at this double-bind give way to the image of a prisoner paralysed by indecision when his cell door is opened, and the understanding that 'I couldn't leave her' (Ilse) 'because I was frightened that my mother wouldn't be there to replace her . . . The role of prisoner was more profitable than the alternative' (99).

Before the scene develops into its second stage, when Fraser feels the cords come undone but is still unable to move, P. suggests that it is 'a screen memory which can suggest many things'. Fraser responds: 'It's not a memory at all. I didn't know about it until I interviewed Ilse' (98). Here he seems to be using 'memory' in the very limited sense of an event which has always, or already, been remembered: what takes place in this session is a different kind of 'memory', Bollas' 'unthought known' which has persisted as a 'structure of feeling' with no clear point of origin. Fraser's comment – 'I don't know if it really happened, but it feels like it' – raises the question of the truth-status or veridicality of what might be defined as memory, or alternatively as fantasy which nevertheless embodies the affect of cumulative experience which has persisted in the unconscious. In his *HWJ* interview Fraser (now aware of the psychoanalytic position that the truth of the event is less important than what is felt to have happened) explains: 'I feel also that an unnecessary dichotomy is sometimes created between the event and the fantasy. It's not usually the event itself – unless, of course, it's traumatic – that's significant, but the meaning we give to it' (1985: 184). Fraser seems to imply that a 'traumatic' event is one of a separate and special kind which is easily recognised as such, and also that the events of his childhood were not traumatic.[4] Lyotard, Cathy Caruth, Dori Laub and others have also suggested that the event – not registered by the infant who experiences it – becomes traumatic, or is constituted as such, when it is re-experienced or reawoken some time later: that trauma is constituted by its belatedness. Objectively described, Fraser's early experiences (verified by Ilse herself and by others) do seem the material of possible trauma and it is in the analysis that their full effect is registered as if for the first time. What he seems to be reliving or reconstructing in the analytic session is not one discrete memory or experience of being tied to the pot (he experiences himself as lying down in this scene) but a composite 'event' which embodies or makes concrete the entirety of his infantile feelings of passivity, ambivalence and divided loyalties. The ternary temporal structure of *Nachträglichkeit* is evident in terms of the 'original' event, the child being tied to the pot; the reminder of this in the interview with Ilse, where the affect is absent; and the reconstruction and re-experiencing of the event within the analysis. It is this reconstruction that enables Fraser to realise fully and for the first time what it really meant to have two mothers. When he leaves P.'s room on this occasion, 'time suddenly reassembles as present. I am a man, nearly fifty, where a minute ago I was a child' (99).

The composite and partly imaginary nature of this scene may be what P. is referring to when he calls it a 'screen-memory': a screen-memory as described by Freud is usually vivid but trivial and apparently meaningless, screening the memory of another more disturbing, traumatic or sexual event.[5] The memories embodied in this scene seem significant enough not to be the screen for anything else, but Fraser's meeting with his brother and their recall of the war years at Amnersfield do stimulate the memory of another scene with which the first memory is closely linked. The reconstruction and interpretation of this second memory offer the possibility of a further retranslation of the first. Fraser's talks with Colin extend and confirm his memory of his mother as 'at once elusive and inescapable', offering and then withdrawing her attention and her power to rescue them from painful situations, such as the boarding school they both hated. During the war, with their father absent, the boys experience a new freedom to form friendships across class barriers and a new closeness with their mother, but the narrative – composed now of short juxtaposed sections of Colin's memories, servants' interviews and Fraser's analysis – moves towards the revelation of Janey's affair with Wing Commander Teddy Leroy, experienced as a betrayal not only of her husband but of her sons, Fraser now being forced to admit his own desire for her. The end of their childhood and life at Amnersfield is referred to by the brothers and the servants as 'the crash', linking it to a dream Fraser has whilst staying with Colin.

He recalls this dream when his analysis resumes:

I was in a room separated from another by a narrow passage. Outside, the night sky was suddenly filled with planes in combat. As I struggled to shut the window there was a loud crash in the other room. A pilot, evidently wounded or shocked, appeared and I went across to comfort him. As he turned his face to me, I returned, still solicitous, to the other room. In the corridor a woman stood silently watching. (176)

Free association – and a sudden desire to urinate – connect this adult dream with a newly recalled childhood memory:

Floating off the back wall of my mind a memory forces its way through the words and I find myself saying that after my return from Pinewood [Fraser's boarding school], I would often wake in the middle of the night and be unable to find the door to the bathrooom. 'Although I'd slept in that room half my life by then, it was as though I was shut up in a dark box and couldn't see my way out' . . . Out there, in the corridor beyond the bedroom, there's a darkness so intensely black and threatening that in my mind I recoil from it. Who or what do I fear meeting out there? My mother in a hidden role? The darkness seems totally taken up by her menacing presence. (176)

Like the 'memory' associated with Ilse and being tied to the pot, this scene seems to be a moment reconstructed within the analytic session which embodies the fears and fantasies of the child. It echoes the feeling of entrapment experienced in the earlier scene and intensifies its ambivalence towards the figure of the mother. A little later Fraser produces what seems to be a more 'realistic', less fantasised version of this memory: 'Then I see the corridor outside the guest bedroom along which I cautiously tread in the night so as not to be heard, wanting not to hear and yet fascinated by what I heard' (177). The good and bad mother is no longer split between two but embodied in one woman, the mother who was often inaccessible to him and who is now betraying his father, away fighting in the war. Ilse's German nationality, the cause of her separation from Ronnie at the outbreak of war, is echoed and doubled by Janey's own divided loyalties: she spent much of her youth in Germany and maintained that 'if the Germans won the war it wouldn't be the tragedy the English imagined. She knew the Germans and was quite ready to live among them again' (148). As a young child Fraser used to imagine that she was a spy, a traitor; as an adolescent, he experiences her as split between 'a witch waiting to annihilate me' and a 'fairy godmother' who rescued him from boarding school. He is forced to acknowledge her sexuality when he becomes aware of her affair with Leroy, and his own Oedipal desire for her – '[y]ou wanted her totally, didn't you?' (183) – which will now always remain unfulfilled.

The behaviour of Janey – a much younger wife of an authoritarian husband – to her elder son corresponds quite closely to Laplanche's description of the adult who is inevitably unconsciously seductive towards the child:

> In the primal situation we have, then, a child whose ability to adapt is real but limited, weak and waiting to be perverted, and a deviant adult (deviant with regard to sexual norms, deviant or split with regard to himself) . . . given that the child lives on in the adult, an adult faced with a child is particularly likely to . . . perform bungled or symbolic actions because he is involved in a relationship with his other self, the other he once was.[6]

This kind of behaviour, suggests Laplanche, transmits 'enigmatic signifiers' to the child, messages which bear unconscious sexual signification but which the child is incapable of interpreting as such. Breastfeeding is for Laplanche the paradigm of the 'enigmatic signifier': we learn that Janey only breastfed Ronnie for two weeks and that much of his early care was provided by Ilse. But his entire early experience of Janey is one of alternating closeness and distance, intimacy and withdrawal, so that, as P. suggests, he never fully made the 'long journey of disillusionment from a magical to a real world' (169), expecting Janey to remain the 'miracle-worker' of his early childhood. As the mother of an adolescent with an absent father, P. says that '[h]er demands on you were sometimes mischievous, perverse', and her behaviour 'collusive'. 'Sometimes', Fraser recalls, 'sitting by the fire, she would talk to me as though I were a man. And at other, more important times, she told me nothing' (176). When, during a game of chess, she tells Ronnie that she is going to marry Leroy, he senses that she wants his approval. His reply, 'It's your move', is interpreted now, in the analysis, as his realisation that it was 'her responsibility, her choice what she did' (182) and nothing to do with her son's wishes or approval. P. interprets the telescope Janey gave

the adolescent Ronnie instead of the glasses he needed in a classi-
cally Freudian manner: '[s]he gave you a telescope-penis to overcome
your weakness . . . the penis perhaps that would compensate for
yours which was smaller than your father's' (168–9). Although Fraser
resists this 'translation', the telescope does seem to have functioned
as a particularly concrete 'enigmatic signifier', whose meanings for
Janey we can only assume to have been unconscious. Despite his
reluctance, it is during this discussion that Fraser experiences a
'guilty sensation of pleasure flowing like warm water through me'.
The language evokes the always-already lost imaginary 'oceanic'
union with the body of the mother, suggested a few moments earlier
by P. – 'the original state of bliss, the Garden of Eden from which we
are all banished'.

As an adult, and by means of memories reconstructed in analysis,
Fraser is able to recognise his sexual desire for his mother and understand that the split he initially formulated in terms of class has a
more complex psychic dimension. His social reality was clearly split
in obvious ways – two mothers, one German, the other American
with German affiliations; the alternating closeness and distance of the
upper-class 'society' mother; an upper-class British father, surrogate
working-class fathers – but this was also a psychic process by which,
he acknowledges to P., 'I split them! Not they me' (97).

In the last analytic session used in the book Fraser describes his
father's recent funeral, and P. mentions the Freudian idea that 'the
ego is a graveyard scattered with the headstones of lost objects' (183).
Fraser still feels that they are '[t]oo many . . . all fractured', just as he
was fractured into a different 'I' for each of his parents and parent-
surrogates. Wondering if writing could be a way of 'recuperating
what's lost', he recognises that 'I have to make good all those broken
and scattered tombstones inside myself first' (186). Towards the end
of this last session he experiences the imaginary wholeness he lacked
as a child:

In the inner darkness where I'm confined, where nothing now moves, I see
myself looking back down at my childhood, as though through a glass funnel
that narrows at the far end, and silently I feel them gathering, coming together,
until they fill the emptiness around me, and in their eyes, unimaginably, I
see an indestructible love, in their bodies touching each other, an unsurpassable assurance, and I stand there, my hands by my side, like a child
overwhelmed with wonder. (186)

This scene combines the elements of darkness and entrapment from
earlier memories with the object/symbol of the telescope (the 'glass

funnel') in a moment of reconciliation rather like that experienced by Sylvia Fraser when she is finally able to forgive her father for the sexual abuse which she has recently remembered. The important differences are that Fraser acknowledges the reconstructive nature of his 'memories', their complex blend of truth and fantasy, and that he preserves in the structure of his text the incompleteness of his 'story' and the ongoing process of 'retranslation' in which he is engaged. '[A]ll we've done here', he tells P.' 'is to pick up the bits every now and again. Examine the fragments. We've never seen the totality, the causal relationships between them' (186). In a sense, Fraser *has* suggested and possibly even highlighted the 'causal relationships' between the elements of his past and present by means of a process of selection and juxtaposition from interview transcripts and notes of his analytic sessions: the reader is also in the position of 'historian' in his or her reading and interpretation of the fragments Fraser has chosen to include. Fraser brings to his analysis the 'hard evidence' of the servants' interviews and a particular version and interpretation of his past: in the analysis dreams, memories and the reconstruction of partly imaginary moments are translated and retranslated to provide a 'more complete, more comprehensive, less repressive' account of his childhood. As suggested earlier, Fraser tells us almost nothing about his life in the present and we get very little sense of the person he now is from a reading of his text: 'in writing', he tells P., 'I choose to stand outside myself, as though I'm talking to an intimate other – which is how I feel to myself' (109).

Asked in his *HWJ* interview what kind of book he would have written had he found the 'I' he was looking for, he replied: 'A book which would have been a finished object, a literary work, instead of this desperate rummaging among the fractured objects of the past. A seamless totality: a work of art, in other words, dead before its birth.' The text of *In Search of a Past* is, nevertheless, a 'work of art' or at least of writing, but one which problematises 'art' as much as it does 'history' or 'autobiography'. It is a construction wrought out of the 'fractured objects of the past', one which refuses to produce a completed subject, a 'finished object', but which traces the journey of the subject towards a fuller understanding of the interplay of forces which have produced him.

MEMORIES BROUGHT FORWARD: STEEDMAN'S INTERPRETATIVE DEVICES

Steedman's autobiography also attempts to preserve the status of her memories as 'traces, as open signs', making 'the work of interpretation manifest, provisional, and open-ended' (Sheringham 1993: 314). Her use of the form of the psychoanalytic case-study suggests a certain objectification of the self as subject, but we are not witness here to the *process* of psychoanalysis as we are with Ronald Fraser. Rather than the recovery or reconstruction of early childhood memory within the analytic session, Steedman presents key memories as if they have always been present to consciousness and then records the way in which they have developed in meaning over time. Two memories have accumulated the status of founding moments in the formation and subjectivity of the writer – one of a dream she had at the age of three about a woman wearing a 'New Look' dress, and one of a visit to a bluebell wood with her father. Both memories articulate the child's limited awareness of complex family dynamics as well as class relationships: Steedman presents them as formative of class consciousness whilst acknowledging that these meanings have developed along with her own growing political understanding.

The dream is recounted at the beginning of the second section of the book, subtitled 'Exiles':

It remains quite clear across the years, the topography absolutely plain, so precise in details of dress that I can use them to place the dream in historical time. We were in a street . . . Here, at the front, on this side of a wide road, a woman hurried along, having crossed from the houses behind . . .

She wore the New Look, a coat of beige gaberdine which fell in two swaying, graceful pleats from her waist at the back . . . a hat tipped forward from her hair swept up at the back . . . She hurried, something jerky about her movements, a nervous, agitated walk, glancing round at me as she moved across the foreground. Several times she turned and came some way back towards me, admonishing, shaking her finger.

Encouraging me to follow in this way perhaps, but moving too fast for me to believe that this was what she wanted, she entered a revolving door of dark, polished wood, mahogany and glass, and started to go round and round, looking out at me as she turned. I wish I knew what she was doing, and what she wanted me to do. (1986: 27–8)

The way this dream is narrated gives it the quality of one only just dreamed and recalled: we have no way of knowing how 'accurate' the account is, and neither does Steedman at the distance of over thirty years. Unusually, she sees herself in the dream, wearing 'one of my two summer dresses, one of green, one of blue gingham' (31). She says that '[m]y understanding of the dream built up in layers over a long period of time . . . The dream is not a fixed event in the summer of 1950; it has passed through many stages of use and exploration, and such reinterpretation gives an understanding that the child at the time can't possess' (28–9). Although a child of three would not have recognised or named the woman's style of dress as 'New Look' – 'I understood what I had seen in the dream when I learned the words "gaberdine" and "mahogany"' – it is not suggested that these later understandings have modified the memory of the content, the material details of the dream.

The dream is later used as an 'interpretative device' for women's longing for the material goods, including clothes, which are simulta-neously offered to them by advertising and denied them by their cir-cumstances, including their children. It is as if Steedman is suggesting that this dream gave her an early and unconscious understanding of such longings and exclusions, developed and brought to consciousness by her later experience and education: 'That dream is the past of what lies at the heart of my present' (28). The dream could also be described as an 'enigmatic signifier', as Steedman herself suggests when she says that the only '*evidence*' provided by the dream is 'the feeling of childhood – of all childhoods, probably – the puzzlement of the child watching from the pavement, wondering what's going on, and what they, the adults, are up to, what they want from you, and what they expect you to do . . . as an area of feeling it is brought forward again and again to shape responses to quite different events' (29). The central enigma is only solved much later: 'it's only recently that I've come to see who the woman in the New Look dress actually was' (29). Steedman is suggesting that the three-year-old child had an unconscious or semi-conscious knowledge of the fact that her father had left a wife (and a baby daughter) behind in the north of England who was 'responsible' for Steedman's own illegitimacy and the rela-tive poverty of her father's second family: it is clearly only later that she is able to identify this first wife with the woman in the New Look dress of her dream.

Steedman describes the moment when the final identification was made:

Just before my mother's death, playing about with the photographs on the front bedroom mantelpiece, my niece discovered an old photograph under one of me at three. A woman holds a tiny baby. It's the early 1930s, a picture of the half-sister left behind. But I think I knew about her and her mother long before I looked them both in the face, or heard about their existence, knew that the half understood adult conversations around me, the two trips to Burnley in 1951, the quarrels about 'her', the litany of 'she', 'she', 'she' from behind closed doors, made up the figure in the New Look coat, hurrying away, wearing the clothes that my mother wanted to wear. (39–40)

The juxtaposition of the two photographs is striking but not commented upon: it is as if the existence of the wife and baby has been hidden by the existence of the child of the second relationship – the history of the first family occluded by that of the second, but lying in waiting to be discovered. The layer of the past represented by the photograph of the wife and baby also suggests the unconscious knowledge of the child who Steedman then was – the same age at the time of her photograph as she was when she dreamed about the woman in the New Look coat whom she later identified with her father's wife. The discovery of the photographs functions as the second 'time' within the structure of *Nachträglichkeit*, the moment when the latent meaning of an early memory becomes clear. Steedman's was a family characterised by the existence of secrets – chiefly that of her illegitimacy, which she only discovered in 1977 – which could only be transmitted unconsciously and enigmatically to the child: she suggests that 'such secrets can also produce myths of origin that serve both to reveal and conceal what is actually hidden from view' (66).

The memory just discussed is of a dream; another, also formative of the child's identity and her understanding of gender relations, is of a fantasy. As a child Steedman interpreted the mysteries of her parents' relationship through the 'interpretative device' of fairytales, and this conjunction of the imaginary and the partially-apprehended reality provides the material for a fantasy remembered and reconstructed in vivid detail. What we are not told is when and how the writer realised that it *was* a fantasy. 'The Snow Queen' was her favourite fairytale: 'Kay was my name at home, and I knew that Kay, the boy in "The Snow Queen", was me, who had a lump of ice in her heart' (46). She remembers reading Andersen's tales in the summer of her seventh year, and '[t]he feeling of nostalgia and regret for how things actually are was made that June as Gerda . . . looked for Kay along the river banks' (53). She recalls the smell of the roses outside her bedroom window, which she connected with the roses the witch of the story made to disappear underground so that Gerda would not be reminded of her brother.

I lay on my bed, and read, and imagined what it was they were doing downstairs . . . I saw this picture: they both sat naked under the whitewood kitchen table, their legs crossed so that you couldn't really see what lay between. Each had a knife, sharp-edged with a broad yet pointed blade, and what they did with the knife . . . was cut each other, making thin surface wounds like lines drawn with a sharp pencil, from which the blood poured.

A reference to Gerda's encounter with the Little Robber Girl who takes a knife to bed with her suggests where elements of this scene might have originated, and the account continues:

Downstairs, I thought, the thin blood falls in sheets from my mother's breasts; she was the most cut, but I knew it was she who did the cutting. I couldn't always see the knife in my father's hand. (54)

This is the memory of a fantasy, and one which articulates in symbolic form the power relationship between her parents of which Steedman only later became fully aware: 'The fairy tales always tell the stories that we do not yet know' (55). The child's fantasy suggests her unconscious knowledge of the fact that her mother was the active, powerful partner within the relationship, and somehow the agent of her own suffering, not simply a victim. Here the phallic signifier is not attached to the father: the image of the knife in her mother's hand becomes an 'interpretative device' which instigates and enables a rethinking of the supposed 'law of the father' within theories of patriarchy based on orthodox psychoanalysis. Unable or reluctant to marry the mother of his second family, the father is marginalised and de-powered within that family, an emasculation echoed in terms of class in his humiliation in the bluebell wood. Later Steedman longs for her mother to 'get rid of my father, expel him, kill him, make him no more, so that we could lead a proper life' (55). But the imaginary violence is not only directed against the father: her mother's harshness and ambivalence towards her daughters persist as the image of the knife even for the adult Steedman: 'I accept the idea of male power intellectually, of course', but 'in the dreams it is a woman who holds the knife, and only a woman can kill' (19). The fantasy also articulates the ambivalence and over-identification within the mother–daughter relation dramatised so powerfully (and in very different historical circumstances) in Morrison's *Beloved*. Here 'the thin red lines drawn across her breasts' display 'the mutilation involved in feeding and keeping us' (82), and their mutual (but once again ambivalent) desire to expel the father leads to Steedman's later belief that 'my identification was entirely with her, that whilst hating her, I was her, and that there was no escape' (55).

Steedman's central memory of her father, an encounter with a gamekeeper in a bluebell wood, is described with the clarity of the 'New Look' dream: again, we are not given the circumstances of its first recall, so it is as if it has always been available to memory. Although there are a couple of gaps and one significant distortion of which Steedman is aware, the scene is presented as if immune to change over time and subsequent rememberings. She is able to place the scene precisely in time: she was four and her sister had just been born – in retrospect, the event which began the process of her father's 'expulsion from the domestic scene', and which links it closely with the content of the memory. The scene in the wood is not a scene of seduction or abuse (which the reader might expect from its setting and from within a climate of heightened awareness of the prevalence of sexual abuse in childhood): apparently more 'innocent', it becomes an 'interpretative device' which underlies Steedman's political consciousness whilst also suggesting some latent sexual content.

My father started to pick the bluebells from in between the ferns, making a bunch. Did he give me some to hold? I can't remember, except how else to know about their white watery roots, the pale cleanness pulled from the earth? . . .
    The arrival of the forest-keeper was a dramatic eruption on this scene . . . He was angry with my father, shouted at him: it wasn't allowed . . . He snatched the bunch from my father's hand, scattered the flowers over the ground and among the ferns, their white roots glimmering, unprotected; and I thought: yes; he doesn't know how to pick bluebells.
    My father stood, quite vulnerable in memory now. He was a thin man. I wonder if I remember the waisted and pleated flannel trousers of the early 1950s because in that confrontation he was the loser, feminised, undone? . . . In remembering this scene I always forget, always have to deliberately call to mind the fact that my father retaliated, shouted back; and that we then retreated, made our way back down the path, the tweed man the victor, watching our leaving. (50)

Steedman suggests that such memories are vulnerable to change over time by the fact that she 'always forgets' that her father retaliated, her image of him now being one of powerlessness. The detail of his clothing reinforces this, suggesting that memory selects and preserves the elements which sustain a particular – and possibly partial – interpretation. The phrase 'vulnerable in memory' suggests both that she remembers him as vulnerable on this occasion and that her memory of him is vulnerable to change – his vulnerability at this moment increasing over time as Steedman's perception of it is augmented by subsequent experience and growing political understanding. It is immediately claimed as the founding moment of her political consciousness: 'All the charity I possess lies in that moment. Any account that presents its subjects as cold, or shivering or in any way unprotected recalls the precise structure of its feeling' (50). The vulnerability of the exposed bluebell roots, connected first with that of her father, is transposed on to Henry Mayhew's little watercress seller (discussed more fully in the penultimate section, 'Histories') and later on to John Pearman, the socialist and republican policeman whose memoirs she edited. Raymond Williams' phrase, 'structure of feeling', is used to indicate a continuity between the child's feelings for her humiliated father and the adult's political allegiance, although her feelings then included the somewhat less sympathetic 'yes; he doesn't know how to pick bluebells'. Something in the young child – now also exposed and unprotected by her father's power – was also reassured by this confirmation of her mother's view of her father as incompetent.[7]

When Steedman returns to this scene some twenty pages later, it is to assert that 'the official psychoanalytic myths ignore the social powerlessness that the scene in the bluebell wood reveals, speak to other matters: to the illegal picking of the flowers, the vulnerability of their white roots' (74). Here she narrates part of the story of John Pearman, whose children were forced to watch his humiliation when he was ordered out of Eton when his youngest child contracted scarlet fever, and questioned by the roadside by a 'gentleman on a horse'. 'The point of the symbolic scene' (the episode in the bluebell wood) 'lies at the moment of its use, not in historical time; its point is perhaps the place where it enables me to watch John Pearman's children watch the play of class relations on the road to Winkfield in 1867' (74–5). Throughout the text the scene is used as an 'interpretative device' by which the writer reinterprets the theory of patriarchy for working-class subjects, but the detail of the 'shivering' bluebell roots recurs in a way which suggests that the 'official psychoanalytic myths' are not entirely irrelevant. In the initial account of the memory Steedman refers to 'a more difficult charity . . . pity for something that at the age of four I knew and did not know about my father (know now, and do not know), something about the roots and their whiteness, and the way in which they had been pulled away, to wither exposed on the bank' (51).

It seems presumptuous – and problematically biographical – to suggest that more might be lurking in this memory than the writer remembers or admits, but a link is surely being suggested between sexual and political impotence, both of which were only partly, or unconsciously, perceived by the young child. The adult still senses something which she does not 'know' about her father, and which the reader is not in a position to reconstruct. At the end of the section about her father, subtitled 'A Thin Man', Steedman evokes the power of the father and the daughter's desire embodied in fairytales and 'modern psychoanalytic myths' in order to mark their absence in her own case: 'But daddy, you never knew me like this; you didn't really care, or weren't allowed to care, it comes to the same thing in the end. You shouldn't have left us there . . . You left me alone; you never laid a hand on me: the iron didn't enter the soul. You never gave me anything: the lineaments of an unused freedom' (61). Here she expresses a regret for what her father did not provide: the seductiveness of power, the possibility of the daughter's desire for the father, and the separation from the mother which he might have enabled her to achieve. Instead of the phallic power of the knife, this scene offers only shivering white bluebell roots, inadequate signifiers of the father's power and for Oedipal desire, which also leave *her* exposed and vulnerable. The traces remain of a fantasy, or of regret for a fantasy, thwarted by the absence of an adequate object of desire, but the traces are elided in favour of a more securely political retranslation of the scene. Earlier in the text Steedman suggested that 'if we do allow an unconscious life to working-class children, then we can perhaps see the first loss, the earliest exclusion (known most familiarly to us as the oedipal crisis) brought forward later, and articulated through an adult experience of class and class relations' (14). This is the process at work in her ongoing retranslation of this scene: 'the earliest exclusion' occurs at the moment of her witnessing her father's social humiliation, and the destruction of any power she may have been attracted by. What her retellings of this memory reveal is that its psychic meanings have not been entirely eclipsed by the socio-political.

'Worked upon and reinterpreted, the landscape' of childhood 'becomes a historical landscape; but only through continual and active reworking' (98). In the section of the book subtitled 'Interpretations', Steedman rehearses and analyses the places and moments where the memories of her childhood gathered meaning and became 'historical', as she does in the case of the bluebell-wood scene, interpreted now through the lenses of John Pearman and Mayhew's watercress girl. Having clearly evoked the exclusions and deprivations of her own childhood (and that of her mother), Steedman moves away from them to other, 'historical', lives, principally those of the watercress girl and of Freud's Dora. In this context she describes 'child analysis' as 'a late manifestation of the romantic quest to establish childhood as an area of experience lying within us all, not as a terrain abandoned, but as a landscape of feeling that might be continually reworked and reinterpreted . . . childhood *is* a kind of history, the continually reworked and re-used personal history that lies at the heart of each present' (128). In contrast to Sylvia Fraser, whose *Memoir of Incest and Healing* will be discussed in the next chapter, Steedman envisages the past not as a 'terrain' abandoned and waiting to be rediscovered intact, but as a 'landscape' subject to continual reinterpretation. As such, no complete or final story of this past can be told: she quotes Stephen Marcus on the assumption within psychoanalysis that 'a coherent story is in some manner connected with mental health . . . On this reading, human life is, ideally, a connected and coherent story, with all the details in explanatory order and with everything . . . accounted for, in its proper causal or other sequence' (131). Ronald Fraser resists the desire for a fully 'connected and coherent story' whilst also suggesting, and producing in his analysis, clear causal connections between childhood experience and his adult identity. As Steedman shows, Freud tried to construct such a story out of the fragments and dreams communicated to him by Dora, accusing her of the hysteric's 'failure of narrative' which was, in fact, as much a failure of his own 'interpretation'. Steedman suggests that in his later case histories Freud acknowledged that 'narrative truth, order and sequence does not much signify in the eliciting of a life history, for it must remain the same story in the end, that is, the individual's account of how she got to be the way she is' (132) – as this text is Steedman's account of how *she* came to be her present self. 'To concentrate on narrative sequence is to ignore the transactional nature of individual narratives' (132). Although 'it must remain the same story in the end' seems to contradict what Steedman demonstrates throughout the book, that 'story' and 'interpretation' are indivisible and the establishment of identity an ongoing process, she is here claiming the right of the subject to tell the story of her own formation. Steedman's narrative is a process of 'transaction' between past and present, between individual memory and the broader 'history' in which it is located, between experience and theory, in which these complex movements are more important than the production of a 'connected and coherent story'.

It is not narrative inconsistency which problematises the story of the little watercress girl: Mayhew allows her to tell her own story, which displays a high degree of coherence and order. It is the child herself, and the material of her life, who discomforts Mayhew: with 'the blank absence of childhood from her face' (134), he 'did not know how to talk with her' (126). The child has already evaluated and interpreted the material of her own life: 'the point of her story was herself, and how that self had been made' (135). The connections between the elements of her story, the material of her life, Steedman suggests, 'remain unrevealed by our reading' because they do not carry the meanings the late twentieth-century, (probably) middle-class reader expects. Steedman contrasts this life with Ronald Fraser's, as reconstructed in *In Search of a Past*. She acknowledges the place he gives to the voices of the servants, but claims that otherwise he tells 'a story that we know already', constituted as it is by the figures of classic psychoanalysis – the nursemaid, the absent mother, the Oedipal father. She may be right in that the childhood Fraser painfully reconstructs does seem to rehearse the Oedipal story, but she does not acknowledge the provisional, transactional and ongoing nature of his reconstruction, and the fact that the reader experiences it as something painfully discovered rather than already known and understood.

The little watercress girl sees and narrates herself in economic terms, of her value to her family in terms of how much money she can earn babysitting, or selling watercress: 'I am a capital hand at bargaining . . . For a penny I ought to have a full market hand' (136). 'In this situation her labour was not an attribute, nor a possession, but herself,' comments Steedman. 'It was in the face of this integrity of being that Mayhew was undone' (136). It is an integrity which Steedman acknowledges and respects by allowing her 'to slip [. . .] away into the darkness, as she turned into the entrance of her Clerkenwell court' (139). At the end of her text Steedman insists on 'the irreducible nature of all our lost childhoods: what has been made has been made out on the borderlands'. The 'irreducible' is what cannot be reduced to its social or historical context, though it must acknowledge it; it also suggests the core of truth, of memory, at the core of all our rereadings and retranslations of the past. Finally Steedman asks for 'a structure of political thought that will take all of this, all of these secret and impossible stories, recognize what has been made out on the margins; and then, recognizing it, refuse to celebrate it; a politics that will, watching this past say "'So what?" and consign it to the dark' (144). The lives of the marginalised, Steedman suggests, need to be remembered, acknowledged and reconstructed, but not preserved like monuments or relics in a museum case. The autobiographies of Fraser and Steedman resist monumentalisation or crystallisation because, as we read them, we are witness to lives and identities still in the making, in the active process of retranslating the past.

Notes

1. Fraser's previous work included an oral history of the Spanish Civil War, *Blood of Spain* (1979).
2. In *Past Tenses* (1992) Steedman includes an essay on the writing of *Landscape* entitled 'History and Autobiography'.

3. As with my analysis of the structure of Sylvia Fraser's memoir in the next chapter, I here use and adapt Peter Brooks' schema for his analysis of Freud's 'Wolf Man' case history (in *Reading for the Plot*, 1984: 272).
4. The'Diagnostic and Statistical Manual of Mental Disorder' published by the American Psychiatric Association in 1987 defines trauma rather illogically as 'an event which is outside the range of human experience'. See Laura S. Brown (1995), 'Not Outside the Range' in Caruth (ed.), 100–12.
5. Freud (1899: 301–22), 'Screen Memories'.
6. John Fletcher quoting Laplanche in 'The Letter in the Unconscious: the Enigmatic Signifier in the Work of Jean Laplanche' in Fletcher and Stanton (eds), *Jean Laplanche: Seduction, Translation, Drives* (1992: 111).
7. Steedman's articulation of her sense of her father's absence and powerlessness is strikingly echoed in *Daddy, We Hardly Knew You* (1989), Germaine Greer's account of her quest to find her father's origin and identity: absent during the war and suffering from 'anxiety-neurosis' after it, he seemed incapable of forming any relationship with the daughter who, likewise, 'did not recognise him' (194).

3

'A life entire':
Narrative Reconstruction in
Sylvia Fraser's *My Father's House*
and Margaret Atwood's *Cat's Eye*

INTRODUCTION

In this chapter I examine two texts, one a novel 'whose form is that of an autobiography' (Atwood) the other an autobiography which uses 'many of the techniques of the novelist' (Fraser, 'Author's Note'), which are predicated on the assumption that memory of childhood trauma can be repressed and (almost) completely recovered, enabling the reconstruction of the past 'as it really was'. The concept of memory they employ thus differs radically from the idea of memory and of identity as a continual process of 'retranslation' in the autobiographies of Ronald Fraser, Carolyn Steedman and Georges Perec, which acknowledge the provisionality and incompleteness of memories of childhood. *My Father's House*, Sylvia Fraser's *Memoir of Incest and Healing* (1987) and Margaret Atwood's novel *Cat's Eye* (1988) both represent the recovery of memory of trauma: Fraser's of prolonged sexual abuse by her father, and the severe psychological bullying suffered by Atwood's protagonist Elaine Risley as a young child. Both are predicated upon Freud's belief that the 'burial' of the past entails its 'preservation', that the unconscious is 'that part of the self which had become separated off from it in infancy' (Freud 1909: 57–8). These texts embody an assumption about the process of memory which has been thrown into question by recent work on the later Freudian notion of *Nachträglichkeit*: that 'it is not simply a matter of recovering a lost memory, but rather of the restructuring which forms the past in retrospect as "the original site [. . .] comes to be reworked"' (Nicholls

1996: 54). My readings of these texts will show that the 'truth' about the preserved and rediscovered past only emerges as an effect of narrative itself. Reading the two texts side by side is not intended as a denial of the difference between fiction and autobiography, but rather as a means of highlighting the fact that the creation or impression of truth is an effect of language and narrative.

The main focus of this chapter will be Sylvia Fraser's 'memoir', which exposes quite clearly the contradiction between the idea of 'reconstruction' as the accurate archaeological re-creation of the past and as the 'mark of the fictionality' (Møller 1991: xi) of any such re-creation. She makes explicit use of the archaeological metaphor, comparing her resurrected memories of sexual abuse to 'smashed hieroglyphic tablets', which, when she 'finally began excavation', had to be 'fitted into patterns and dated' (218). At a stage prior to the writing of the text, she reread her life in the light of the 'evidence' produced by this excavation: her reconstruction of this rereading within the text employs, as she readily admits in her 'Note', many of the 'techniques of the novelist' in order to 'provide focus and structure'. But within the text the final literary reconstruction has come to stand in for the complex psychic reconstruction which must have preceded it (although Fraser does give us *some* account of this), and the structure she has produced is so highly and tightly *con*structed, and the recovery and representation of memory so apparently complete, that doubts arise about the truth status of the events she reconstructs and the appropriateness of these novelistic techniques for this material. The text obviously *is* a reconstruction of her past in the light of certain beliefs she has come to hold about it, but I shall argue that it is a reconstruction which the text largely effaces. My analysis of her autobiography is not an attempt to disprove the facts of her sexual abuse, but an examination of the way in which narrative is used to establish that truth.

Although *My Father's House* could be seen as a landmark text for those (including survivors) who have fought for the recognition of child sexual abuse as an important and neglected reality, the 'novelisation' of Fraser's experience now also reads like a paradigm of the kind of memory recovery of which many – and not only accused parents – have become wary.[1] Roberta Culbertson's account (1995) of her memories of sexual abuse provides a useful alternative model, one which draws attention to the huge difference between the child's experience and the adult's understanding and description of that experience. The notion of *Nachträglichkeit* is here both instructive and problematic: it alerts us to the fact that, as Laplanche and Pontalis explain, '[e]xperiences, impressions and memory traces may be revised at a later date to fit in with fresh circumstances or to fit in with a new stage of development' (1973: 111), but also throws the 'original' scene into doubt in a way that might be judged dangerous by those dealing with victims of sexual abuse. The two Freudian cases cited by those who have found the structure of *Nachträglichkeit* useful – the Wolf Man's witnessing of his parents' intercourse and the assault on Emma – are far removed from the severe and prolonged sexual abuse to which Fraser was subjected, although the creation of her 'other self' could be read as explaining how the trauma was 'not experienced' by the subject.

Culbertson draws attention to the way in which extreme victimisation and the experience of powerlessness dislocate memory and the sense of self. Fraser describes the emergence of another 'self' during her experience of abuse, and Atwood's Elaine finds ways of disassociating herself from the bullying to which she is subjected. The splitting of the subject, and the 'preservation' of the past from the consciousness of the present, are represented in the narrative structure of the texts: both employ narrative techniques which attempt to hold past and present apart, so that the past can be represented as if uncontaminated by the consciousness of the remembering subject. They thus both adhere to the 'philosophy of representation – of the original, the first time, resemblance, imitation, faithfulness' – which postmodernism, and the memory-structure of *Nachträglichkeit*, disrupts (Foucault, quoted in Nicholls 1996: 53). Nicholls goes on to explain how the 'modernist' idea of temporality is characterised by a 'tendency to conceive the past as a phantasmic space to be reinhabited and repossessed (historical events become the object of a desire which promises to draw them into some sort of symbiotic union with the present)' (56) – the process we see at work in these two memory-texts. Fraser uses italics to represent the 'space' of her forgotten childhood, and Atwood's Elaine tells two stories which never quite meet, one reconstructing her past, including the forgotten traumas of childhood, the other narrating the events of a brief period in the 'present' when she revisits Toronto for a retrospective exhibition of her paintings. But Elaine's 'reconstruction' cannot avoid the incorporation of later knowledge and insight; her account of her childhood frequently incorporates the knowledge of what she 'didn't know then', whilst also 'preserving' the pain and immediacy of the experience of the tormented child. In Fraser's text, full recovery and narrativisation of memory is equated with the reintegration of the self and with healing; Elaine reaches a moment of understanding and reconciliation with her childhood tormentor, but her story also acknowledges gaps and losses which cannot be restored.

Atwood's Elaine recovers her memory of the forgotten and traumatic past by means of a novelistic device, the rediscovery of her cat's eye marble which enables her to 'see [her] life entire' (398); Fraser also experiences a sudden moment of revelation which is prepared for by means of an intricately plotted chain of events and coincidences. Over-determined or highly coincidental *fictional* plots may be unconvincing, but they obviously do not create the same kinds of doubt about the truth of the events being narrated as can arise in texts which claim autobiographical status. In certain genres, in fact, plot depends precisely upon what Mark Freeman has called 'the reciprocal determination' of 'endings and beginnings' (1991: 176). Peter Brooks describes the detective story as 'using the plot . . . to find, or construct, a story of the crime which will offer just those features necessary to the thematic coherence we call a solution, while claiming, of course, that the solution has been made necessary by the crime' (1984: 29). Fraser compares herself to a detective, and my analysis of her text will demonstrate exactly this 'double logic' of plot, which makes memory itself the agent and effect of a closed system of determination, in which 'final scene returns to first scene' (Greene 1991b: 307) both as a measure of difference in understanding, but also as proof and solution. The text also demonstrates the powerful appeal of the model of memory as total recovery of the past; even when the past is traumatic this model is nostalgic in its comforting assumption that nothing is lost and that wholeness and reintegration are possible. This is not to deny, of course, the psychological importance of the restoration of a sense of wholeness to lives and identities shattered by trauma.

In first-person fictional narrative, we also accept the convention that the narrator has a much more complete and detailed knowledge of her past life than is usually the case in reality. The rediscovery of the past and its re-creation in full detail is a popular narrative trope; in both texts under discussion the experiences of the past which have been 'forgotten' and those which were presumably always available to memory are reconstructed with equal fullness and 'fidelity'. Paradoxically, the 'thickening' of detail which provides the texture of reality in a novel seems unconvincing in a text which purports to be autobiographical, and is problematised even further when much of the narrator's past was supposedly forgotten for forty years. Fraser's use of the 'techniques of the novelist' evades the question of the unreliability, fluidity and 'retranscription' of memory. In *Cat's Eye*, the double narrative frequently obscures the position of the narrating subject; we are often unsure from which point in time the subject is speaking, as Elaine does not tell her story from the point in time at which it was supposedly remembered, the finding of the cat's eye marble. This aporia reveals the difficulty any first-person narrator has in stabilising the position from which she speaks: past and present cannot be held apart, in spite of the narrative strategies used by Atwood and Fraser in an attempt to do so. This instability is signalled by Fraser's awkward question, posed just before she recovers her memory of abuse: 'How would I feel to discover that the prize, after four decades of tracing clues and solving riddles, was knowledge that my father had sexually abused me?' (211). Here the subject-narrator wonders how she is going to feel when she 'finds out' something that she knows already, signalling the circularity of the text's narrative strategy.

FRASER'S 'AUTHOR'S NOTE' AND THE QUESTION OF POINT OF VIEW

Fraser's 'Author's Note' highlights several potential problems with the technique she has chosen to use in order to tell her story. 'The story I have told in this book is autobiographical', her 'Note' begins: 'As a result of amnesia, much of it was unknown to me until three years ago.' The use of the term 'amnesia' suggests a clinical authority for her experience of forgetting: it sounds even more 'medical', susceptible of objective diagnosis, than the usual post-Freudian term 'repression', and makes clear that Fraser is not talking about Christopher Bollas' 'unthought known', or Freud's later idea that 'forgetting impressions, scenes or experiences nearly always reduces itself to shutting them off . . . failing to draw the right conclusions and isolating memories' (1914: 148). Although survivors of accidents or violent assaults often attest to a 'blacking out' of some details of the traumatic event, 'amnesia' is the kind of forgetting which few survivors or therapists claim or describe, talking rather in terms of isolated and often meaningless visual images which cannot be articulated, or affectless narratives which hold memory at a distance.

The statement about amnesia is followed by a comment on technique: 'For clarity, I have used italics to indicate thoughts, feelings and experiences pieced together from recently recovered memories, and to indicate dreams.' The split text is, to some extent, a narrative reconstruction of the split which she claims was the result of the abuse, a split between the 'child who knew' and the conscious self who had no knowledge of the abuse. In fact, this division does not make for as much 'clarity' as she claims: in the first few pages there is indeed a clear and marked separation between the story of the child who 'did not know' and the experiences of the child who 'did', but later it is often unclear whether what is being reconstructed in the italicised sections is a recovered memory, a dream or a fantasy, or from which period of her life these date. Italics are also used to express adult understandings or interpretations of the experience of abuse as well as the unmediated experience of the child. Mark Freeman, in his analysis of this text, says that taking Fraser's advice and keeping 'this device in mind' will help us to 'acknowledge throughout that the story being told is a reconstruction' (1991: 151). In fact, although this is in one sense obviously true, as I read the text I feel that the reader is often being invited to assume just the opposite: that is, that the past, bracketed off in italics as it is, has been recovered 'pure' from the timeless dimension in which it waited until recovered by the subject. When we read in the first section of the text '*I lie naked on my daddy's bed, clinging to the covers. His sweat drips on me. I don't like his wet-ums. His wet-ums splashes me.* (10), we are very well aware that this is a *literary* reconstruction, but at the same time we are expected to believe in it as an exact account of the child's experience, in the present tense and in her language and mode of perception. This is very much as the adult Fraser re-experiences these moments through hypnosis, which seems to give her direct access to a repressed experience unmediated by time and changing understanding. By contrast, an italicised comment on the feelings of the child who has just been 'saved' by her father from having to kiss her dead grandmother's cheek is clearly an adult reconstruction: '*In those few seconds, my other self reconfirms – if she ever doubted it – the wisdom of serving power in a precarious world*' (23). Other reconstructions and interpretations, such as the first paragraph of the section entitled 'The Other' (15), are not italicised; this gives an account of the 'splitting' of Fraser's personality and the creation of her 'other self', something which she obviously only realised once the memory of her abuse had been recovered. If the 'piecing together' is, as claimed in the 'Note', only represented in the italicised sections, the implication follows that the roman sections must have the status of the 'always known', the past unproblematically remembered, and this is clearly not the case with the account of the creation of the 'other self' who remembers what the conscious self has forgotten. The fact that both italics and roman are used for the interpretation of past experience is a textual acknowledgement of what the text otherwise denies, that memory as such cannot always be distinguished from the ongoing process of 'retranslation'.

Cat's Eye also employs a double narrative structure, not marked typographically, but alternating sections in which Elaine tells the story of her childhood with sections describing her visit to Toronto some forty years later for her 'retrospective'. The childhood sections are narrated with the full knowledge of what she later remembered, and because there is no typographical distinction as in the case of Fraser's narrative, it is not always clear what has always been remembered and what was forgotten, and when that forgetting occurred. Although the visit to Toronto, when she revisits the sites of her childhood experience, provides the occasion for an *intensification* of memory, it is not the time or place when she first 'remembers'. This occurred some years earlier, with the finding of the cat's eye marble, although the *effect* is that she is remembering during her visit to Toronto. The narrative technique enables the *reader* to see Elaine's life 'entire', with the forgotten elements of the past reinserted into the narrative of that part of it which had always been available to consciousness. The forgotten past is not narrated from the point in time at which memory was supposedly recovered, but from several intermediate points which are impossible to 'place' exactly in time. Although the past as narrated to us has been supposedly 'forgotten' by the self who narrates it, nevertheless it is already marked by a degree of retrospective interpretation which creates the effect of the narrator knowing and not knowing about the past at the same time. Although this could be seen as a demonstration of a psychoanalytic truth about traumatic and 'forgotten' experience, here, as in *My Father's House*, it is also a specific effect of narrative. As Freeman puts it, 'I cannot speak of that of which I *am* unconscious, but only of that of which I *was*. Hence the narrational dimension of the notion of the unconscious itself' (1991: 152). One clear example of this indeterminacy is Elaine's account of her first meeting with Cordelia, an account which preserves its innocence – she is standing in an apple orchard with two other little girls who were already Elaine's friends – but also 'reads' the scene in the light of later knowledge when she adds the comment that it was 'empty of premonition' (69). The fact that she felt no premonition then is worthy of comment now because of what followed, the bullying to which Cordelia subjected her: her memory of the scene includes a sense of what she would have felt then had she known what she knows now. The poignancy of this moment arises from the meeting and mutual transformation of past and present: the instability of the position of the speaking subject demonstrates that our readings of the past are in a continuous process of retranslation, a process denied or hidden by the comparative rigidity of Fraser's typographical separation of past and present.

When Fraser claims in her 'Note' that 'I have not exaggerated or distorted or misrepresented the truth as I now understand it', she is

clearly referring to the 'truth' of her abuse which it seems presumptuous to question, but which is also brought into question by the
highly 'reconstructed' or novelistic nature of that truth. Her last
phrase embodies a recognition that 'as I understand it' may not be the
same as 'as it actually was', although this is one of the few recognitions within the text of that possibility. Towards the end of the book
Fraser refers to the process she underwent '[t]hree years ago', when
'I decided to retreat to a place where I could heal and integrate, and
perhaps write a book' (245). Although the text seems painfully honest
about the experiences of the abused child and the adult who suffered
as a consequence, and about *some* of the processes of remembering
and reconstructing, this last stage of 'integration' and 'piecing together'
is omitted, leaving us with the text which is the *result* of that integration. In an *Observer* interview with Scarlett McGwire in 1989
Fraser said: 'Writing was a natural way of discovering more about
what had happened': it is not clear here whether she is referring to
earlier novels, including *Pandora*, which is mentioned and used in
My Father's House, or to the *Memoir* itself. If the latter, then this is a
stage which the text effaces, there being no reflection on the way in
which the writing of the text transformed or developed the memories
with which it deals. The second and third stages suggested in my
analysis of the autobiographical texts of Ronald Fraser and Carolyn
Steedman – the memory of the event and the writing of (the memory
of) the event – are here elided: indeed, we are asked to accept the
event, its recall and its representation as identical.

The italicised sections in the first chapter, 'Secrets', give us the
'truth' which the adult Fraser only realised some three or four years
before the writing of the book, her sexual abuse by her father. Towards
the end we are told that this began in tenderness: 'In my earliest
memory' (although we are not told how or when *this* was recovered)
'I am an infant lying on my father's bed, being sexually fondled but
blissfully unaware of any deception. Then I was treated with tenderness. That was my Garden of Eden. As in Genesis, pain came with
knowledge and expulsion' (241). The italicised sections trace the
development of the abuse from this early bliss through enforced
masturbation and attempted penetration, accompanied by threats of
destroying her beloved cat, and of not being loved herself. There
are also hints – choking fits, and more explicit details of having her
head forced down towards her father's genitals (103) – at what we
later realise is oral abuse: although the narrator is telling her story
from the beginning with the full knowledge which she has acquired
by the end, these hints function as a kind of titillation, the promise
of further shocking details to come. Full narrative gratification is thus

postponed until near the end of the text, when Fraser finally remembers 'through the body', re-enacting the most extreme violation involved in the abuse: 'my head bends back so far I fear my neck will snap, my jaws open wider than possible and I start to gag and sob, unable to close my mouth – lockjaw in reverse. These spasms do not feel random. They are the convulsions of a child being raped through the mouth' (220). The narrative is thus structured by means of a partial concealment of the full facts of the abuse which is supposedly fully available to the consciousness of the narrating subject: as in the case of *Cat's Eye*, there is a sense in which the text wants to have it both ways, to reveal and not to reveal, the narrator knowing and yet not knowing at the same time. In the cases of Ronald Fraser and Perec, it is the *subject* who both desires and fears to be found: in these texts, we are more conscious of this simultaneous revelation and evasion as an effect of a narrative which wants to keep us reading.

FOUR NARRATIVE ELEMENTS: A PARALLEL WITH FREUD'S 'WOLF MAN' CASE HISTORY

Using the formalist distinction between *fabula* ('the order of events referred to by the narrative') and *sjuzet* ('the order of events presented in the narrative discourse') (1984: 12), Peter Brooks analyses Freud's case history of the Wolf Man in a way that is also useful for an understanding of the narrative technique of *My Father's House*. Brooks distinguishes four narrative elements in the case history of the Wolf Man:

(1) the structure of the infantile neurosis (the history of the neurosis);
(2) the order of event in the past providing the cause of the neurosis (the etiology of the neurosis);
(3) the order of emergence of past event during the analysis (the history of the treatment);
(4) the order of report in the case history. (272)

(4) is the *sjuzet*, and (1), (2) and (3) are, at different points of the text, the *fabula*. In Fraser's case, the four elements of the text need to be defined slightly differently. (I use the term 'neurosis' for convenience and to establish a parallel structure, not as a clinical definition.)

(1) the story of her childhood and adolescence ('the order of event in the past providing the cause of the neurosis');
(2) the emergence of symptoms which hint at the truth behind (1), ('the history of the neurosis');

(3) 'the order of emergence of past event', the way in which Fraser remembers or reconstructs her past by interpreting the symptoms in (2) and by means of various therapies;

(4) 'the order of report', the text itself (the *sjuzet*).

In *My Father's House* Fraser takes the roles of analysand *and* analyst, interpreting dreams, symptoms and fragments of memory in order to provide the 'etiology' of her own 'neurosis', also writing as the child who experienced the events which the adult subject has forgotten. In the text level (3) is already inserted into level (1): the italicised sections provide the reader of (4), the *sjuzet*, with the 'evidence' of the 'cause of the neurosis' as the story of her childhood is being told. Here the supposed defence against an intolerable reality – the splitting of the subject into a self who knows and a self who does not know – provides the means by which the 'past event' is allowed to 'emerge' within the narrative while the subject is simultaneously ignorant of it. It is useful to distinguish these four narrative elements because they are so often elided within Fraser's text: she is 'reading' her own life, interpreting her own symptoms, in order to find the 'primal scene' that leads to the given outcome, which, in the end, seems *over*-determined because of the high degree of narrative coincidence. Given that she is reading her *own* life (and every reading of a life *is* the construction of a *sjuzet*), it could be said that she is deriving her *fabula* – the 'real' story, the 'truth' – from her *sjuzet* – the plot, or construction – as the reader of any narrative must do. In 'Constructions in Analysis' Freud writes: 'The path that starts from the analyst's construction ought to end in the patient's recollection; but it does not always lead so far.' Instead of recollection of the repressed, the analysis may produce in the analysand 'an assured conviction of the truth of the construction which achieves the same therapeutic result as a recaptured memory' (1937: 265–6). Citing this passage, Brooks suggests that this conviction is close to that of the detective who feels that he has successfully solved a case: 'it is the conclusion that a *sjuzet* has been so well formed, so tightly enchained, that the *fabula* derived from it must be right' (1984: 322).

'MY OTHER SELF': THE SPLITTING
OF THE SUBJECT

At the beginning of the second chapter of *My Father's House* the voice of the narrator, who 'now' has full knowledge of the abuse, tells us: 'When the conflict caused by my sexual relationship with my father became too acute to bear, I created a secret accomplice for my daddy by splitting my personality in two. Thus, somewhere around the age of seven, I acquired another self with memories and experiences separate from mine, whose existence was unknown to me' (15). Mark Freeman claims that 'this "other" and her activities are strictly (and avowedly) constructions' (1991: 153): it is not clear what he means by this, since although Fraser could not, by definition, have 'known' about this 'other self' at the time, she is presented as the only possible explanation of the amnesia. The use of italics to indicate the memories and experiences associated with her does, however, make her at least in part a *textual* construction. But the reader is also being asked to accept this 'other self' as a psychic reality, 'constructed' by the psyche as a defence mechanism in response to the radical assault on the child's sense of self. Throughout the text she is referred to as a twin, 'my other self', the child who needs to be comforted when the adult Fraser 'remembers': she lives a hidden but parallel life which occasionally 'leaks' messages and emotions into the conscious subject through dreams and somatic symptoms.

The creation of this other self could be interpreted as a response to trauma which the psyche cannot register: her father's sexual assaults are traumas not registered as such by the conscious self as a pre-pubescent child. Roberta Culbertson suggests that '[w]ounding produces in the body particular neurological responses' which limit the experience

sometimes merely to the reflexes; siphoning senses of fear and panic off into other parts of the brain so as not to destroy the potential for action as required. Thus events and feelings are simply not registered, but this does not mean they are forgotten; they are located in other parts of the mind and the parts of the body affected as well, though separated from the continuing integrated story of the self. (1995: 175)

Her analysis of the experiences of survivors of severe trauma is close to the process observed by Dori Laub in Holocaust survivors: she describes the 'simultaneous existence of a more or less functional self and the truncated, surviving self' (178), the latter being that aspect of the self which 'remembers' the trauma which the 'functional' self has forgotten. She makes it clear that she is not talking about the controversial question of 'multiple personality', but an 'existential division' such as that described by Fraser and also by Charlotte Delbo, who experiences her present-day functioning self as fundamentally different from the self who experienced Auschwitz – although this experience has not been 'forgotten'.[2] Abraham and Torok have formulated a very similar psychic process, an 'internal psychic splitting', as a result of which 'two distinct "people" live side by side, one behaving as if s/he were part of the world and the other as if s/he had no contact with it whatsoever' (1994: 100). If the trauma occurs when the subject is a very young child, the process is further complicated by the fact that she does not have the language or the understanding to represent to herself what is happening.

To narrate a child's memory is . . . to construct a culturally acceptable narrative unavailable to the child, to create in some sense . . . a fiction, a story the child never knew, from a perspective that was not part of the original scene or experience . . . [T]he demands of the adult in whom such memories appear to reside require that they be bundled into narratives constructed from chaotic and branching sets of facts, essentially as fiction masquerading as objective truth, rather than recounted as truth finally set down. (Culbertson 1995: 181–3)

There is a sense in which Fraser acknowledges this 'masquerade' by the very act of turning her experience into the form of a novel; when she 'relives' the experience of abuse under hypnosis, she also ackowledges that: '[m]ostly my feelings can't be classified because I have no framework of experience in which to place them or to judge them' (226). Her use of the language of the four- or five-year-old who was first abused is, on the one hand, an attempt to represent the confusion of the child, but on the other hand suggests that the adult can have direct and unmediated access to this experience – that it is, precisely, 'truth finally set down'. Culbertson does not make this claim: in her discussion she includes several quotations from her own auto-biographical writing which represent 'the movement of one sort of truth to another . . . [f]rom reconstructed memory to true memory, to fragments without meaning, or with meaning layered on only in the telling'. She does make a claim for 'true memory', but suggests that it is only 'true' in so far as it remains wordless and fragmented, the 'feelings, smells, sounds, movements, images' first experienced by the young child. She is 'aware that [her] childhood memories may have been refigured over time, reshaped, embellished by subsequent memories gathering on them like dust from then to now'. Culbertson also acknowledges that a child's early memory of painful or confusing experiences will inevitably be intermingled with fantasy – in her case 'black cloaks and talons and knives and witches and my own white knights' (181–3). Her scrupulous analysis of her own memories of sexual abuse is instructive for those on both sides of the 'recovered' or 'false memory' debate in its insistence on the elusiveness of the notion of 'truth' when dealing with very early experience and memory. Sylvia Fraser's account, although clearly part of her own process of 'healing', lays claim to 'objective truth' albeit in the guise of fiction.

Fraser's second 'self' also brings into focus the difficulties inherent in the complex term and idea of 'repression'. Although in the 'Rat Man' case history Freud talks in terms of the repression of a part of the self, in the 1915 paper 'Repression' he talks rather of the repression of 'an instinctual representative', by which he means an 'idea' or representation (*Vorstellung*) which is invested with 'psychical energy coming from an instinct' (152). 'Repression' here clearly means not the forgetting of a painful experience, but an internal operation of the psyche. In the second of the 'Three Essays on Sexuality', however, repression is clearly linked to '[h]ysterical amnesia, which occurs at the bidding of repression', and 'is only explicable by the fact that the subject is already in possession of a store of memory-traces which have been withdrawn from conscious disposal, and which are now, by an associative link, attracting to themselves the material which the forces of repression are engaged in repelling from conscious-ness' (1905: 91). In 'The Aetiology of Hysteria' the term 'defence' is used interchangeably with 'repression', and Freud writes: '*The defence achieves its purpose of thrusting the incompatible idea out of consciousness if there are infantile sexual scenes present in the (hitherto normal) subject in the form of unconscious memories*' (his italics) (1896, 211). In both these accounts, repression is 'actually an after-pressure' (*Nachverdrängung*) in that it depends upon the prior existence of 'memory-traces' or 'unconscious memories' associated with the instincts of the ego or with premature sexual experience. Freud seems to be suggesting that repression 'proper', in the sense of '*turning something away, and keeping it at a distance, from the con-scious*' does not occur without 'primal repression', 'which consists in the psychical (ideational) representative of the instinct being denied entrance to the conscious' (1915: 147). But now repression, rather like the 'primal scene', seems to retreat forever backwards, in the sense that it cannot happen unless it has already happened. As Lis Møller puts it: 'Repression is thus always already anticipated by repression, by a mythical moment of original repression that constitutes the condition of possibility of repression proper, but which can only be hypothetically deduced from the phenomenon of after-pressure' (1991: 64). In 'Repression', Freud explains that

[t]he process of repression is not to be regarded as an event which takes place *once*, the results of which are permanent, as when some living thing

has been killed and and from that time onward is dead; repression demands a persistent expenditure of force . . . the repressed exercises a continuous pressure in the direction of the conscious, so that this pressure must be balanced by an unceasing counter-pressure. (1915: 151)

Although Freud is here talking about the repression of 'instinctual impulses' and not of painful memories, this process seems close to the continuous work of repression necessitated by prolonged and repeated abuse. It also requires the psychic mechanism of Elaine's account of forgetting: 'I've forgotten things, I've forgotten that I've forgotten them' (Atwood 1988: 200). If repression does require an 'original' moment of 'turning away' an impulse, then in *My Father's House* this might be represented by Fraser's 'original' moment of *jouissance*, the 'Garden of Eden' where she was 'sexually fondled but blissfully unaware of any deception' (241). Internal conflicts within the ego, or messages unconsciously picked up from the world outside, might have resulted in the repression of the instinct which sought or responded to this pleasure.

Roberta Culbertson and Judith Lewis Herman both link the kind of forgetting characteristic of childhood experience of severe trauma with what Culbertson calls 'transcendence' and Herman 'trance states' or 'dissociation'. Herman explicitly links dissociation with the splitting of the self and even with the formation of multiple personality, using Fraser's own account – 'I unscrew my head from my body as if it were the lid of a pickle jar' – as an example (Fraser 1987: 221; Herman 1992: 103).[3] Both Fraser and Atwood employ this idea in the response to trauma: during her father's assaults, Fraser's '*mind goes away like when the big boys . . . push you too high on a swing and you scream to get down*' (10). She relives the experience under hypnosis, describing how 'I hold my breath a lot and that makes me dizzy, or light-headed, as if I were swaying in a hammock outside time and space' (226). Elaine describes her ability to dissociate from the experience of being tormented by Cordelia in similar terms, and also as a kind of 'doubling' of the self: 'fainting is like stepping sideways, out of your own body, out of time or into another time. When you wake up it's later. Time has gone on without you . . . At those times I feel blurred, as if there are two of me, one superimposed on the other, but imperfectly' (173, 184). Culbertson suggests that '[t]hose who find themselves now and again having "gone blank", particularly after a triggering event of some sort, might indeed be having a memory, revisiting a time in which they "went blank" in the midst of terror, entered another level of experience retained elsewhere in the mind and triggered by other stimuli' (1995: 175). Such states might contribute to the experience of the self as fragmented and discontinuous, represented concretely in *Cat's Eye* by the 'black hole' in which Elaine is buried by Cordelia: 'I have no image of myself in the hole; only a black square filled with nothing . . . Perhaps the square is empty; perhaps it's only a marker, a time marker which separates the time before it from the time after' (107). Culbertson also describes a more positive version of what she calls 'transcendence', often described by children as 'being in a golden light, in forests and castles, floating above themselves, being among the stars' (1995: 176). Elaine seems to experience a version of this when she nearly freezes to death in the ravine and is 'saved' by her vision of a black-cloaked lady on the bridge. The relationship between reality and fantasy in this memory will be discussed later: it echoes Culbertson's reconstruction of a memory in which, during or after the experience of sexual abuse, she feels 'another presence – arms around me from behind, big skirts surrounding me and a sense of skimming just above the ground . . . it is clear to me then that there must be some other force beyond my own body which keeps me alive' (1995: 187). Such experiences are clearly connected with the mysticism to which Fraser is later attracted and upon which Atwood draws in its connection with the 'new physics': the idea that 'time is not a line but a dimension' (3) provides a 'cosmic' dimension to the operations of memory to which I will return.

Freud's later cases, and the theory outlined in 'The Aetiology of Hysteria', presuppose more or less isolated incidents of infantile abuse which cease long before puberty and before the child becomes aware of their full meaning. Abraham and Torok's formulation of the 'crypt' as the site of 'preservative repression', which, as Nicholas Rand explains, 'seals off access to part of one's own life in order to shelter from view the traumatic monument of an obliterated event' (Rand 1994: 18) also seems predicated upon the occurence of a unique and isolated event, not repeated traumatic experience. The structure of *Nachträglichkeit* also supposes a singular 'later' event in which the latent traumatic force of the 'original' is felt as if for the first time. In Fraser's case the abuse was more or less continuous for approximately ten years, with a brief respite at around the time of puberty. When it resumed, both her conscious self and, we are told, her 'other' were more fully aware of its meaning and the betrayal it involved: '*She is old enough, now, to know about blood and babies*'. Here the language of the 'other self' has also changed in order to express the developed understanding of the adolescent: '*For the first time, penetration is attempted, though it is by no means completed . . . She feels used, not as one person exploited by another, but as a condom is used then discarded in the gutter*' (43). But in spite of the increased awareness attributed to this older, other self, we are still being asked to believe in her separate existence, although Fraser does acknowledge the increasingly fragile boundaries between her two selves: 'Just as the emotions of my other self often leaked up into my life, now my moral values began seeping down into hers' (39). The repression of the memory of a few isolated incidents of infantile abuse is much easier to accept than the idea of the conscious and repeated repression of the knowledge and memory of a more or less continuous experience. The idea of a second self which 'takes over' and even participates in the sexual relationship could be seen as a construction which overcomes this difficulty whilst also creating others in its place.

REPETITION TOWARD RECOGNITION

As already suggested, in *My Father's House* Fraser represents both the forgotten events of the past *and* the process by which she recovers her memory of them. The text enacts a search for what might count as truly authentic memory, as full 'proof' of what she increasingly suspects must have happened in the past. Unconscious repetition, (semi-)automatic writing, dreams, body memory, visual memory recovered under hypnosis; all are experienced and interpreted in the narrator's reading of her hidden early life. The narrative Fraser constructs out of these memories and experiences is marked by a high degree of narrative coincidence, which also seems to function as proof of their point of origin. Modelling his concept of narrative on a reading of Freud's *Beyond the Pleasure Principle*, Peter Brooks claims: 'Repetition toward recognition constitutes the truth of the narrative text': the 'middle' is 'the place of repetitions, oscillating between blindness and recognition, origin and ending' (1984: 108). Fraser's text embodies this 'oscillation', but because the narrator has already 'recognised' the truth and recovered her memory of the 'origin', and revealed that origin to the reader, the series of events which constitute the 'middle' of her plot are reconstructed as repetitions of an originating event for which they also provide the evidence. Repetition is also a textual device which reinforces the pattern of narrative determination: significant sections of the text are literally repeated at the points where the events or dreams they describe inform the understanding of the remembering subject.

The first element of the narrative – 'the order of event in the past providing the cause of the neurosis' – could be said to end when the adolescent Fraser is finally able to say 'no' to her father, to resist and deny him.

As daddy pushes her head down to his crotch, she at last gets out the words:
'I hate you!' She smashes her left fist into his belly. 'Touch me again, and I'll
kill you!' She punches and punches like her mother kneading bread dough.
He doesn't resist. He doesn't fight back.
   So that is all it took, would have taken. (103)

So Elaine finally refuses the domination of Cordelia: 'I turn and walk
away from her ... I see that I don't have to do what she says, and
worse and better, I've never had to do what she says. I can do what I
like ... They need me for this, and I no longer need them' (193). In
Fraser's case it is significant that the power and action of refusal is
ascribed to the 'other self', not to the conscious subject, which we
might expect if we see this refusal in terms of a spell being broken.
But the continued existence of the second self is necessary for the
maintenance of the structure of repression. In future she will be
brought into play in order to suggest the underlying and hidden
cause of the subject's 'symptoms': her defensive retreat into the logical and intellectual, her fear of having children, her compulsive
insecurity with her boyfriend Danny before their marriage, and her
increasing depression after it, and what she interprets as a repetition
– an attempt to 'reunite with daddy' – in her affair with Paul Lawson,
the father of one of her high-school friends.
   We are even told that her 'other self' takes over on her wedding
day, so that she *'will have no memory of the wedding ceremony'* or
'of the wedding night ... It will never be written on my consciousness
any more than a hand inscribing water produces a record' (141). The
wedding night is thus distinguished from early childhood experience
of trauma, in that the text is clearly claiming that memory-traces of
the latter *are* 'written on' the *un*conscious, and potentially available
to consciousness. Here a voice from the future tells us that this event
will *'never'* be remembered. Neither does the *'sexual initiation'* which
occurred on her wedding night function as the trigger for her
repressed memories: instead we are told that this *'is the territory of my*
other self' (141) so that the event seems to function as the occasion
for a further and more thorough repression. It is unclear from the text
whether sex continued to be the 'territory' of her 'other self': if so, all
of her sexual life must have remained on the level of the unconscious,
which seems unlikely. When she first visits Paul, knowing that a
sexual relationship is likely to develop, the words of her 'other self'
from the first chapter of the book are repeated and juxtaposed with the
account of the later encounter in order to reinforce the interpretation
of this affair as an unconscious repetition:

Hitching at the strap of my sunsuit, I scrape my foot back and forth over the metal band marking the threshold of my daddy's room ... Again I'm turning towards the steps when a male voice barks through the door: 'I'm coming. Hold your horses'. Paul opens it, wearing a white terry bathrobe ... *My daddy sits on the bed in his undershirt* ... (171)

Italics are thus used to signify *both* the 'return' of an unmediated and as yet unrecognised 'repressed' memory (in the voice that says 'no' to daddy) *and* the voice of the subject reconstructing her experience in the light of present knowledge: this suggests the impossibility of holding apart the memory of an event and its interpretation.

The affair with Paul is not the first 'symptom' to emerge after her marriage and to be in need of later interpretation: her depressions are interpreted as '*experiencing the unexpressed sorrow of my other self* ... *It is precisely because my life is tranquil that she is staking her emotional claim*' (146). Here the 'other' voice is also used to provide information which 'explains' the recurring image of a hangman's noose which begins to haunt her dreams: '*Though I don't yet know it, my maternal grandfather hanged himself, age forty-four, and a maternal aunt soon would*' (146). That which she 'didn't know yet' is transmitted almost telepathically from the future in order to provide the imagery of her dreams and fantasies *and* to provide the means by which she interprets them. A ragamuffin child, obviously an image of her 'other self', keeps appearing in her dreams and fantasies, demanding attention and recognition: towards the end of the text she visualises a 'five-year-old child with matted hair and blue fangs' with 'the bloody mark of a broken leash' around her neck' (227), and is forced to recognise the co-identity of this child with the adolescent who was also abused and with her adult self. As the ragamuffin child first appears and demands attention, so Fraser feels drawn to her childhood haunts: the pictures she finds in trunks at her old home, of fairytale heroines defaced and marked by signs of violence, do not trigger conscious memories, but surface in the violent, stream-of-consciousness narratives her 'other self' begins to write. Repetition here takes the form of an unconscious representation in writing produced almost 'automatically', effecting a re-entry into the world of childhood, although not yet with full memory of her relationship with her father:

My other self has learned to type. She presses my keys, throwing up masses of defiant memories – stream-of-consciousness stuff without punctuation ...
It's as if I have fallen down the Alice-in-Wonderland hole into that detailed child's universe below an adult's kneecaps ... *My other self leads me to the*

edge of her secret world, offering up murky clues without taking me over . . . (149–50)

Fraser tells us that the material of the unrecognised unconscious – 'a gush of primordial pain from a part of me I never knew existed' – is eventually reworked into a text called *Pandora*, in which, at some point, she made a transition between the 'first person hysterical' and the third. This semi-autobiographical text seems to have functioned as an earlier version of *My Father's House*, expressing knowledge not yet fully available to consciousness. Fraser wonders: 'Why did I give my fictional father a hooked arm? . . . Why did I suggest incest in my father's family?' (151–2). The process of reworking which this text underwent seems to have functioned both as a revelation and a concealment of the truth, and stands as another 'repetition': it is a text that Fraser herself comes to 'read' in the light of later knowledge, and is also itself the catalyst for the revelation of the truth.

This 'automatic writing', and her increasingly explicit dreams, perform a similar function to the pictures Elaine begins to paint when she is pregnant, long before she has recovered her memory of her childhood experience. Her first paintings are of 'things that were actually there, in front of [her]' (337); she is attracted to early medieval paintings, 'with their daytime clarity, their calm arrested gestures', to 'objects that breathe out light; a luminous flatness'. She is looking for a mode of representation which is 'innocent', transparent and clear, with no shadows or hidden corners – a visual equivalent of the version of the past she has created for herself. But when she is pregnant she finds herself painting 'things which aren't there' (337), things which the reader, but not the Elaine who paints them, recognises as memories of objects associated with her forgotten childhood. The silver toaster and glass coffee percolator were minutely observed by the young child at breakfast time as a way of avoiding the moment when she would have to leave for school and face Cordelia; she even paints a jar of deadly nightshade, with the 'eyes of cats' in the 'tangle of the glossy leaves', an unconscious memory which transposes images associated with the ravine with her burial in the 'black hole'. The Elaine who paints these pictures realises that 'these things must be memories, but they do not have the quality of memories . . . I have no image of myself in relation to them. They are suffused with anxiety, but it's not my own anxiety. The anxiety is in the things themselves' (337). As she remembers these objects in the process of painting them, she re-experiences the anxiety associated with them as external to herself, projected on to the objects in a way which also makes it convincing that she should now 'remember' them so vividly.

The objects have almost become screen-memories, standing in for the painful experiences with which they are linked but which have not yet been remembered.

Elaine also paints her friend Grace's mother, Mrs Smeath, who 'floats up without warning, like a dead fish, materializing on a sofa I am drawing'; she is 'smiling her half-closed smile, smug and accusing. Whatever has happened to me is my own fault, the fault of what is wrong with me. Mrs Smeath knows what it is. She isn't telling' (338). As a child Elaine was fascinated and repulsed by Mrs Smeath and the idea of her 'bad heart'. When she is first described, from the point of view of the child, the narrator goes on to reflect: 'This is how I will see her forever: lying unmoving, like something in a museum.' When she adds: 'She is ten years younger than I am now. Why do I hate her so much? Why do I care, in any way, what went on in her head?' (58) the perspective of the narrator has clearly shifted to the 'future', but the subject who speaks at this point has clearly not yet 'remembered', otherwise she would be able to associate her hatred of Mrs Smeath with the fact that she knew about, and colluded in, the bullying to which Elaine was being subjected. It is the reader who makes the connection between Elaine's paintings of Mrs Smeath and the role she played in her childhood: when Elaine reviews these paintings at her retrospective her hatred is transformed into understanding. 'I used to think these were self-righteous eyes, piggy and smug . . . And they are. But they are also defeated eyes, uncertain and melancholy, heavy with unloved duty . . . the eyes of a small-town threadbare decency. Mrs Smeath was a transplant to the city . . . A displaced person, as I was.' She is also able to see herself through Mrs Smeath's eyes, 'a frazzle-haired ragamuffin from heaven knows where . . . And yet she took me in' (405). Reviewing her paintings as versions or representations of the past enables Elaine to retranslate the meanings of the reality of that past.

Elaine's paintings are visual equivalents of the way in which we rework and re-represent elements of the past, and her reinterpretations acknowledge the complex processes of condensation, displacement and fantasy which produce what we call 'memory'. Fraser's stories and dreams are interpreted more crudely as 'symbols' or evidence, and her earlier novel, *Pandora*, initiates a chain of events which leads to the revelation of the truth about her past, the most contrived and novelistic element of the text. Fraser is interviewed about *Pandora* on a TV show by Joker Nash, a member of her old high-school gang. He reads aloud a section in which Pandora is sexually assaulted by the bread delivery man and dismisses it on the grounds that ' [s]ome little girls can be seductive at an early age. I think your book is typical of the kind of hysterical imaginings we're seeing too much of thei days' (158). Both the 'breadman' who assaults Pandora and Joker himself are described as having 'pointy teeth' (156, 158); the intertextual echo raises the question of how far each text has 'rewritten' the other. Joker plays a key role in the revelation of the truth about Fraser's past: he becomes the comic-strip figure who haunts her dreams – '*Joker Nash, dressed as a magician in whiteface, top hat and tails, perches on the railings of my father's house*' (221) – and is the indirect catalyst for the final recovery of Fraser's memory of abuse, when her friend Babs, who has recently married him, tells her that he has molested her daughter. It is this kind of narrative coincidence which makes the reader aware of the construction of a sequence of events almost *too* tightly plotted to be convincing as truth. The second 'encounter' with Joker Nash is a means by which Fraser is able to reinterpret the meaning of the first, that is, the strength of her reaction – trembling and speechlessness – when he denied the reality of events such as those described in *Pandora*. In the second scene, italics are used for repetitions of Joker's earlier statements of denial, juxtaposed with the revelations Babs is making, suggesting an unconscious memory and reinterpretation of the earlier scene. The two scenes thus stand towards each other in the relationship of *Nachträglichkeit*, with the first scene, that of Fraser's own abuse, standing behind these two. This primal scene is then re-enacted in the responses of Fraser's body to Babs' words.

DREAMING AS REPETITION

Repetition towards recognition also takes the form of a series of obviously symbolic dreams which Fraser says she 'learned how to interpret . . . as messages from my unconscious' (211), a rather crude formulation of the possible significance of dreaming. In the 'Wolf Man' case history Freud claimed that 'dreaming is another kind of remembering': 'It is this recurrence in dreams that I regard as the explanation of the fact that the patients themselves gradually acquire a profound conviction of the reality of these primal scenes' (1918: 285). Fraser does recover memory independently of her dreams, but they are so tightly constructed, or reconstructed, and so obviously symbolic, that it often seems as if they have been either dreamed in response to recovered memory or even constructed in order to provide evidence for it.

The ending of Fraser's relationship with Paul Lawson and the death of her father are reconstructed in a sequence which incorporates several dreams which encode or predict events in this obvious way. Her father is taken ill just before she and Paul are due to take an illicit holiday. As Fraser discusses her father's condition with her mother over the telephone she notices a previously unnoticed resemblance to her father in a photograph of Paul. She goes to sleep uneasily, thinking of her Aunt Estelle, her father's sister; just before her affair with Paul began she visited her father in his nursing home and he called her 'Estelle'. She now has a dream in which Estelle figures prominently, and which she remembers ten days later when she goes home for her father's funeral:

I am a princess lying on a bier in the forest. Aunt Estelle cuts a swatch of my hair and presents it to my father. Now I am standing beside the bier, holding the blond hair, looking at the princess. Through the glass floor of the forest I see a ticktacktoe game, marked with Xs and Os. Pointing to the princess, Aunt Estelle announces: 'She is not dead yet, but she is dying.' (205)

The dream only develops its full meaning much later, after her father's death, when, as a result of another dream, she 'knows' that her father and Aunt Estelle must once have been lovers: at this point, it is clearly connected with the ending of her relationship with Paul, her own contemplated death by suicide, and the death of her cat which functions as a substitute. The next evening Fraser attends a Halloween fancy-dress party as a cat and meets Paul there: when he tells her that he has to spend the week with his wife instead of on vacation with her, she ends the relationship in a way which explicitly echoes the way in which she finally managed to resist her father: ' *"Touch me again and I'll kill you!" He doesn't resist. He doesn't fight back. So that is all it took, would have taken*' (195). This is clearly the conscious reconstruction (level 4 of the narrative) of a then unconscious repetition (level 2) which also functions as a step towards level 3, 'the order of emergence of past event'. Haunted by the image of the noose with which her grandfather hanged himself, she sees suicide as the end for which she is destined. She dreams: '*I am curled in a tight ball, still wearing my cat costume ... Now I am a cat with a red leash wound like an umbilical cord around my neck ... I'm looking down a long dark tunnel, and I'm choking*' (198). The next day she finds her cat, choked to death on its collar. The echoing of event – loss of a beloved cat, the ending of an abusive relationship – and imagery – the leash around the neck – again reinforces a too-insistent pattern of repetition, as if the story of the discovery of the truth of the past is being deliberately constructed as an echo of the story of the past itself.

When Fraser receives the news that her father is dying she decides not to catch the first plane home, thus missing the chance of seeing him whilst he is still alive. Instead, the shrieking of a train whistle at the precise hour of his death establishes a 'telepathic' connection with him, of a kind she will later come to accept as part of a vision of the world as 'infinite' and 'full of wonder' (253). Ferenczi suggested a possible explanation for telepathy precisely in terms of the kind of abuse Fraser suffered as a child: '[p]eople who claim to be clair-voyant . . . have been forced into a kind of hypersensitivity from childhood. That is, they have been the victims of such cruelty on the part of their parents that in order to survive they had to develop a remarkable sensitivity to determine what their parents were really feeling, so that they could avoid their murderous rage' (in Masson 1992: 184). Fraser remembers her dream about Aunt Estelle when her mother shows her a lock of her father's baby-hair just after his death, and the account of the dream is repeated at this point (205). It is one of many such dreams in which the events and images of her life are reworked and represented in a way which symbolise the hidden truth in a manner almost too direct to be plausible. Here the Xs and Os echo the game she used to play with her father as a child, described on the first page of the text; the princess is the fairytale heroine with whom she identified as a 'special' child; she has recently established a connection with Aunt Estelle; the bier is a premonition of death; Aunt Estelle's words are a reference to the 'other self' who is on the way to being recognised and hence to her 'death', and to the conscious self who will die unless the hidden self is recognised.

After her father's death Fraser becomes seriously ill following a hysterectomy and has a series of dreams whose obvious symbolic content make them difficult to credit if we are reading the text as autobiography. The imagery of caves, demon-monsters, white larvae, a blonde child giving birth to Satan's baby, devil-masks, snakes, rocky passageways, impenetrable castles, a 'joker in a deck of cards', of blindness and death (212–17), is too obvious to need interpretation, and gives the unfortunate impression of having been invented for the purpose. Ultimately we do not know whether these dreams were actually dreamed at the time and possibly written down immediately, dreamed in response to ideas suggested in analysis, or more or less constructed either at the time of the recovery of memory or in the process of writing the text – or any combination of these. Culbertson suggests that the young child who is being sexually abused might construct around the events fantasies incorporating images of evil from fairytales, but in Fraser's case these fantasies only seem to emerge in her adult dreams as part of the process of 'remembering'.

Culbertson's suggestion provides a possible explanation for some cases of supposed 'satanic' abuse (although in her account the paedophiles who abused her *did* use 'parlor occultism', 'ritual and dress-up' (1995: 184) as a cover for their activities); Fraser's use of such images seems sensational given the concern of some therapists that the quest for evidence of 'satanic' abuse might be a diversion from more 'ordinary' and genuine cases.

In spite of the precision and 'relevance' of these dreams, and the growing feeling that 'I seem to be on the verge of remembering something sexual to do with my father', Fraser states: 'I was never going to believe anything I dreamed to have literal truth, no matter how persuasive. *My insight and intuition could only prepare me to remember. They were my detectives who could uncover clues, but who couldn't deliver a confession. That had to come from my other self*' (217). Here she further subdivides herself and objectifies elements of her psyche into separate agents; 'insight' and 'intuition' are seen as distinct from the repressed unconscious which holds the memory of the trauma, and function as 'detectives' looking for a 'confession'. The 'other self' finally emerges physically and emotionally, when her body re-enacts the experience of the abuse, but this kind of memory is further distinguished from 'verbal or visual' (225) memory which she seeks via hypnosis as stronger or more valid evidence. She uses a mechanical model for the memories which seem to count as the most valid evidence, explaining that '[l]ike a small child playing hide-and-seek, she often tried to conceal herself by closing her eyes so that visual memories were sometimes not recorded' (218): this could be read as another way of describing the kind of dissociation discussed earlier, but also suggests the idea that memory functions like a video camera, filming what is 'there' for future review. After 'remembering through the body' her experience of being 'raped through the mouth', she says: 'One startling piece of information has been fed into my head like a microchip into a computer: I KNOW my father raped me.' The image used here puts this new information in terms of scientific fact: except, of course, any 'fact' can be fed into a computer in order to effect what Fraser calls a 'drastic shift' in 'history' (221). An italicised dream or fantasy which uses the image of '*Joker Nash, dressed as a magician*' retextualises the memory, and the voice of the conscious narrator comments: 'The Joker on my father's porch has at last delivered. And the true villain of the piece? Not the breadman, as I wrote in Pandora, but the breadwinner with the devil's hooked hand' (221). Dreams or fantasies are once more brought into play in order to reinforce the 'evidence', reinforcing even further the closely constructed network of proofs and connections.

The final stage in the process of Fraser's remembering is via hypnosis: it is significant that this therapy is only resorted to at the end of a long process of the recovery of memory by other means, given the controversy over the use of hypnotherapy in cases of 'recovered' memory. Here, hypnosis gives Fraser access to the 'visual' memories she has been looking for: under hypnosis she is able to 'see' herself as a young child hanging around outside her father's bedroom door, and then to 'watch' the sequence of abusive actions. Hypnosis itself does not produce the experience of 'remembering through the body', but is experienced as more convincing 'proof'. When she 'blocks', her therapist encourages her to use images or fantasies: she imagines herself in a 'fairytale forest' with her mother 'dressed like the witch in Snow White' (226), and then sees herself in a mirror in the moonlight. Here she is using the fairytale as a mode of narrative visualisation by which she is able to insert herself into a story of persecution: it thus becomes an 'interpretative device' by means of which she is able to remember that her father also abused her as an adolescent. The child in the mirror is 'too old' – eleven or twelve – and Fraser later continues the guided fantasy to produce the image of the five-year-old child with matted hair and blue fangs already referred to, and who she finally accepts is also her adolescent and adult self. This realisation of the continuance of the abuse into adolescence is almost harder for Fraser to accept than her rape as a young child; as suggested earlier, the continued repression of the knowledge of the experience into adolescence also becomes harder for the *reader* to accept.

'LIFE DOES HAVE A SHAPE . . . '

The final move of Fraser's story is that of understanding and forgiveness. She sees her journey as one of moving from darkness into light, both in terms of knowledge and psychic health. As Mark Freeman points out: 'The narrative Fraser elects to tell . . . is a function of the very beliefs she holds about what human beings ultimately are . . . The very way one understands the past . . . is the product of a narrative choice which, in turn, may issue from the most fundamental beliefs, values, and ideals one holds' (1991: 173). Fraser partly 'explains' her ability to forgive and even love her father in terms of the notion of 'readiness to remember': 'I did not remember the past . . . until I was stable enough and happy enough that sorrow or anger or regret or pain was overwhelmed by joy at my release' (252). For Fraser, 'truth', the solving of a mystery, has therapeutic value in itself: 'Finally, truth is the only thing worth saying' (233). 'Life does have a shape and maybe even a purpose' (253), she claims: hers was a life which 'was structured on the uncovering of a mystery' (252). Her narrative, as I have shown, is itself highly 'shaped' by the 'reciprocal determination' of ends and beginnings. As she reads and rewrites her own life, and we read that rewriting, 'we read only those incidents and signs that can be construed as promise and annunciation, enchained towards a construction of significance – those markers that, as in the detective story, appear to be clues to the underlying intentionality of event' (Brooks 1984: 94). Fraser's understanding of her parents' failures is framed in terms of their own deprivations: her mother's displacement from England to America, the deaths of her sisters from diseases of poverty, her father's suicide, her sexual ignorance and the need for respectability. Her own father's life was one of loneliness and frustration: 'My father's rage was an impotent rage. He shouted and waved his fists like a child in a high chair. I know that now. He demanded and was obeyed, but was never heard' (239). She even wonders whether he was 'as profoundly split as I. Was there a Daddy Who Knew and a Daddy Who Did Not Know?' (240).[4] This kind of 'explanation' is part of Fraser's acceptance of a particular model of causality of child abuse: 'Children who were in some way abused, abuse others; victims become villains. Thus, not to forgive only perpetuates the crime, creates more villains' (252). Fraser sees herself as blessed with the ability to understand and forgive in order to break this cycle: she knows that it was her parents' determination to give her an education and a 'better chance' than they had had that enabled her to gain the insight, understanding and resources to survive. Like Carolyn Steedman, she is the middle-class daughter of working-class parents who is able to bring the insights of intellectual work and psychoanalysis to bear on the problems and traumas of her parents' lives, and to use writing as a mode of exploration, explanation and, for Fraser, catharsis. 'Children are always episodes in someone else's narrative,' suggests Carolyn Steedman (1986: 122), and Fraser agrees: 'All of us are born into the second act of a tragedy-in-progress, and then spend the rest of our lives trying to figure out what went wrong in the first act' (241).

Sylvia Fraser's rewriting of her life is characterised by a need to fashion an 'intelligible, consistent, and unbroken case history' (Marcus 1984: 61) in which all gaps are filled and all clues 'solved'. Her narrative is marked by a search for, and discovery of a primal scene – or series of scenes – that function as a total explanation of the 'symptoms' of her life and her fragmented sense of identity. Child sexual abuse is an important reality, not to be evaded by definitions of the primal scene such as Ned Lukacher's as 'a constellation of forgotten intertextual events offered in lieu of a demonstrable, unquestionable origin' (Lukacher 1986: 24), despite the usefulness of this concept as a tool for the analysis of narratives in which such an origin is postulated and sought. Fraser's search is marked by nostalgia for an originary memory and presence, not of abuse experienced as such but of the original tenderness and bliss of the child still in the Garden of Eden of innocent infantile sexuality.

'TIME IS NOT A LINE . . .'

Fraser's reconstruction of her life depends upon a 'law of human nature, as compelling as Newton's, that whatever is hidden in the psyche will struggle to reveal itself' (153). This assumption about the nature of the psyche is given a 'cosmic' dimension by the idea Elaine takes over from her physicist brother Stephen in *Cat's Eye*, that '[t]ime is not a line but a dimension' still existing 'somewhere' and potentially available for the kind of revisit created by these two narratives. Elaine says at the beginning of the book that 'I began then to think of time as having a shape, something you could see, like a series of liquid transparencies, one laid on top of another... Sometimes this comes to the surface, sometimes that, sometimes nothing. Nothing goes away' (3). What does become available to consciousness is imagined as random and involuntary; Elaine comes to think of the past as 'discontinuous, like stones skipped across water, like postcards' (302). Although we are asked to imagine that Elaine is suddenly able to 'see [her] life entire', the narration preserves some of this discontinuity, telling a story which is roughly chronological but in short disjointed sections which also reflect the sense of disconnection Elaine feels from earlier versions of her 'self', the idea that 'there is never only one, of anyone'. Cordelia, increasingly insecure as a teenager, is told by Stephen that she only has 'a tendency to exist' (242), and Elaine describes how 'her face goes still, remote, unreflecting. It's as if she's not inside it' (221) 'She's mimicking something... some role or image only she can see' (244). Cordelia now begins to manifest the absence of self, the 'nothingness' which, as a child, she projected on to Elaine and which persists in her as an adult: '*What do you have to say for yourself?* Cordelia used to ask. *Nothing*, I would say. It was a word I came to connect with myself, as if I was nothing, as if there was nothing there at all' (41). Elaine also imagines several future identities for the grown-up Cordelia she never actually meets: in one sense Cordelia has escaped the future by her absence, whilst on the

other she is stuck in time as a nine-year-old bully just as a part of
Elaine is stuck in the past as her nine-year-old victim. When she
revisits their old school playground in the present time of the narrative,
she suddenly feels 'ill will' surrounding her: 'it's hard to breathe. I
feel as if I am pushing against something, a pressure on me, like
opening a door against a snowstorm. Get me out of this, Cordelia. I'm
locked in. I don't want to be nine years old forever' (400). A little
later she feels that Cordelia is vanishing and escaping while 'I'm
headed for a future in which I sprawl propped in a wheelchair, shed-
ding hair and drooling . . . and I stand in the snow under the bridge,
and stand and stand' (413). Here the 'I' is imagined as split between
the ageing self and the child who is stranded in the past, the self of
the present absent. The novel also dramatises the doubling of the
self, the 'invasion by and loss of the self to a malignant other' in
Elaine's internalisation of Cordelia 'as an aspect of her own personality' (Brooks Bouson 1993: 160). The novel is full of doubles and
twins, Elaine tormenting the teenage Cordelia with the idea that she
is the vampire twin of a human girl who sleeps in 'a coffin full of
earth' (245), suggesting an unconscious memory of her burial in the
black hole. When, as a young woman, Elaine paints her one and only
'portrait' of Cordelia, she realises that she is 'afraid of being Cordelia.
Because in some way we changed places, and I've forgotten when'
(239).

It is the episode which marks the end of the bullying and the
beginning of Elaine's 'forgetting', the time when she nearly freezes to
death in the ravine and is 'saved' by a 'dark lady', that enacts the most
complex revisiting of the past and its reinterpretation in the light of
later understanding. When Elaine tells the story of what happened in
the ravine it is with full memory of what the child of nine *believed*
to have happened, although, as with the rest of her memory of childhood, it is not clear when it was remembered, and it is immediately
problematised by the subject's uncertainty about what she really
'saw'. Elaine's hat is thrown down into the ravine by Cordelia, who
then orders her to retrieve it; she climbs down the steep and frozen
bank and walks out on to the ice. Her boots fill with water and she
struggles to get out, sitting and then lying down on the bank, convinced she will be unable to climb back up again with her frozen feet.
Her head fills with 'black sawdust' and she imagines that the rustling
of the sleet through the branches is the voices of the dead people
gathering around her. Cordelia has long since abandoned her there,
but when she looks up she sees a figure standing there on the bridge,
which now looks quite different: 'it seems higher above me, more
solid, as if the railings have disappeared or been filled in. And it's

glowing, there are pools of light along it, greenish-yellow, not like any light I've seen before' (189). What she 'sees' is a lady in a black cloak who walks or floats down towards her, holding her arms out so that she can see a patch of red, 'her heart, on the outside of her body, glowing like neon, like a coal'. She hears her voice telling her: '*You can go home now . . . It will be all right. Go home*' (189). As she makes her way back up the hill she 'knows' that '[i]t's the Virgin Mary, there can be no doubt' (190). The memory of this episode and its representation are complicated not only by the process of forgetting, which began after this episode, but also by the fact that a few days afterwards she became unsure of the identity of the 'dark lady', though she still 'believes' it was the Virgin Mary, and by her final realisation, when she goes back to the ravine during the Toronto visit, that 'there was no lady in a dark cloak bending over me' (418). What was 'remembered' when Elaine saw 'her life entire' was thus a fantasy, but it is only when she revisits the ravine that she realises it *was* a fantasy, whilst at the same time the dark lady comes 'back to me now in absolute clarity, acute in every detail' (418).

When Elaine describes her visit to the ravine in the 'present' we become aware that as a nine-year-old lying there she was 'remembering' or 'seeing' the future when she saw the concrete, lighted bridge which she now walks across. The Elaine of the present asserts '[n]evertheless it's the same bridge' (418). An event already remembered is now re-remembered with the immediacy of place: 'That's where I stood, with the snow falling on me, unable to summon the will to move. That's where I heard the voice,' although at the same time she realises '[t]here was no voice', that there was no dark lady, although she can now 'see' her in clear detail: 'There was only darkness and silence. Nobody and nothing' (418). The effect is of a memory being re-created and destroyed at the same time. At this point Elaine becomes aware that if she turns around she will see someone waiting for her ahead on the path: at first she thinks it will be her nine-year-old self in her blue knitted hat, but then turns to see the nine-year-old Cordelia, looking at her:

There is the same shame, the sick feeling in my body, the same knowledge of my own wrongness, awkwardness, weakness; the same wish to be loved; the same loneliness; the same fear. But these are not my own emotions any more. They are Cordelia's; as they always were. (419)

This awareness of Cordelia's *own* sense of failure and fear of rejection, projected on to and internalised by Elaine, is a complex interpersonal psychological process which the text subtly suggests to the reader at the time of its occurrence, when Elaine is too young and vulnerable to realise it. It is the counterpart of Elaine's teenage internalisation of Cordelia's defensive childhood cruelty. Cordelia's fear of her father, the violence that is only hinted at, is never developed into the kind of over-determined explanation which we see at work in *My Father's House*. The climax of *Cat's Eye* is a cathartic moment of repetition-with-a-difference, a final 'meeting' between the adult Elaine and the child Cordelia which could not have occurred in reality; the text sets up a framework of reference for this in terms of Stephen's ideas about time so that understanding and acceptance comes about not as an effect of memory alone, nor as the result of a long process of construction and reconstruction in therapy, but by means of a supposed re-creation of an earlier moment as time 'doubles back' upon itself. Here again the 'end writes the beginning' in the suggestion that the earlier event – the ravine episode – was 'created' or determined by the end – this final meeting on the bridge. Elaine now feels that 'I am the older one, now, I'm the stronger', and Cordelia is the child in danger: 'If she stays here any longer she will freeze to death; she will be left behind, in the wrong time . . . I reach out my arms to her, bend down, hands open to show I have no weapon. *It's all right*, I say to her. *You can go home now*' (419). One interpretation of this, suggested by the black dress she is wearing, the gesture and the echoed words, is that the child Elaine was 'saved' by a vision of her adult self, an idea that belongs to the realm of the mystical and irrational if taken literally: Elaine grows up to become the woman who saves her own life as a child. But this moment also metaphorically suggests the way in which the adult who has fully remembered and come to terms with the past frees the part of the self which is still 'stuck' there. This also necessitates a 'letting go' of the Cordelia who tormented her, a gesture which symbolically redeems the lonely and frightened child who Cordelia also was, but which also accepts that she is gone. Elaine's recognition of their mutual identification, the process of projection and internalisation which made them 'others' to each other, gives psychological conviction to the mystical or telepathic connections established here, so that they are 'of the psyche' as well as 'psychic'.

Elaine's paintings rework in symbolic form the elements of the past which her narrative reconstructs; they are also reviewed in the light of fuller understanding – and of recovered memory – when she reviews them at her 'retrospective'. *Unified Field Theory* suggests the 'unified field' of moments in which past and present are held together; the moment when she 'meets' the past on the bridge, and the moment when she rereads the painting which is a reworking of that moment.

The 'Virgin of Lost Things' stands on the bridge over the ravine, holding an oversized cat's eye marble; beneath the bridge is the night sky, full of stars: 'galaxy upon galaxy: the universe, in its incandescence and darkness'. Looking more closely, one also sees 'beetles and small roots', because this is also 'the underside of the ground'(108) suggesting the beetles collected by Elaine's father, the earth under which she was buried and the 'underside' of unconscious memory. This painting functions both as a representation of a memory which was in part a fantasy, the ground in which past and present meet, and an image of the future, the meeting on the bridge in which Elaine 'becomes' the dark lady of her memory.

As Elaine looks once more at these paintings, she acknowledges that they have escaped her control: 'I can no longer . . . tell them what to mean. Whatever energy they have came out of me. I'm what's left over' (409). It is as if the past itself, and her efforts to rework it, has used her up. She realises 'I may have thought I was preserving something from time, salvaging something', but is now tempted to 'destroy the lot', thus raising very explicitly the complex questions of our relationship to the past and the function of memory itself. She here rethinks her mental model of time: it is 'not a place' but 'only a blur, the moving edge we live in', a phrase which precisely evokes our tenuous sense of inhabiting the present moment. She goes on to evoke time as something 'fluid, which turns back upon itself, like a wave' (409), suggesting the way in which she 'meets' past versions of both herself and Cordelia, and the structure of the novel itself.

Her understanding of the past includes a recognition of loss: flying home to the west coast Elaine sits next to two old ladies who are enjoying their friendship and the freedom of old age: 'They're rambunctious, they're full of beans; they're tough as thirteen, they're innocent and dirty . . . now for a short while they can play again like children, but this time without the pain' (420). Now Elaine realises that she misses 'something that will never happen' – close female friendship as she grows old, the friendship she might have had with Cordelia. In spite of this recognition of loss, the ending of the novel is not as negative as is suggested by Gayle Greene, who ignores its final paragraph in stating that the novel ends with repetition of the word 'nothing' (Greene 1991b: 321): in fact, it ends with a description of the night sky full of stars, 'echoes of light, shining out of the midst of nothing. It's old light, and there's not much of it. But it's enough to see by' (421). It has enabled Elaine to 'see' what was really going on in her relationship with Cordelia and to recognise their mutual need. It is an echo of her realisation that '[a]n eye for an eye only leads to more blindness' as she looks again at her paintings of

Mrs Smeath, which also suggests the kind of forgiveness reached by Sylvia Fraser and the breaking of a cycle of victimisation. Atwood's novel ends on a note of cautious and qualified optimism, in contrast to Fraser's 'I have burst into an infinite world full of wonder' (253) – although *My Father's House* does actually end on the sadder note of the death of Fraser's mother. In spite of the trope by which the narrator-subject is imagined as seeing 'her life entire', both narrative and sense of self are left more fractured and discontinuous, less 'complete' and resolved, than Fraser's autobiography which (almost) ends with a dream/fantasy in which she says goodbye to her father in his coffin, is 'joined' with her lost 'inner child', and turns into a seabird on its way to the ocean with a quill in her mouth 'to be dipped into the sun' (242). Here recovered memory is put to the service of a fully 'integrated' and reconstructed identity. Although the resolution of Atwood's novel is more provisional, both texts provide the reader with the vicarious satisfaction of the experience of trauma and the comfort of recovery, as well as the narrative satisfaction described by Peter Brooks and by Stephen Marcus: 'What we end with, then, is a fictional construction which is at the same time satisfactory to us in the form of the truth, and as the form of the truth' (Marcus 1984: 62).

Notes

1. The British False Memory Society has a well-documented and researched file of cases of 'recovered' memory of sexual abuse which they believe to be false, claiming that no confirmed case exists. This side of the debate is outlined in Frederick Crews (1995), *The Memory Wars*: the most influential book in the recovered memory movement was *The Courage to Heal* by Ellen Bass and Laura Davis (1988). Much of the debate centres around the opposition between the two models of memory outlined in the first chapter.
2. Culbertson uses Lawrence L. Langer's discussion of Delbo's account in *Holocaust Testimonies* (1991).
3. Both Culbertson and Herman use Fraser's account in their discussions of sexual abuse and its after-effects without acknowledging it as a literary reconstruction in which 'truth' is produced as an effect of narrative.
4. Robert Jay Lifton cites evidence for this kind of splitting on the part of perpetrators in his *The Nazi Doctors* (1986). In *The Drowned and the Saved* (1988), Primo Levi also describes how the perpetrators of atrocities in the Nazi camps used a '*cordon sanitaire*' in order to 'impede the entry' of 'burdensome memories': 'it is easier to deny entry to a memory than to free oneself of it after it has been recorded.' They subsequently 'built a convenient past for themselves and ended by believing it' (17–18).

4

Myths of Origin:
Identity, Memory and Detection in
Barbara Vine's
A Dark Adapted Eye and
Asta's Book

INTRODUCTION

In the previous chapter I explored the narrative strategies by which Sylvia Fraser constructs the story of her past as the excavation of a hidden truth and a doubled identity. She explicitly compares her quest for the truth as an act of detection; her narrative satisfies the reader's desire for resolution and certainty, and the writer's for wholeness and integration. The narrative draws attention to the highly reconstructed nature of her memories, but the reader is not expected to doubt their veracity. Fraser reads her own life as an act of detection; the reader reads *her* reading, realising that 'prior events, causes, are so only retrospectively, in a reading back from the end' (Brooks 1984: 29). An exploration of two popular fictional works of detection will further highlight the strategies that Fraser employs to establish the truth of her origin.

In 1986 the popular and successful crime writer Ruth Rendell published her first novel under the pseudonym Barbara Vine. As Vine, Rendell has developed a kind of fiction which uses the strategies of detection to explore and problematise the notion of identity; the processes of memory – of character, narrator and reader – are also employed in the reconstruction of the past, which, in the novels under discussion, preserves the 'doubt at the heart of things' (*A Dark*

Adapted Eye 1986: 291). Rendell soon admitted that she was 'Barbara Vine', but continues to write under both names; this doubling and disguise of name and identity is a central trope of many Vine novels. Their complex narrative structures frequently revolve around the identity of a child – killed, stolen, abandoned or exchanged – and explore the relationships between motherhood, memory and author-ship. Swanny, the protagonist of *Asta's Book* (1993), maintains: 'Our need to know our origins is deep-seated, is at the root of personality' (303), and the trajectory of Vine's novels is frequently this search for origins – sometimes of an individual, and sometimes of a sequence of events, a chain of cause and effect. The search for origins, for the truth about the past, takes place in large part through the processes of writing and of reading: the central text of *Asta's Book* is the diary kept by Asta which conceals – and reveals – the identity of her elegant upper middle-class daughter Swanhild or Swanny. Swanny is made to doubt her identity in late middle age by means of an anonymous letter; Ann, her niece, reconstructs her own attempts to discover Swanny's true identity, mostly by means of meticulous read-ing and rereading of the diaries, which were themselves discovered as a result of the anonymous letter which prompted Swanny's search for her origins. In *A Dark Adapted Eye* (1986), it is the truth-status of memory itself that is at issue. Some thirty years before the present time of the narrative, a five-year-old child, Jamie, is the object of a struggle for possession between his mother and his aunt. He remains convinced – partly through a memory which is later brought into question – that Vera, who raised and breastfed him, and finally mur-dered her sister Eden in the struggle for possession, was his real mother, and this becomes a key factor in his sense of identity. Letters and documents, as well as memories, are produced as evidence, but the narrator remains unsure of Jamie's true parentage and the narrative leaves the question open.

In Vine's novel, *The Chimney Sweeper's Boy* (1998), the daughter of a famous novelist, Gerald Candless, discovers, just after his death, that he had assumed a false identity as a young man. The narrative reconstructs her attempts to discover his origins, finally revealed in the pages of a missing and unpublished novel. Candless' publisher mentions Germaine Greer's *Daddy, We Hardly Knew You* (1989) as an example of the kind of family memoir which has recently become popular: in this text Greer also reconstructs her discovery that she only knew her father under an assumed name and identity. Vine's fictions are popular versions of the need to know our origins, the temptation to create myths around them, and the fascination involved in the works of detection to discover them. Greer's discovery that her father was fostered and semi-literate provokes her pity but also a sense of emptiness: 'In finding him I lost him. Sleepless nights are long' (311).

In Fraser's autobiography, the strategies of detection and of writing are employed to produce 'truth finally set down' (Culbertson 1995: 183); Vine's narratives are structured in a way which problematises and textualises notions of origin and identity. They also employ popular ideas about the functioning, or misfunctioning, of memory: the failing memories of the elderly, with their vivid recall of earlier days; infantile amnesia and the false memories formed in early childhood, as in the case of Jamie; the distortions of nostalgia. Popular fascination with the functions and failings of memory is put to the service of plots which play with the reader's desire for certainty and resolution, and which call upon the reader's *own* memory in the unravelling of plot and the reconstruction of the past. First-person narratives usually invoke the reader's trust in the reliability of the memory of the narrator; this is clearly problematic when the writer, like Fraser, claims to have repressed the memory of significant chunks of her past. Ann and Faith (the narrator of *A Dark Adapted Eye*) are presented as reliable, detached and more-or-less objective narrators even though, in Faith's case, she is dealing with traumatic material – the murder of one aunt and the execution of the other. Her name also suggests that we should trust her as a narrator, whilst also drawing attention to her own (possibly misplaced) 'faith' in what she remembers and what she is told.

Both narrators are dependent on their own memories, the memories of others, and on a wide range of texts and documents for the reconstruction of the stories of their subjects, members of the previous generations of their respective families. In the preface to *Asta's Book*, Ann describes the book she has written as: 'A collection of papers and memories: my grandmother's diaries, an account of a crime and a transcript of a trial, letters and documents and the things I remember'. She works, appropriately, as an 'author's researcher', describing herself as 'only the watcher and the recorder, the notetaker, the privileged insider' (44), often treated by others 'like a private detective' (124). She admits, however, that although it is not her story, 'the difficulty is that it's I who tell it and the things that happened to me affect it' (202). This awareness functions in terms of the gaps in her knowledge – caused by her youth or absence – but is not used by Vine to suggest an emotional bias which might make her an unreliable witness. Her involvement both enables and prolongs the revelation of the truth, but is not seen as fundamentally distorting that truth. Faith, who begins by collaborating with a writer who is working on a book about her aunt, refers to 'the real book that is Vera's life recorded on a tape run only in my own consciousness' (25). This suggests a more personal relationship to her subject, and a direct access to the 'reality' of Vera's life, but her narrative is nevertheless partly composed out of the memories and written evidence of others. It also leaves her, and the reader, with a radical uncertainty as to Jamie's origin.

Vine's novels are precisely set in time and place. The key events of *Asta's Book* take place just before and during the First World War, which is finally revealed to have an intimate connection with the lives of the family. In *A Dark Adapted Eye*, the lives of two middle-class women living in a Suffolk cottage just before and during the Second World War are closely observed, and their sexual lives bound up with the changes brought about by the war. In these novels, disputed identity also involves the question of class. Possession of the infant Jamie is contested by two sisters, originally lower middle class, who now have rather different class affiliations: Vera's life is almost a parody of middle-class obsession and ritual, and of post-war ideologies of femininity, whilst class mobility during the war and her marriage place Eden rather precariously in a class several notches higher. The upper middle-class Swanny is made to doubt her parentage by means of an anonymous letter based on class envy, and is finally revealed to be the child of a servant and a working man. Here class snobbery is also inflected by national identity. Asta and her husband are Danish, living in London in the early years of the century; Asta retains an acute sense of national superiority whilst her husband does his best to become English. In *The Chimney Sweeper's Boy*, the origins of the novelist Gerald Candless are revealed as working class, but here the motive for a change of identity is sexual: an encounter in a bath house between Gerald and his brother, both unacknowledged homosexuals at a time when this would have been a matter of shame and concealment. All three works of detection reveal and reconstruct stories of other families – several rungs down the social ladder – whose lives are intimately connected with, and sometimes echo, the lives of their middle-class protagonists. Most importantly, the texts of Asta's diaries and Ann's work of detection are intertwined with texts that relate the story of a 'famous' turn of the century murder, that of a working-class woman, Lizzie Roper, apparently by her husband, and the disappearance of their baby daughter Edith. For much of the novel Swanny believes herself to be the missing Edith and constructs a provisional identity based upon that belief.

The reader of Vine's novels becomes a participant in the quest for truth: as Peter Brooks puts it, reading becomes an act of detection in which we 'read in a spirit of confidence, and also a state of dependence, that what remains to be read will restructure the provisional meanings of the already read' (1984: 23). In *Asta's Book*, reading is multi-layered: we read the extracts from Asta's diary that Ann has chosen to include, and also Ann's account of her reading and rereading of the diaries in her search for clues to Swanny's identity. 'Memory... is the key faculty in the capacity to perceive relations of beginnings, middles and ends through time' (Brooks 1984: 11). It is only with hindsight that apparently irrelevant details reveal their significance, and just as Ann keeps going back to the diaries to search for half-forgotten, possibly relevant details, so the reader flips back and rereads in order to confirm or contest Ann's interpretations. Rereading a Vine novel is like being vividly reminded of a previous half-forgotten experience or dream, sometimes with surprise at what has been forgotten and sometimes with heightened understanding of what has turned out to be significant. As John Forrester suggests, on rereading, we revisit events which '*would have been* recognized as a purpose and *would have* determined the action, had it been anticipated' (1990: 18).

The fascination of Vine's plots is a function of the gap between the *szujet* – the events *referred to* by the narrative – and the *fabula* – the way the events are *reconstructed by* the narrative. Peter Brooks suggests that 'plot could be thought of as the interpretive activity elicited by the distinction between sjuzet and fabula, the way we *use* the one against the other' (1986: 13). In *Asta's Book* and *A Dark Adapted Eye*, this is at least a double process. Like all detective fiction, – and like Fraser's memoir – these novels tell two stories, that of the crime (here broadly defined) and of the investigation. Faith and Ann tell their own stories of the process of detection: they are engaged in reconstructing the *sjuzet* out of the *fabula* of their own and other peoples' memories, memoirs, letters and diaries. The reader follows and echoes this process but also reconstructs the *sjuzet* of the work of detection: we may also be tempted to construct another *sjuzet*, the stories of Faith and Ann which, they insist, are not the subject of their narratives.

ASTA'S BOOK: ORIGIN AND ORIGINAL

Brooks suggests that the nineteenth century was characterised by 'the need for an explanatory narrative that seeks its authority in a return to origins and the tracing of a coherent story forward from origin to present' (1984: 6). The detective story is paradigmatic of this narrative structure and desire, as demonstrated by Fraser's use of the strategies of the genre; the Freudian psychoanalytic case history also attempts to reconstruct an originating cause. Vine draws on both the strategies of detection and the case history whilst also bringing into question the very idea of 'origin', and of the 'original' – the 'original' story, and the 'original' text. The 'real' reader is inserted into an already existing textual history – the story of the discovery and publication of the diaries – the history of a text and the text of a history, a history still in the making. Intertextuality is woven into the dynamics of the plot: Asta's own favourite writer is Dickens, and Swanny's husband suggests at one point that Asta may have invented the 'plot' of the mystery of Swanny's parentage under the inspiration of stories of orphans and changelings in *Bleak House* and *Great Expectations*.

The text of *Asta's Book* includes a series of inter- and sub-texts which foretell, echo, illuminate or obscure the 'ur-text' of the 'original' story of Asta's life and the birth of her daughter. Asta herself is obviously a fictional construction, and the central text, her diary, is of course *her* reading of her life. Ann, and the reader, reconstruct the *sjuzet* of Asta's life from her own reading of it – Asta herself, she tells us, never rereads her diaries. Ann describes the aura of the original diaries when she first sees them: she looks at them 'as at objects rather than books. They smelt of mildew . . . Their covers were spotted like a mosaic with ineradicable mould marks, a soft pinkish-grey marbling' (275). After Swanny's death she inherits her house and the diaries, and feels 'a certain awe' and 'a little shiver' when she first opens their covers. What might have remained 'an old woman's jottings' had 'undergone a metamorphosis, not only their contents but the materials of which the notebooks are made too, their physical substance, so that this has somehow been hallowed and taken on the quality of a First Folio or a copy of the Vulgate' (32). The authentic, almost mystical aura of these originals suggest that they must contain the truth about Swanny's origins, but Ann, and the reader, are disappointed: crucial pages have been removed, and when they are recovered, the relevant entry is still missing.

Vine also builds into her narrative the idea of the postmodern multiplication of images for popular consumption – Asta's diaries have been serialised on radio and dramatised for television, Ann's friend Cary is producing a television play about the Roper murder – and blurs the distinction between 'story' and 'history'. Ann addresses the reader directly in her preface, invoking the 'paperback editions' of 'Parts I to IV' which 'you may have on your shelves', suggesting that 'if you want to put them [the extracts she quotes] in context you have simply to consult your own copies'. This extra-textual move – Ann also mentions Jane Asher taking the part of Asta in a TV adaptation – suggests that Ann is, in fact, referring to a real or original story which has been reproduced for consumption and which can be used as part of the work of detection. She describes and quotes from an account of the Roper case in a 'green Penguin paperback in the *Famous Trials* series', again suggesting that this story is 'real' history. The relationship between the real and the fake, the original and the reproduction, is thus frequently evoked within the text and implicitly connected with the idea of 'true' origin and identity: Swanny's origins are sought in the original diaries, but cannot be found there as the crucial pages are missing. The different versions of the diary – the original notebooks, the translation, and the first published edition – are read, reread and compared by Ann and by others in an attempt to locate the missing pages and clues to Swanny's identity; Cary searches them for references to the Ropers in order to reconstruct the murder and trial for TV consumption.

Towards the end of the novel, and towards the end of Ann's work of detection, the missing pages are sent back by the woman to whom Asta gave them, for a reason quite unrelated to the question of Swanny's identity: they contained an account of the sinking of a ship, the *Georg Stage*, useful to the woman in question because she was writing a book on Danish naval history. Ann is convinced that the lost pages must contain the truth about Swanny's birth. On reading them she realises that one entry is still missing, but manages to work out the truth without this piece of textual evidence. The 'original' does not, therefore, reveal the 'origin'. The last line of the novel evokes what Ann and the reader will never see or read – 'a page destined for no one's eyes but her (Asta's) own, never to be known and never to be read' (437). The author, Rendell writing as Vine, is concealed behind Asta and Swanny and Ann; and behind these layers of text, of notebook, diary and reproduction, of acts of construction and reconstruction, lies the 'original' story as Vine first conceived it, or rather the question of which came first: *fabula*, the concealment of identity within the missing pages of a diary, or *sjuzet*, the story of a stillbirth and a 'borrowed' child.

The text also offers a visual or material variant on the idea of the relationship between original and copy. Whilst Asta, as a youngish, rather unhappily married woman and mother, is writing her diaries in secret, her husband spends hours of his time building a doll's house for his youngest daughter Marie, mother of Ann. This doll's house is a meticulous reconstruction of Padanaram, their real house in Hampstead, the grandest of the houses the family owned as they climbed the social ladder. Ann unearths the fact that the 'real' Padanaram is a village in Scotland named after a 'plain of Syria' in the Book of Genesis, providing another ironic and playful reflection on the idea of origins. Ann inherits the doll's house, which even contains a 'real book' lying on a table, a half-inch square cut from the thickness of a notebook. 'One of hers?' (Asta's) wonders Ann, 'but the tiny pages of [t]his book were blank' (33), eching the 'blank' or missing page which might have revealed Swanny's identity.

Ann and Cary Oliver visit the house where the Roper family lived to see whether it is suitable for the set of Cary's film. They find that it is now divided up into flats, and that the couple who live on the top floor, where Lizzie Roper was murdered, have created a pastiche of what the 'original' might have looked like. Things 'had been very deliberately and self-consciously retained or the originals copied . . . all the lighting was made to look as if the power which came through was from late-nineteenth-century sources', and the rooms are full of old sepia portrait photographs of 'no-one in particular' (332), except for two of Lizzie and Arthur Roper above the bed. Cary resists the landlord's attempts to rent her the flat for the shooting of her film, choosing instead a 'cheap and ugly' house made of 'brown brick with heavy plaster trimmings . . . more the sort of house Maria Hyde' (Lizzie's mother) 'ought to have lived in than the one in which she actually did live' (339). Cary is thus 'rearranging history' (327), creating a reconstruction which will be accepted as more 'authentic' than the 'original', as in much postmodern cultural reproduction for film and television, museum and heritage site.[1] The question of truth, authenticity and the original is thus echoed in the material settings of the novel.

ASSUMING AN IDENTITY

Swanny's own search for her identity also raises the question of what it is that constitutes the 'real' or 'authentic' self. When she is in her fifties she receives an anonymous letter from someone who clearly envies her for her wealth, beauty and upper middle-class security. The letter claims: 'you are really nobody. You are not your mother's child or your father's. They got you from somewhere when their own one died. Off a rubbish heap, for all you know' (77). Thus Swanny, and later Ann, are plunged into a distorted version of Freud's family romance, in which the child fantasises that he or she is really the child of noble or royal parents. Swanny is forced to doubt her parentage and identity in middle age: 'What had happened to her, though inevitably an evil, more *suitably* happened to children and adolescents' (95).

What Ann finally deduces is that Swanny was the child of an

unmarried servant, Florence Fisher, a friend of Hansine, servant to Asta and Rasmus Westerby. Florence was a servant in the household of the Roper family, where a murder was committed just before the birth of the child who became Swanny. Arthur Roper was acquitted of the murder of his wife Lizzie; their fourteen-month-old daughter Edith disappeared on the day of the murder and was never found. When Ann finds a copy of the Penguin *Famous Trials* account of the case in Swanny's study after her death she realises that towards the end of her life Swanny came to believe that she was the missing Edith. As a younger woman Swanny had been an obedient and submissive daughter and wife; in middle age an abyss opens under her feet and she becomes obsessed by the question of her true identity, a question which her mother refuses (or is unable) to resolve. After Asta's death and the discovery of the diaries she finds a new, more secure and independent identity as 'guardian of the diaries and their editor, the keeper of the shrine, the confidante of the living and the spokeswoman of the dead' (289).

As such, the doubt over her identity has to be put aside, but in her mid-seventies the question seems to resurface unconsciously, and Swanny 'mastered the handling of a split personality' (303), assuming, when she is alone, the personality and behaviour of the woman Edith might have grown up to be. She assumes a working-class north London accent, refuses to bathe, wears old skirts and slippers, takes up knitting, and turns a tiny red blood vessel on her face into the mole that was Edith's distinguishing feature. Ann knows that Swanny could not have been Edith, who was fourteen months older; but perhaps, she thinks, 'believing herself to be Edith Roper, she *wanted* to be her, she had found an identity at last, and if it wasn't the one she would have chosen, it was all she was going to get' (309). By the time Swanny is dying, of a series of strokes, 'the reign of Edith Roper was over'. Swanny thus assumes an identity unlikely to be hers rather than remain without one – an identity which would have affronted the acute class-consciousness of her adoptive mother. When Ann refers to 'the real Swanny, whoever and whatever that real woman was' (370), she is suggesting that the fact of her birth, not her upbringing and life's experience, is what constitutes 'real' identity. When Swanny compulsively questions Asta about the truth of her origin, she insists on its irrelevance and on the fact that she always loved Swanny best. Asta also casts doubt on the common assumption that children inherit features and characteristics from their parents, suggesting instead that 'children copy their parents and behave the way they've seen them behave' (315). Here Asta is used to question the conventional definition of 'origin', replacing it with the idea of the 'copy'. The novel thus opens up the question of what constitutes the person as a unique individual, but does not allow us to enter Swanny's consciousness to explore her dilemma from within. The doubling of personality is here caused not by childhood trauma, as in the case of Sylvia Fraser, but by the need for a firm identity which cannot be fully adopted because of its social unacceptability.

WRITING AND 'TRUTH'

A diary is, in a sense, a 'copy' or at least a representation of a life, and Asta's diaries contain frequent reflections on the process of keeping a diary. She keeps it secret from her husband and children, reflecting in November 1905 on keeping 'my best and favourite activity a dark secret the way other women hide a clandestine love affair' (62). We never know what Asta actually wrote about the 'dark secret' of Swanny's identity, and it is even suggested that she did *not* record it when she writes: 'I've put everything down in this diary but one thing' (357). Motherhood, writing and truth are thus intimately linked. The page that reveals the secret is lost or absent; the last page of Ann's narrative reconstructs Asta breastfeeding Swanny for the first time, her own child having died during or just after childbirth some days earlier, and then laying her down to 'do what she has to do. The most important thing, the stuff of life', recording her 'pain and loss and joy' (437). Recording her experience in writing, Ann suggests, is more important to Asta than the experience of motherhood itself.

In old age, Asta reflects: 'your diary is the one person you can say everything to' (357). The most painful realities, however, she finds difficult or impossible to record in writing: when Harry Duke (who won the VC for trying to save Asta's son at the Somme) visits her to tell her about his death, she wants to hear the truth, 'but I can't write it. I wanted to know and I got what I thought I wanted. Better get on quickly and not write that part. Mogens died two days later in the hospital' (275). In November 1905, a few months after the arrival of Swanny, Asta reflects on the relationship between writing and truth:

When I first started writing this diary I told myself I'd write down only the absolute truth. Now I understand that's not possible. It wouldn't be possible for anyone, not just me. All I can do is be honest about what I feel . . . Total openness about facts I can't manage and I've given up arguing with myself about it. I needn't tell lies but I can't tell the whole truth. (65)

Here Asta seems to be confirming the postmodern impossibility of recording the 'whole truth' in general terms, as well as reflecting on the impossibility of writing the facts about Swanny – in case the diary *is* ever read or discovered, or because she could not acknowledge, in writing, even to herself, Swanny's working-class origins. The diaries function both to conceal and reveal the truth, offering transparency whilst also practising concealment.

One of the elements of the text which Ann, and the reader, may forget, half-remember and need to reread, are the stories which Asta writes in her diary and tells to her listeners as an old lady. In her diary she reflects: 'I've always liked stories, telling them to myself, true and made up ... I tell them to myself as a way of getting to sleep, for instance, and in the daytime to get away from reality' (8). These stories are rather like the urban myths which circulate in contemporary culture, things which *may have* happened to somebody's cousin or girlfriend. Ann says that Asta's diaries were her novels in which she improved on the truth: 'She gave it a beginning, a middle and an end. With her it always had a climax' (71). Asta's stories are 'fabrication[s] ... in the heart of which was a tiny thread of fact' (202). Reflecting on the revelation of the truth of the Roper murder and the fate of Edith, Ann says: 'Perhaps such stories proliferated, apocryphal tales founded on a single real instance, and then sometimes they came true. Ironsmith might even have heard such a story himself and made it true' (406). 'History', it is suggested, might imitate 'story': Ironsmith turns out to be the real killer of Lizzie, who had been his mistress, and the father of Edith: his wife was unable to bear children, and Ironsmith killed Lizzie when she refused to give up the child. This story is first mentioned in Ann's narrative early on in the novel, when she overhears Swanny telling Daniel (a psychiatrist who is later to become Ann's lover) 'the story of the man her cousin knew in Sweden who murdered his mistress to get their child for his wife'. Ann goes on to wonder 'if Swanny had speculated about any relevance this story might have had to her own origins' (98), but this sets up a false scent for the reader, since this event turns out to have occurred in the Roper family, whose story, in a sense, echoes and parallels that of the Westerbys in a lower class setting and in more violent mode. 'Drama was what she [Asta] liked, vitality and power. Many of her stories featured violent death' (72), as do those of Rendell and Vine.

Ann reconstructs one of the parties at which Asta held court, even into her eighties, telling stories to Swanny's guests. One of these involved Asta's cousin Sigrid, whose husband took her to an orphanage to choose a child, and led her to a beautiful little boy with whom she fell immediately in love. They adopted the boy, who turned out to be the son of Sigrid's husband by a mistress. Sigrid forgave her husband and kept the child. Asta vehemently denies that this is something she could have done herself, but she offers this story as one possible version of Swanny's origin when she shows her the anonymous letter and asks her for the truth. When Swanny first asks Asta whether the letter is a lie, Asta replies: 'if you want it to be, *lille* Swanny. If that makes you happy it can be. A lie. What is truth anyway?' (87), and she goes on to tear up and burn the 'evidence', the anonymous letter. She continues to offer different versions of the truth to Swanny, once insisting that 'I thought of you as mine. I forgot you were someone else's' (90). Ann reflects on the difference between the kinds of stories Asta liked to tell and the story she herself is telling, which is of course the 'truth' as she believes it to be: 'If this had been one of Asta's stories it would have involved a tremendous scene with a climax, an opening of the heart and ultimately some sort of confession. But it wasn't, it was life itself, which she so loved to embroider' (84). A wilful old lady is thus made the vehicle for a blurring of the boundaries between truth and fiction and for a radical uncertainty about identity and origin.[2]

Although at one stage Asta tells Swanny: 'I made it all up because I'm a bad old woman who likes to tease', towards the end of her life she does begin to lose her memory: 'In her mind the past was either lost or terribly distorted, so that she would confuse the stories she told, mixing up the one about going to the orphanage with the one about mushroom poisoning. The result was a garbled tale of her cousin going to the orphanage on her own and returning home to find her husband dead of fungus toxins' (202). In her 4 June 1966 entry, Asta writes: 'I hate this forgetfulness. Whole decades have slipped away from me.' She can remember her childhood, but 'it is the middle years which are gone'. This was the period when Swanny was desperate to know the truth of her origins, and Asta's admisssion of memory failure makes the reader (and possibly Ann, as these last diaries were not translated until many years after the events took place) re-evaluate Asta's behaviour. Asta writes: 'She refuses to believe me when I say I can't remember. Some, of course, I remember, the fact of it, but not who and when and how. I resolved once never to write of it but I could laugh when I think how little that resolution matters now. I couldn't write of it if I chose because I've forgotten nearly everything' (363). This amnesia is also Asta's reason for giving up her diary: 'It's pointless trying to keep any sort of record when you can't remember what's happened five minutes ago' (363). The writing of a diary both depends upon memory, and is one way of attempting to preserve it, although Asta herself has no desire to preserve the past and would have preferred to have the diaries destroyed.

Asta's story as she narrates and conceals it is thus dependent upon both remembering and forgetting: the final realisation of the truth of Swanny's parentage comes by means of a meticulous rereading and reinterpretation of the diaries and the documents which reconstruct the Roper case, and through an act of memory and recognition on the part of Ann. Rereading and the work of memory – and translation – establish the link between Harry Duke, whom Asta first met when he came to tell her how her son Mogens had died on the Somme, and who becomes her close companion after the death of her huband, and Florence Fisher, servant of the Ropers. Florence had been engaged to an Ernest Henry Herzog, and Ann remembers from the diaries that Harry was the grandson of a German immigrant who had changed his name to Duke (English for Herzog) just before the outbreak of war. Ann also (belatedly) sees a resemblance between Harry and Swanny. So Swanny's father turns out to be the man who loved Asta in later life, whom she loved too and wished she could have a child with. Asta (and Swanny) die without the knowledge that she did 'have' Harry's child after all. The final 'page' of her story is one that Asta (and Swanny) could never read, just as Ann (and the reader) never read the missing page that reveals how Asta got her beloved daughter. The 'truth' is thus established by means of a process of construction, of detective work and memory: it is not a truth we are invited to doubt, but it is never 'present' in the narrative or 'proven' in writing.

The identity of lost or changeling daughters is thus linked to the fate of sons: the death of Mogens enables Asta to meet Harry Duke and to have the conversations about his first fiancée and his changed name which help to reveal the truth to Ann and the reader. Asta is interested in the sinking of the *Georg Stage*, and mentions it in her diaries, because she knows a woman whose son was drowned in the accident. When the elderly Swanny begins to assume Edith's identity, she refers to a brother who was killed at Argonne in 1918 (as Edith's brother Edward was), not at the Somme in 1916, as was Mogens. The fate of the *Georg Stage* is also linked obliquely to the theft of Edith. A young woman called Lisa Waring, the great-grand-daughter of George Ironsmith, is determined to prove that her ancestor was central to the case even if it proves him a murderer: she says that Ironsmith went back to America with the child on the *Lusitania*. Cary's more efficient research confirms that he could not have sailed on this ship, which was sunk by a German submarine ten years later than his crossing in the *Lucania*. The identity of Swanny and the fate of Edith are thus linked to political history: Asta's diaries include brief summaries and comments on the course of the war, which seem like 'thickening' until the reader sees the connection between the events of the Great

War and the story of Swanny – Harry Duke's change of name, the death of Mogens – and, of course, the intimate connection between a middle-aged woman's crisis of identity and a scandalous 'true crime'.

The narrative of *Asta's Book* is thus a process of both concealment and revelation. A diary is often assumed to reveal the 'truth' about the writer and his or her life: Asta's reflections on keeping a diary suggest something more complex and less transparent. The discovery of her diary promises the revelation of a truth which is then evaded and denied, a process by which the novel itself also teases and misleads its readers. 'The desire of the text (the desire of reading) is . . . desire for the end, but desire for the end reached only through the least minimally complicated detour, the intentional deviance, in tension, which is the plot of narrative' (Brooks 1984: 104). The nature of the Westerby women themselves serves this narrative deviance: Ann comments that Swanny

always appeared frank and open, as all three women did, expansively ready to speak of anything, to air their emotions and open their hearts. This is the insidious kind of frankness, more deceptive and finally maddening than true transparency, the apparent artlessness that seems impulsive and spontaneous, yet masks an ingrained passion for privacy. (43–4)

The apparent clarity and transparency of the style of both the diaries and Ann's narrative masks the art, or the process of conceal-ment, by which the narrative is constructed. Ann, and the reader, read the diaries and the other narratives which compose the novel in order to find the truth, to satisfy the desire for completion and closure, whilst also desiring to postpone the end. Swanny, who begins the quest after receiving the anonymous letter, is also afraid or reluctant to discover it: 'You have to understand that Swanny . . . wanted to know the truth and . . . was at the same time afraid to know it' (124). In this she is a fictional version, in popular detective mode, of Ronald Fraser and Georges Perec, who both want to be found and need to stay hidden, and the narrative of which she is the centre both conceals and reveals her.

A DARK ADAPTED EYE:
'THE DOUBT AT THE HEART OF THINGS'

In *A Dark Adapted Eye* the truth of the identity of the child at the centre of the plot is never conclusively discovered or revealed. The plot of this novel hinges upon 'a bizarre point of genesis', producing 'the doubt at the heart of things' (291) which prevents *one* possible version of this story from being written or published. A writer named Daniel Stewart, who has 'made a speciality of reassessing murder cases, looking at them afresh and from the point of view of . . . the perpetrator' (23), approaches the narrator, Faith, for help with a book he is planning to write about Vera Hillyard. Vera was the narrator's aunt, hanged some thirty years earlier for the murder of her sister Eden. The genesis in question is that of the child Jamie, apparently Vera's son, although not by her husband; but possibly Eden's, named as his mother on the birth certificate. Disputed possession and 'the terrible pressures of love' are the reasons for the murder: the final 'doubt at the heart of things', and the discovery of the truth about another murder, the reason for Stewart's decision not to write this book. But his initial efforts are the 'genesis' of the book we do have, a 'transcript' of what Faith describes as 'the real book that is Vera's life recorded on a tape run only in my own consciousness' (25), as opposed to the edited version of events she writes down for Stewart. This suggests that, through Faith, we do have direct access to Vera's life (whose name also suggests a truth to be revealed or discovered) – although she frequently acknowledges the 'great gaps, the spaces in the past', some of which are filled by the memories of others, by letters and documents, whilst others remain permanently empty.

A Dark Adaped Eye is thus a novel which foregrounds the process of its own narration and the question of identity. Even more than *Asta's Book*, it is crucially concerned with the processes of memory, and Vine signals many of the questions about memory which psychoanalysis and conventional psychiatry address, and which have also become part of popular discourse. Although the narrator, now a middle-aged, happily married woman, had a youth and adolescence marked by unspoken secrets, bizarre family relationships, and finally by violence, Vine uses her as a basically reliable narrator whom the reader can trust to tell the truth as far as she knows it. The gaps are not those of traumatic memory, but of fact and the silences of others. When Faith insists (talking about Jamie's happy early childhood) that 'I know I have not falsified the past . . . No trauma has distorted my memory, no bias or fear altered what I saw and heard' (139) the psychoanalytically-inclined reader may be inclined to doubt her, especially as she did, just a little later, experience the trauma of murder and execution in the family. But a witness and narrator with a memory distorted by this trauma would not serve Vine's purpose; if anything, the experience has produced in Faith a slightly remote air of detachment which invites the reader to trust her as a narrator. Her clear, matter-of-fact and direct style contributes to this, as does her reliance on other witnesses and her acknowledgement of the distortions to which memory of the past *is* subject. She is aware of the possible effects of hindsight in her reconstruction of Vera's life, wondering whether 'I am projecting what I certainly later knew and felt onto that time' (51). When she describes Vera awaiting Eden's return from work, '[i]t was as if her body could not contain so much, such compression, such screwing up, so that the stress overflowed into the air around her. Can I really remember that?' (51). She also reflects upon the functioning of memory in old age and in infancy. It is a commonplace that the elderly forget what happened yesterday whilst, like Faith's aunt Helen, older half-sister of Vera and Eden, they 'can remember . . . perfectly what happened forty years ago'. Helen's recall of the more distant past becomes a convenient narrative device for filling in the gaps in Faith's knowledge.

PRIMAL SCENES

More interestingly, the question of memory-formation in the young child complicates the notions of witnessing and of parentage, of truth and identity. At the beginning of Chapter 9, Faith reflects: 'It has been said that we can remember only from the time when we first learned to speak. We think in words, so memory also operates in words, and we can remember nothing of those first two or three years before we could speak. On the other hand, there is a school of thought which would have it that recall is possible from our time in the womb' (139). This formulation sums up, rather crudely, the cultural struggle over memory and its relationship to the possibility of knowing the truth about the past. Towards the end of the novel Faith reflects: 'Memory is an imperfect function. We are resigned to not remembering things. It is the knowledge, imparted to us by unshakeable outside authority, that an incident we remember never took place, which we find hard to accept' (291). When she first meets the grown-up Jamie she notices an instinctive gesture he repeatedly makes, 'a flicking movement with his right hand towards his left shoulder' (19). She explains:

Jamie told me . . . that Eden's blood had flown at him that day splashing onto his clothes. It was the only thing he could remember. But when he read the trial transcript he saw that he had been mistaken. He remembered something that had never happened, for Mrs King had carried him away before Vera struck out with her knife, seconds before. So the mannerism he has kept, the flicking at blood, is founded upon illusion. (291)

Jamie's adult identity is marked by an unconscious gesture which signals the formative event of his life, a life 'spoiled and incomplete' (19). Later references to the murder, which Jamie could not have completely avoided, have provided a violent detail which he now 'remembers' instead of the events leading up to the murder – including separations from Vera and a kidnapping by Eden – of which he seems to have no memory. A screen-memory[3] conceals the memory of a more significant or painful event than that which is superficially remembered: here the 'memory' of a moment of violence screens the memory of the conflict between his two mothers over the well-behaved and passive child he then was. Early childhood memory of trauma is seen to be vulnerable to change over time and cannot be relied upon as 'evidence' : here bodily memory, often assumed to hold truths inaccessible to consciousness, is also shown to be fallible.

Jamie claims that he has no memories of the time before he was six – 'except of something that never happened' – because 'he was too unhappy. His psyche, defending itself from further pain, blocked off the memories' (139). Faith, who remembers 'his early years, or episodes in them, very well' – principally the 'unwavering, devoted love' he received from Vera until the reappearance of Eden – disputes this broadly accepted psychoanalytic truism and offers an alternative explanation: 'Is it perhaps that knowing what happened and how he was used as a pawn in a game, he believes his early childhood must have been wretched?' (139). Again what he was told has become part of what he thinks he remembers, or else the memory of the feelings aroused when he was a 'pawn in a game', if not the actual events, has been projected backwards and become attached to the whole of his early childhood. At their first meeting, Jamie tells Faith that he wouldn't mind if anyone wanted to write a book about 'all that . . . As a matter of fact, I'd welcome it to put the record straight, I'd like to see the truth'; but, as Faith points out, 'you say you don't remember' (22), thus signalling the complex relationship between memory and truth upon which the narrative is built.

Two other 'primal scenes' are brought into play in order to explain, or further problematise, the questions of Jamie's parentage and of the functioning of memory. As an adolescent Faith saw Vera breastfeeding Jamie (an act that in 1940s middle-class England would usually be performed in private). 'She sat upright, her legs spread apart, her head bent as she contemplated the steadily sucking child. He lay in the crook of her arm. Her other hand was lightly closed round the back of his fair, downy head. The look on her face I had never seen before, it was so young, so tender, so infinitely sweet and adoring' (148). 'Memory . . . operates in words', Faith claims, but this is a visual memory and one which recurs in her dreams: 'Or I open a dream door into a dream room and Vera is sitting there, Madonna-like, tranquil and splendid, her breasts bare and the suckling Jamie in her arms' (15). She now describes this scene in words, but at the time she was too embarrassed to speak: with hindsight she wishes 'that we had spoken of what she was doing. It might have made things clearer, it might have helped' (148).

Laplanche describes how breastfeeding functions as an 'enigmatic signifier' to the infant, who picks up the unconscious sexual desire of the mother[4] – here it is another kind of 'enigmatic signifier' for the teenage Faith, who later reflects that, if they had spoken of it at the time, it might have helped to clarify whether Vera had really given birth to Jamie, or whether she had induced lactation in order to feed a child not biologically hers. At the time when this memory was formed, Faith and the rest of the family had no reason to doubt that Jamie was Vera's child; although they might have suspected that Gerald, Vera's husband, could not have been the father as Jamie was born ten months after his last leave, this was not something they would ever have commented on. After the murder Faith assumes that Eden must have been his biological mother, and that Vera brought him up as hers in order to conceal the fact that her sister had had an illegitimate child. When she meets the adult Jamie for the first time she is shocked by his unswerving belief that Vera was his mother: she decides that his unconscious memory of this early intimate relationship with her must be the foundation of this conviction. It must, she thinks, be 'based solely on an inclination of the heart, on nostalgia for an adored and adoring presence that he sees in dreams but of which he has no waking recollection' (26–7). Here very early 'memory' of the pre-Oedipal dyad of mother and child is taken as 'proof' – by the child now grown-up – of biological, 'real' motherhood. The breastfeeding scene poses the complex question of what constitutes motherhood: nurture (Eden shows no interest in Jamie until it becomes clear that she cannot have any – or any more – children) or the fact of giving birth. It also suggests the unconscious sexual desire of the mother for the male child and the exclusive, almost obsessive nature of Vera's relation to Jamie, which Faith describes approvingly but which the psychoanalytically informed reader might see as part of the problem which leads to murder.

Faith also denies that she was a 'traumatized witness' of a further primal scene: she sees Chad (apparently a rejected suitor of Eden's, later a close friend of Vera's) making love to Francis (Vera's older son) in the hut at the bottom of Vera's garden. Of this scene she writes: 'So much was changed. I was no Go-between, though. I was no traumatized witness of a primal scene . . . it had been a shock, what I saw, but it was rather an interesting, a fascinating shock than an unpleasant one' (198). What is changed is her idea that Chad (with whom she also thought herself in love) might be the father of Jamie, but the real shock is the realisation that Eden must have played the 'go-between', introducing Chad to her thirteen-year-old nephew and concealing, or even encouraging, their sexual relationship, possibly in order to hide one of her own. These revelations – of Chad's homo-sexuality and Eden's complicity in his relations with Francis – cause Faith, and following her the reader, to revise and reinterpret what she saw as a young girl in Vera's house. When she first saw Eden and Francis together she tells us, in retrospect, that she experienced 'a sinking of the heart, something not far from panic, an idea that all would now be spoiled'. The exchanges between Eden and Francis function as 'enigmatic signifiers' to the young girl who feels confused and excluded by them: 'Years were to pass before I could analyse and solve the mystery. It was that they behaved like secret lovers' (71), which is what they were, vicariously, Francis also, possibly, paying later for Eden to have an abortion. The potentially traumatic sexual scene functions not to distort memory but to clarify the past and the plot.

FORGETTING AND NARRATING

Although Faith does revisit and reinterpret past traumas, stimulated by Stewart's request for information, the process is not strictly speaking one of *Nachträglichkeit* or afterwardsness, as the events of the past do not become traumatic when they are revisited, although it does seem as if they have been incompletely processed. The narrative begins at the 'end', on the morning of Vera's execution. Brooks suggests that 'It is the role of fictional plots to impose an end which yet suggests a return, a new beginning: a re-reading' (1984: 109) . . . 'prior events, causes, are so only retrospectively, in a reading back from the end' (29). The end is narrated first in order to signify the necessity for rereading the events which led up to it: because she knows how it ended, Faith also reconstructs the story which leads up to that end in the light of later knowledge.

The novel begins with an evocation of the effect of the murder and execution on Faith's respectable middle-class family. This morning of the execution seems to have been imprinted on Faith's memory as her family wait for the moment of Vera's death, her father John (Vera's twin) reading aloud from the newspaper and pausing in the middle of the phrase 'In the Far . . . East', so that the words 'In the Far' res-onate in Faith's memory: 'this geographical common-place . . . I have never been able to see or hear without remembering my father on the morning of Vera's execution reading aloud in the toneless and sense-less voice of a mynah bird. "In the Far . . ." he said and stopped and folded up the paper and sat silent' (23). The news of the murder insti-gates a long process of repression on the part of Faith's father, who has made 'a monstrous effort . . . if not to forget, at least to behave as if all was forgotten' (10). On hearing the news, 'silence and conceal-ment fell like a shutter', lifting briefly when Josie, chief witness at the trial and Vera's only close friend, told him and Faith what hap-pened that day. 'He never spoke of it again. His twin was erased from his mind and he even made himself – incredibly – into an only child.' Just before his death, a stroke 'as if by some physiological action stripping away layers of reserve and inhibition, . . . released an unre-strained gabbling about how he had felt that summer. His former love for Vera the repressive years had turned to repulsion and fear, his illusions broken as much by the tug-of-war and Eden's immorality – his word, not mine – as by the murder itself' (11).

This repression is symbolised within the novel by a box into which John places all the photographs, letters and other momentoes of his sisters the day after Vera is charged with murder. It is also echoed by John's daughter Faith, who, she tells us, got a poor degree and made a hasty and mistaken marriage to her cousin Andrew in order to 'keep it in the family'. She and her second husband (son of Vera's friend Josie) never speak of Vera, who, 'in all that time, made herself known to me only in dreams, when I would be a child again' (15). The story and the 'facts' have not been forgotten, but deliber-ately not thought about, becoming like Bollas' 'unthought known'. Faith describes how, at some point during the thirty-five years between the murder and the present, she found a book about women murderers in a public library, with *Vera Hillyard* printed on the spine. When she reads it, she is annoyed that the author has 'missed the point', but more than this, '[a] kind of catharsis had taken place, an exorcism, making me look things in the face and tell myself: she was only your aunt, it touches you only at a remove, you can think of it without real pain' (14). By this we infer that she was previously unable to think of it at all, or without pain: belatedness has produced the detachment that makes it possible for her to narrate the story, and to become a reliable narrator. 'Only time bleaches away' the 'Mark of Cain' branded on the foreheads of the family in which murder has taken place, 'and makes it possible to reach back into the past in a kind of tranquility' (276).

She describes a similar process taking place in Jamie after he has read the trial transcript: she quotes a passage from Dante in which he 'sees' Beatrice again, and wonders: 'Has Jamie, too, been overthrown, his mind in a turmoil, through being shown once more what haunts him? Through seeing and not seeing?' This proves not to be the case:

Without subscribing to specious psychotherapeutic doctrines of the let-it-come-up-and-it-will-go-away school, he tells me he is glad he read the transcript. At least it has made him face it. Ceasing to be a bugbear, a chimera, a half-imagined thing, it has come out into the open, no worse than he imagined and no better, but the thing itself, the real thing. To use the jargon of those doctrines, he has confronted it. (292)

This is an ambiguous disclaimer: is it Jamie, Faith or Vine herself who does not subscribe to 'specious psychotherapeutic doctrines' whilst also invoking them and employing them in the dynamics of the narrative? Faith's account of this 'doctrine' is crude, but she admits that confronting the truth has been therapeutic in Jamie's case, as it also seems to have been in hers. Prompted by Stewart's request for information, his sample chapter providing a family history, and a visit to Jamie, Vera comes 'back into my life after an absence that extends over more than a third of a century . . . she is here in the house, the awkward guest she always was when she stayed in the homes of other people. I almost fancy that I can see her . . .' (25). This suggests a closer involvement than Faith has admitted, and accounts for the vividness of her re-creation of the years when she, Faith, was a vistor in Vera's house during the war. Later Faith wonders: 'What was I then, or at any time, but a figure in one of Vera's dreams?' (242) Now Vera has become the *unheimlich*, the ghost to be exorcised again through the process of re-remembering and writing.

When Faith first opens her father's box, she finds a photograph 'taken for no purpose one can imagine unless to record how on a certain hot day in a certain summer a crowd of relations gathered together in a particular garden' – like thousands of photographs, pored over later with the hindsight of what happened to these people, how their lives unfolded. It is after looking at this 'innocent' photograph, and putting everything back into the box, that Faith finds herself crying: 'The tears are running down my face, a curious thing, for it was all so long ago and I had loved none of these people except my father and mother. Oh, and Chad, of course, but that was different' (45). This is one of the moments where we wonder whether Vine is hinting at denial or repression on Faith's part: she had a schoolgirl crush on Eden, longed to be accepted by Eden and Vera on her visits to their cottage during the war, thought herself in love with her cousin Andrew, and adored her aunt Helen (who is still alive). The narrative is also a process of realisation on Faith's part that she *was* more deeply affected by the events of the past than she has cared to admit, her remarks about the 'Mark of Cain' coming towards the end of her story. In terms of structure, this photo and other memorabilia prompt Faith's recollection of her first visit to Great Sindon, which she then reconstructs. When she has told the whole story (and when Stewart has decided not to write his version of it), he sends the contents of the box back to her, and the narrative comes full circle: as she looks at the photographs and letters again, 'this time there are no tears, only a feeling of rueful nostalgia, of folly and of waste'. She puts everything back, 'placing on top of the pile, the picture of us all in Vera's garden in summertime, a united family, wearing our innocent smiles, not yet imagining those births and marriages and deaths to come' (299–300). 'Any narrative', suggests Brooks, 'wants at its end to refer us back to its middle, to the web of the text: to recapture us in its doomed energies' (1984: 109) – an apt description of the trajectory of this plot and these lives.

TRAGEDIES OF CLASS

'Those births and marriages and deaths to come', and the question of identity itself, are, as in *Asta's Book*, closely entwined with the issue of class. Stewart's second chapter is a family history of the Longleys, Vera's parents and grandparents, and, like the memoir of the Roper family in *Asta's Book*, is a story of shifting class identifications and mobility. Vera's grandfather was a shoemaker in Colchester: his son Arthur had been given a 'considerably superior education to that his father enjoyed, but [was] still destined to follow him in the family business'. However, 'he had other ideas. The lure of middle-classdom, so tempting to the Victorian working man of that particular stamp, the leaning towards what we today call the "upwardly-mobile", had ensnared him' (28). It is this 'lure of middle-classdom', and middle-class envy and imitation of the class just above, which is so deeply implicated in the tragedy of Vera and Eden. Their father Arthur woos and marries (much against her father's will) Maud Richardson, only daughter of a local landowner. When Maud dies in childbirth, her daughter, Helen, is sent to live with her maternal grandparents, and thus belongs to a higher social class than her half-siblings. Vera, John and Edith (Eden) are the children of Arthur's second marriage to a governess to a local family who were 'seed merchants with pretensions' (31). This insecure class identity in one generation leads to exaggerated class identifications in the next: Faith writes: 'My father considered himself middle class. He was always saying so with a kind of shameful pride. What he never said was that the middle class don't commit adultery whatever the upper and lower may do, but it was a deeply felt aspect of his creed' (163) – hence the inability to make open the question of Jamie's parentage which may have averted the tragedy.

Vera marries Gerald Hillyard, a man 'several cuts above' her, belonging to the same social class as her half-sister Helen, through whom they meet in India: Gerald's sister decribes Vera as 'ladylike in the wrong way' (37). Reflecting on her experience of the lives led by Vera and Eden just before the war, Faith writes: 'They had the power, those two, of making their world – narrow, confined and bourgeois, as I now see it – an esoteric, intensely desirable place, rather like an exclusive club with unimaginably strict rules no outsider could live up to' (54). Themselves almost a parody of the rituals that govern middle-class identity – not eating with the right hand, for example – they are parodied on another level by Vera's older son Francis. In order to torment his mother he decides that he can only eat yellow foods on Tuesdays and red on Wednesdays, and leaves the 'ie' or 'ey' ending off every word after hearing Vera tell Faith that 'auntie' is vulgar and she should call her 'Aunt Vera' instead. Vera's way of life is also almost a parody of 1940s and 1950s femininity: she spends her days cooking, especially huge and delicious teas, and her evenings sewing, and her house is spotless. With her husband in India and her son at boarding school she devotes herself to her younger, more beautiful sister Eden, and it is the intensity of this relationship that also leads to tragedy.

The war provides the opportunity for the selfish and ambitious Eden to broaden her horizons. She joins the Wrens and embarks on a series of love affairs which lead to an abortion and (possibly) the birth of Jamie. Eden also comes into contact with members of a higher social class, becoming after the war a companion to one Lady Rogerson, through whom she meets her future husband, Tony Pearmain – 'one of *the* Pearmains, you know' (162), as she delights in telling Faith. It is a miscarriage and her subsequent inability to provide Tony with an heir which lead to her appropriation of Jamie. Her class identification is exposed as precarious in her reaction to an unexpected visit from Faith and Andrew: 'I am sure she didn't expect to see us . . . and was unpleasantly surprised by the sight of us. Nor could she quite disguise this. She had not been born to this style of life or nurtured in a tradition of social grace, the concealment of feeling, the putting on of an artificially welcoming face' (229). As for Vera, even in the midst of her despair at getting Jamie back (he has been staying with Eden and Tony whilst Vera is ill with flu), she boasts: 'Eden has kindly invited me to stay with them at Goodney Hall . . . Tony is sending one of the cars for me tomorrow.' 'Poor Vera!' comments Faith. 'Even in the extremity of her dread, snobbery – in this case vicarious snobbery – was not forgotten' (240). Acute class sensibility and resentment and the obsessive maintenance of class identity produce the exclusivity and secrecy which is integral to the plot, both in terms of the series of events that lead to the murder, and the way in which those events are narrated – as the excavation and revelation of those secrets.

As with the 'excavation' of the truth about the murder of Lizzie and the disappearance of Edith Roper in *Asta's Book*, there is another mystery to be solved in *A Dark Adapted Eye* which provides an intertext and the material for the book which Daniel Stewart *does* decide to write. This story also involves class relations and is finally shown to be linked to the trauma of the First World War. When Vera was a teenager, a two-year-old, Kathleen March, disappeared whilst in her care, her body being discovered many years later. The mystery was never solved but many commentators attempted to link this probable murder with the later murder of which Vera was guilty. The baby's father, Albert March, had suffered a serious head wound in the war but managed to hold down a job as a railway signalman. Kathleen's mother, being interviewed by Stewart some fifty years later, says: 'in those days a man who'd worked in insurance and who lived in a detached house with electricity laid on was miles above us, there was no comparison . . . I really thought Vera was condescending coming to my house' (93–4). Stewart's researches lead him to discover that five female children under the age of three went missing from 1920 to 1940 in that part of Essex; he also becomes interested in the case of Sonny Durham, youngest child of an upper class family in Norfolk, apparently murdered by her sister May. His investigations reveal that the gamekeeper on the estate had some relatives staying with him at the time of the murder – his sister and brother-in-law, Adele and Albert March, who had lost their child two years before. Stewart now wonders whether Albert March's head wound, which left him subject to severe migraine, might also have 'caused brain damage of another kind, so that while afflicted with this almost intolerable head pain he was driven to commit acts . . . which he forgot once the headache was past?' (178–9). Physical trauma and its consequences are thus woven into the texture of the plot. Faith comments on the 'stealthy convergence of human lots' (179) when she realises that Sonny Durham's brother had been best man to Tony Pearmain (Eden's husband), but this connection is not fundamentally significant in the way that the story of the Ropers was so entwined with that of the Westerbys in *Asta's Book*. What the story of Albert March and the murdered children provides is the narrative gratification of a mystery solved, which is denied in the case of Jamie and his finally undetermined parentage. Stewart's researches exonerate Vera of a crime of which she was suspected: both novels involve the disappearances of little girls and the uncertain identity of a central character, all linked to the two world wars by which their lives were transformed.

'Narrative', suggests Peter Brooks, in a discussion of the first scene of *Great Expectations*, when Pip meets Magwitch by his parents' grave, 'would seem to claim overt authority for its origin, for a "primal scene" from which – as from the scene of a crime in the detective story, "reality" assumes narratibility, the signifying chain is established' (1984: 96). The 'original' 'primal scenes' of Vine's narratives – the births of Swanny and of Jamie, the origins of these characters – are concealed within incomplete or inaccurate written testimony or are irretrievable now that their parents are dead. Swanny's is revealed by means of a complex act of rereading and detection, whilst Faith ends her narrative with two possible explanations of Jamie's origins. Eden seems the more plausible mother, but Jamie believes that he was Vera's child; *A Dark Adapted Eye*, like *Asta's Book*, questions the foundation-stone of the biological fact of motherhood in the formation and construction of identity. In these popular but complex novels concealed or disputed identities are problematised by the fallibility of memory, embedded in the writing and reading of texts, and fatally entwined in the processes of class and of history. Vine employs the tropes of popular fiction in order to explore the construction of plots which make sense of – or construct myths about – our lives and identities.

Notes

1. See Fredric Jameson (1984), 'Postmodernism, or the Cultural Logic of Late Capitalism', *New Left Review* 146.
2. In *Remind Me Who I Am, Again* (1998), Linda Grant wonders when her mother's memory-loss began, and whether she had really forgotten why, for example, there was an eight-year gap between her two daughters, or whether she had simply got into the habit of lying:

   'But you said you had your tubes tied.'

'Rubbish.'
'You *did*. You told me.'
'Did I? I can't remember.' (46)

3. See Chapters 2 and 5 for fuller discussions of screen-memory.
4. See John Fletcher, 'The Letter in the Unconscious: the Enigmatic Signifier in the work of Jean Laplanche' in Fletcher and Stanton (1992).

Holocaust, Memory, Representation:
Georges Perec's
W or The Memory of Childhood
and Anne Michaels'
Fugitive Pieces

INTRODUCTION

Quelque part, je suis étranger par rapport à quelque chose de moi-même; quelque part, je suis 'différent', mais non pas différent des autres, différent des 'miens': je ne parle pas la langue que mes parents parlèrent, je ne partage aucun des souvenirs qu'ils purent avoir, quelque chose qui était à eux, qui faisait qu'ils étaient eux, leur histoire, leur culture, leur espoir, ne m'a pas été transmis.

(Somehow, I am a stranger to myself; somehow, I am 'different', but not different from others, different from 'my own': I don't speak the language that my parents spoke, I don't share any of the memories that they may have had, something that was theirs, that made them what they were, their history, their culture, their hope, was not transmitted to me.)[1]

In Elie Wiesel's novel *The Fifth Son* (1987), Reuven, the son of a Holocaust survivor, says: 'I suffer from an Event I have not even experienced. A feeling of void: from a past that has made History tremble I have retained only words' (192). This chapter focuses on two texts which, in very different ways, negotiate the 'crisis of witnessing' produced in Western consciousness by the Holocaust,[2] and more specifically by the broken link between those who experienced or were destroyed by it, and the next generation who had to 'recover the past by inventing it'. Like Reuven, Georges Perec grew up in 'the compact void of the unspeakable': 'What is dead is dead . . . and cannot be resurrected. It can only be invented' (Fine 1988: 42). At the beginning of *W or The Memory of Childhood* (1975) he claims: 'I have no childhood memories . . . I was excused: a different history, History with a capital H, had answered the question in my stead: the war, the camps' (6). The 'void' is filled by the fantasy of W, an imaginary island which Perec invented as a thirteen-year-old, and rediscovered and reconstructed many years later as a gradually emerging allegory of the Nazi death camps. In his reconstruction of the fragments of his childhood, which he always acknowledges is, pre-cisely, a reconstruction, Perec foregrounds the textuality of memory, the investment of fantasy and the inevitability of 'afterwardsness'. In *W* the instability and belatedness of memory is doubly inscribed, in terms of the nature of early childhood memories as such and the specific trauma experienced by the subject. In 1942, at the age of six, Perec was sent away from Paris into the Free Zone, and in 1943 his mother died in Auschwitz – although, of course, he 'didn't know that then'. Perec's representation of his own memories and his mother's story in *W* is oblique and indirect – a technique described by Warren Motte as 'writing under erasure' (1995: 237). 'I know that what I say is blank, is neutral, is a sign, once and for all, of a once-and-for-all annihilation . . . all I shall ever find in my very reiteration is the final refraction of a voice that is absent from writing, the scandal of their [his parents'] silence and of mine' (42).

Anne Michaels' novel *Fugitive Pieces* (1997) also negotiates this 'scandal of silence'. Jakob, its protagonist, is a young child living in Poland when the Nazis invade, killing his parents and – possibly – his sister Bella whilst he hides behind the wallpaper in a cupboard. Much later he writes: 'I have nothing that belonged to my parents, barely any knowledge of their lives' (141). He is haunted by his failure to witness their deaths and by his ignorance of Bella's fate: 'I did not witness the most important events of my life. My deepest story must be told by a blind man, a prisoner of sound' (17). Jakob's notebooks are later found by his student Ben, the son of survivors who have never told him about his lost siblings, and who grew up in a home where there was 'no energy of a narrative . . . not even the fervour of an elegy' (204). The identities of Perec, Jakob and Ben are thus founded on absence and concealment: as a young child Perec has to conceal his Jewishness, and Jakob hides first in the mud of Biskupin, a buried Iron Age city, and then on the Greek island of Zakynthos. Like Ronald Fraser, Perec 'was like a child playing hide-and-seek, who doesn't know what he fears or wants more: to stay hidden, or to be found' (7), realising that his denial of memory 'protected' him from 'my history, the story of my living, my real story, my own story' (6).

Linda Grant has written that 'while all cultures are to do with memory, none more so than the Jewish community in which everything is about what was' (*Remind Me Who I Am, Again* 1998: 269). For Perec the question of identity is intimately bound up with the processes of memory and of writing: memory can only be reconstructed through the writing which inevitably 'retranscribes' it, and is the mark both of absence – the memory of his parents 'is dead in writing' – and of a paradoxical presence – 'I write because they left in me their indelible mark, whose trace is writing' (42). Jakob, who becomes a poet, believes that his 'life could not be stored in any language but only in silence', and searches for a way of writing 'in code, every letter askew, so that loss would wreck the language, become the language' (111). Adorno later modified his view that to write poetry after Auschwitz is barbaric to claim that '*literature must resist this verdict* of silence' (1962: 313). 'The abundance of real suffering . . . demands the continued existence of art [even as] . . . it prohibits it. It is now virtually in art alone that suffering can still find its own voice, consolation, without immediately being betrayed by it' (quoted in Berger 1985: 33). Whilst both writers take on the burden of representation – Perec of his own fractured memories and fantasies, Michaels giving voice to imaginary survivors – both also acknowledge the paradoxical demand for a kind of silence, for 'some sort of narrative margin which leaves the unsayable unsaid' (Friedlander 1992: 17).

The largest part of this chapter is devoted to an analysis of Perec's *W* as a text that 'never forgets that there is the forgotten and never stops writing its failure to remember and to fashion itself according to memory' (Carroll 1990: xxiii). At the end of the chapter I offer a reading of *Fugitive Pieces* as a novel which attempts to provide a 'site of memory' – 'a different way of thinking about it, of moving on without forgetting' (Michaels 1997: 15) – as the generation which experienced the Holocaust directly begins to die out. I suggest that whilst the novel is a moving evocation of loss and absence, Michaels' use of the idea of biological or archaeological memory mystifies human agency and offers moments of false consolation.

THE VIOLENCE INFLICTED ON LANGUAGE . . .

David Carroll has described the Holocaust as an 'extreme limit case of memory' (1990: viii). Habermas evokes the sense of rupture effected by this event in historical terms:

Something took place here which up until that time no one had even thought might be possible. A deep stratum of solidarity between all that bears a human countenance was touched here. The integrity of this deep stratum had, up until that time, remained unchallenged, and this despite all the natural bestialities of world history . . . Auschwitz has altered the conditions for the continuity of historical life-connections – and not only in Germany. (1988: 251–2)

Lyotard has compared the Holocaust to an earthquake so powerful as to destroy all the instruments that might have been capable of measuring it: despite this, 'a complex feeling of something indeterminate having happened would stay in memory' (1988: 56). For the West, it is 'that piece of collective memory which it is hardest for the culture to recall', functioning 'like the return of the repressed: a fragment of the cultural unconscious that will not go away' (Rose 1991: 7–8). Rose's application of psychoanalytic processes to the analysis of culture follows the Mitscherlichs (1975), who wrote of Germany's 'inability to mourn', Eric L. Santner and originally, of course, the Freud of *Moses and Monotheism* (1939). Santner argues that post-war Germany has been unable to

work through the more primitive narcissistic injury represented by the traumatic shattering of the specular, imaginary relations that had provided the sociopsychological foundations of German fascism . . . Nazism had promised a so-called utopian world in which alterity in its multiple forms and dimensions could be experienced as a dangerous Semitic supplement that one was free to push to the margins and finally to destroy. (1990: 32)

Santner's use of psychoanalysis makes it clear that he is not talking about Nazi Germany as a unique abberation, but a potential inherent in any form of social organisation which prevents or impedes the recognition of others as separate but equal identities – a process in operation in Kosovo in the former Yugoslavia as I write. Michaels, through Jakob, explores the Nazi objectification and dehumanisation of the Jews. Perec's text demonstrates the persistence of fantasies of omnipotence and the elimination of difference in its employment and rewriting of his childhood fantasy of the Olympian island of W; it also refuses to impose the trope of a reconstructed identity on to the fragments of memory.

Therapeutic work with survivors demonstrates that the experience of massive trauma disrupts what we think of as the 'normal' processes of memory, altering 'the conditions for the continuity' of personal as well as 'historical life-connections' (Habermas 1988: 252). Dori Laub (who was himself imprisoned as a child) analyses how these processes,

and the ability to use memory in order to bear witness, were specifically dislocated during the experience of the death camps: 'The perpetrators, in their attempt to rationalize the unprecedented scope of
the destructiveness, brutally imposed upon their victims a delusional
ideology whose grandiose coercive pressure totally excluded and
eliminated the possibility of an unviolated, unencumbered, and thus
sane, point of reference in the witness' (Felman and Laub 1992: 81).
Even Primo Levi, possibly the 'sanest' of witnesses, testifies in his
later work, *The Drowned and the Saved*, to the difficulty of bearing
witness to events which disrupt accepted frames of reference. 'In this
case, all or almost all the factors that can obliterate or deform the
mnemonic record are at work'; the violence that is 'inflicted on man'
is also 'inflicted on language' (1988: 12, 76), the medium in which
witness might later be borne. If the subject's sense of identity is
largely dependent upon memory, '[t]he systematic destruction of
self-identity of inmates in concentration camps was also the attempt
to destroy their narrative of themselves' (Funkenstein 1992: 77). The
inmates were 'systematically deprived of foresight' (Hartman 1992:
324): like Leon Greenman, who didn't know that his wife was being
taken to the gas chamber; the child Perec, who didn't know that he
was saying goodbye to his mother for the last time; and his mother
herself, whom Perec claims died 'without understanding' (33). Laub
describes the world of the camps as one in which 'there was no
longer an other to which one could say "Thou" in the hope of being
heard, of being recognized as a subject, of being answered . . . when
one cannot turn to a "you" one cannot say "thou" even to oneself.
The Holocaust created in this way a world in which one *could not
bear witness to oneself*' (82). It becomes vital to Jakob, once he begins
to find out about the death camps, to establish whether the victims
'witnessed' their own deaths, and to establish who exactly can stand
in the place of the witness. Shoshana Felman also claims that the
Holocaust functions as a 'historically ungraspable *primal scene* which
erases both its witnesses and its witnessing' (194). This erasure of the
witness is exploited dangerously by Holocaust 'deniers' and would
seem to concede defeat to the Nazis, who aimed to create 'an event
without a witness':

However this war may end, we have won the war against you; none of you
will be left to bear witness, but even if some one were to survive, the world
would not believe him . . . there will be no certainties, because we will
destroy the evidence together with you. (Levi 1988: 1)

Witnesses survived and the evidence was not destroyed, however problematic the process of witnessing. The practice, rather than the theory, of Laub, Lawrence Langer and others re-creates the witness in the therapeutic setting: 'The emergence of the narrative which is being listened to – and heard – is . . . the process and the place wherein the cognizance, the "knowing" of the event is given birth to' (Felman and Laub 1992: 57), as it is 'given birth to' in Perec's reconstruction of W. Felman and Laub also describe the fractured narrative of witness Simon Srebnik, one of only two survivors of the death camp at Chelmno. He was 'found in Israel' by Claude Lanzmann and inter-viewed in his film *Shoah*. Srebnik was shot in the back of the head two days before the Soviet troops arrived, but again survived: the film provides in history 'the possibility of *seeing again* what in fact was never seen the first time, what remained *originally unseen* due to the inherent blinding nature of the occurrence' (255). When Srebnik returns to Chelmno and sings again the song he sang as a thirteen-year-old prisoner, forced to help burn the still-living bodies brought out of the gas chambers, the film includes 'an element through which the very silencing of Srebnik's voice can be somehow reversed, through which the very loss of Srebnik's testimony can be somehow recovered, or at least resist its own forgetting . . . In spite of his own silencing and of his silence, the return of the witness undertaken by the film nonetheless persists, takes over and survives in the return of the song' (268).

In his analysis of oral testimonies of survivors, Langer has demon-strated that it is difficult for listeners not to construct comforting narratives of liberation or redemption out of fragmented and dislo-cated accounts which bear witness to the co-existence of two selves, the self who experienced the death camps and the self who survived. Stories of suffering, courage and liberation take place in a sequence of temporality contradicted by the a-temporal persistence of the Auschwitz 'self': for Charlotte Delbo, 'the "self" who was in the camp isn't me, isn't the person who is here, opposite you . . . And every-thing which happened to this other "self", the one from Auschwitz, doesn't touch me now, *me*, doesn't concern me, so distinct are deep memory and common memory' (Langer 1991: 5). Taken back to Chelmno, Simon Srebnik says: 'No one can describe it. No one can recreate what happened here. Impossible? And no one can under-stand it. Even I, here, now . . . I can't believe I'm here' (Felman and Laub 1992: 224). For many survivors, it has proved impossible to assimilate the traumatic past into a present which would enable the subject to construct a coherent narrative of the self: 'Testimony seems to be composed of bits and pieces of a memory that has been overwhelmed by occurrences that have not settled into understanding or remembrance, acts that cannot be constructed as knowledge nor assimilated into full cognition, events in excess of our frames of reference' (Felman and Laub 1992: 5).

Perec refuses to construct a coherent narrative of the self out of fragments of memory and fantasy: instead he meticulously charts the retranslations of his memories, and constructs an 'adventure-story' which replaces his own missing 'history', with a 'hero' and a lost child who both stand in for a self who cannot be directly represented. Laub describes how some survivors 'live not with memories of the past, but with an event that could not and did not proceed through to its completion, has no ending, attained no closure, and therefore, as far as its survivors are concerned, continues into the present and is current in every respect' (Felman and Laub 1992: 69). This finds echoes in Anne Michaels' Jakob, who cannot mourn for his sister Bella, only search obsessively for what might have happened to her. David Bellos evokes the 'muffled, displaced, almost absent' quality of Perec's mourning for his mother: for those who had no formal proof of their relatives' deaths after the war, 'their grieving could have no formal beginning: what has no beginning has no end' (1993: 17).

The dislocation of individual identity and memory, of temporality, of ethical categories and of meaning effected by the Holocaust seems to demand recognition in the art which seeks to represent it. In *The Postmodern Condition* Lyotard suggests that the postmodern differs from the modern by projecting 'the unrepresentable in representation itself . . . [it] searches for new presentations, not in order to enjoy them but in order to impart a stronger sense of the unrepresentable' (1984: 79). He later argues that narratives which 'neutralize violence' by recuperating it into chronologies of before and after, cause and effect do their own kind of violence to the event: '[n]arrative organisation is constitutive of diachronic time, and the time that it constitutes has the effect of "neutralizing" an "initial" violence . . . of staging the obscene, of disassociating the past from the present, and of staging a recollection that must be a reappropriation of the improper, achrono-logical affect' – the 'achronology' which results from the shock of unassimilated traumatic experience. His work is a radical critique of 'the limitations of all historicisms and "monumental" or memorial-izing histories that "forget" by having too certain, too definite, too representative, too narrativized . . . a memory' (1988: 16). Gillian Rose (1996) has argued that Spielberg's film of *Schindler's List* falls, in its latter stages, into this trap by sentimentalising Schindler and enabling a too-easy identification with him on the part of the audience, impos-ing a comforting pattern of salvation and redemption. As I go on to show, the structure of *W* represents the belatedness of experience and the 'otherness' of the self in the wake of trauma.

However, just as there are dangers in the view that the Holocaust

was an event which erased its own witnesses, so are there in the con-
comitant notion that the representational functions of language and
of narrative have been irrevocably damaged by this event. As Saul
Friedlander puts it, 'it is precisely the "Final Solution" which allows
postmodernist thinking to question the validity of any totalizing view
of history, of any reference to a definable metadiscourse' (1992: 5).
Some kind of 'historical narrative', however inadequate, is surely
necessary in order to inform those who might otherwise grow up not
knowing of the event, or unable to distinguish it from fictional representations of violence or atrocity. As Langer puts it: 'If "reality" is
not accessible in language it will be made more fully accessible
through blows. The Nazis themselves, prompted by the skeptical
linguisticism of their own time, made the effort to reach beyond
words with their ferocious strength' (1991: 141).

Perec himself, at least in the articles he wrote for the left-wing
journal *Partisans* in 1962–3, disassociates himself from the view that
language cannot represent the world: 'The disease that eats words
away is not inside words ... The "crisis of language" is a refusal of
the real' (quoted in Bellos 1993: 276). However, this apparent faith
in language is undermined later in *W*, in which he includes descrip-
tions of his mother and father, based on photographs and fragments
of knowledge, written fifteen years earlier. These are now heavily
annotated, footnoted and 'corrected', but Perec admits that more
accurate knowledge and exact description bring him no closer to the
reality of his parents:

It is not – as for years I claimed it was – the effect of an unending oscillation
between an as-yet undiscovered language of sincerity and the subterfuges of
a writing concerned exclusively with shoring up its own defences: it is
bound up with the matter of writing and the written matter, with the task of
writing as well as with the task of remembering ... (the unsayable is not
buried inside writing, it is what prompted it in the first place). (42)

There is no 'as-yet undiscovered language of sincerity' which will
recover the dead: the 'unsayable' prompts the attempt to articulate,
to represent, but writing cannot unbury or recover the presence of his
absent parents. Writing performs for Perec the double function
described by Lyotard: it 'always is of some restorative value for the
evil done to the soul because of its unpreparedness, which leaves it
an infant', but reminds us once again 'that there is no salvation, no
health, and that time, even the time of work, does not heal anything'
(33–4). The process of healing is represented in *Fugitive Pieces*,
enacted through the powers of storytelling, of poetry, of love and the

sharing of memory: I argue later in this chapter that on occasions Michaels' uses language, not violence, to 'reach beyond words' in a way that obscures and mystifies the event upon which her novel is based.

The paradoxical absent presence of Perec's parents could also be refigured in terms of the Jewishness which, as a child, he was required to conceal or deny. Jewishness is part of his missing inheritance, making him a 'stranger to himself', to whom his parents' language and memories were not transmitted, but which surface in the signs, fragments, dreams and fantasies of which the text of *W* is composed. His articulation of a sense of 'otherness' from the self could also be read as reinforcing the claim made by Lyotard that 'Western thought . . . attempts to make "jews" of all of us' . . . a 'nonpeople of survivors, Jews and non-Jews called here "the jews", whose being-together does not depend on the authenticity of any primary roots but on that singular debt of an interminable anamnesis' . . . 'as "jews"' we are 'a heterogenous nonpeople obligated to the memory of what cannot be represented, remembered, presented as such, with unpayable debts to a Law that does not tell us what to do but only that we are not autonomous, self-constituting or "self-asserting", but rather "hostage" to it, obligated before being free, other before being same' (Carroll 1990: xii).[3] Lyotard's is one of many attempts to theorise what it is 'in excess' about the Jews as a people which has seemed to necessitate their destruction: such theorisations are problematic in that they appear to universalise, trivialise or even deny the *specific* loss of autonomy and subjection to arbitrary and impenetrable laws experienced by the Jews under the Nazi regime. Lyotard is articulating a sense of postmodern, post-Holocaust identity which does not depend on the 'authenticity' of 'primary roots' – the very 'roots' which Nazism attempted to destroy, but also those which, insisted upon and reinforced in claims to nationhood, perpetuate the separatism which leads to new forms of 'ethnic cleansing'. When Perec describes the Olympian island of W, which is gradually transformed into a concentration camp, he does so in terms which recall the words of Kafka's doorkeeper in *The Trial*, a text which is often read as a premonition of the fate of the Jews in Nazi Europe: 'The Law is implacable, but the Law is unpredictable. The Law must be known by all, but the Law cannot be known. Between those who live under its sway and those who pronounce it stands an insurmountable barrier' (Perec 1989: 117). His book ends with a quotation from David Rousset's *Univers concentrationnaire*: the title of this work recalls the judgement of Tadeusz Borowski, that 'the whole world is really like the concentration camp' (1959: 168) and Binjamin Wilkomirski, imprisoned as a child and unable to understand that he had been liberated: 'nobody ever said right out to me, Yes, the camp was real, but now it's over. There *is* another world now, and you're allowed to live in it . . . The camp's still there – just hidden and well-disguised' (1995: 150).[4] Perec's representation of W raises similar questions of specificity and universality: he implies a continuity of the practice of repression when he says that at the time of writing (1974), several of the islands of Tierra del Fuego (the site of his imaginary W) were being used as deportation camps by Pinochet's fascists.

THE STRUCTURE OF THE TEXT AND THE FANTASY OF W

W consists of two texts, which, as Perec says in his preface, 'simply alternate'. The 'simply' is disingenuous, as is his claim that 'you might almost believe they had nothing in common'; in fact, as he goes on to say, 'they are . . . inextricably bound up with each other . . . as though it was only their coming together, the distant light they cast on each other, that could make apparent what is never quite said in one, never quite said in the other, but said only in their fragile overlapping'. The first is an 'adventure story ' which is further split into two: 'it begins to tell one tale, and then, all of a sudden, launches into another' – the 'other' being the transformed tale of the island of W. In this break – represented in the text by the mark (***) on an otherwise empty page – Perec says 'can be found the point of departure for the whole of this book: the *points of suspension* on which the broken threads of childhood and the web of writing are caught'. The other text is 'an autobiography: a fragmentary tale of a wartime childhood, a tale lacking in exploits and memories, made up of scattered oddments, gaps, lapses, doubts, guesses, and meagre anecdotes'. Perec is a playful and evasive writer who, according to his autobiographer David Bellos, may even leave false clues deliberately as he simultaneously conceals and reveals fragments of his history. My point here is not to attempt a reconstruction of the 'true story', but to show the interdependence of the 'threads of childhood and the web of writing' and of personal history and 'History' in the text. As with Ronald Fraser and Carolyn Steedman, the process of identity formation is hesitant, provisional and incomplete, and, here especially, heavily invested with fantasy.

The 'adventure story' is narrated by a deserter from the army who was given a false identity and the new name of 'Gaspard Winckler'. In the first short section of the text he describes himself in the 'present' as 'impelled by a commanding necessity' to reveal the events to which he was a witness, believing that he was the 'sole depository, the only living memory, the only witness' of a world of which there 'could be no survivor' (3–4). Already the language suggests the need of some Holocaust survivors to bear witness, although the context of Winckler's story is apparently quite different. In the next brief section Perec speaks of his own lack of childhood memories and the story he made up and drew in pictures at the age of thirteen, which he remembered 'seven years ago', and which set 'the snares of writing' – the 'snares' of wanting both to 'stay hidden' and to 'be found'. He 'reinvented and wrote' the story of W, and published it in a journal. 'Today', he says, 'I propose to bring to term – by which I mean just as much "to mark the end of" as "to give a name to" – this gradual unravelling' (6–7). Like Ronald Fraser, Perec is suggesting that writing might be a means of leaving the past behind, but, as *In Search of a Past*, W represents a history in the process of construction, always susceptible of retranslation, not a finished product. Perec confesses: 'W is no more like my Olympic fantasy than that Olympic fantasy was like my childhood. But in the crisscross web they weave as in my reading of them I know there is to be found the inscription and description of the path I have taken, the passage of my history and the history of my passage' (7). We are not witness to the process by which the childhood fantasy became the story of W within the text; nor does Perec tell us how or when he found out how his mother died. But although these omissions could be seen as evasions, they also acknowledge the fact that memory is constructed by means of a process of 'reading' the texts of memory, of retranslating them, and of constructing them as narratives.

Gaspard Winckler is asked by a member of the 'Shipwreck Victims' Relief Society' to undertake a voyage to the islands off the southern tip of South America in order to find the body of the child whose name he was given. This eight-year-old child, the first Gaspard Winckler, was deaf and dumb, for a reason which was never discovered but which 'could only be ascribed to some infantile trauma whose precise configuration unfortunately remained obscure' (23). He was taken on a long sea-voyage by his mother in the hope of a cure, but their ship was wrecked, all on board died, and the body of the child was never found. A lost and traumatised child is thus at the centre of this text. At the point when the second Gaspard Winckler is contemplating this mission, the story breaks off and launches into another, the description of the island of W, located in the region where the child Gaspard was lost, and which is entirely dedicated to the 'Olympian ideal' of highly organised competitive sport. This society is at first represented in utopian terms: in 'cool and happy countryside', W is a 'nation of athletes where Sport and life unite in a single magnificent effort' (65–7). It is a version of the '(always already) lost organic society that has haunted the western imagination' (Santner 1990: 15). When we are told that 'life, here, is lived for the greater glory of the Body', we may already think of the Nazi ideal and Leni Riefenstahl's film of the Berlin Olympics. The reality of W as a brutish struggle for survival under arbitrary laws gradually emerges in details such as a race which culminates in the mass rape of women by the victors, the complex system of handicapping, which means that those who lose have no chance of winning again, and the ritual humiliations to which the losers are subjected – they are given nothing to eat after their failures, the last man in a race sometimes even being stoned to death. Boys are kept in the women's quarters until the age of fourteen (roughly the age at which Perec first invented W); they are then initiated into the athletic rituals, and at the end of their first day see 'the cohort of the beaten returning, the exhausted, ashen-faced Athletes tottering . . . they see them collapse onto the ground, where they lie with their mouths open, wheezing; they see them, a little later, tearing each other to pieces for a scrap of salami, a drop of water, a puff at a cigarette' (139). So the island of W is gradually transformed into the concentration camp itself, with 'Athletes of skin and bone, ashen-faced, their backs permanently bent, their skulls bald and shiny, their eyes full of panic, and their sores suppurating . . .' (161). Roberto Benigni's film *Life is Beautiful* (1999) develops this analogy in reverse: its hero is deported to a concentration camp with his five-year-old son, whom he attempts to protect by pretending that they have come to a bizarre kind of holiday camp where they must collect 'points' by winning races, staying quiet and not asking for more food. The success of this film, I suggest, depends on the viewer's knowledge of the full horror of the camps and the fact that, as David Rousset suggests, in the camps 'anything can be turned to sport: making men turn round very fast, under the whip, for hours on end; organizing a bunny-hop race, with the slowest to be thrown into the pond beneath the Homeric guffaws of the S.S. . . .' (quoted in Perec 1989: 163). In his account of W Perec writes that if, later, 'someone gets in one day to the Fortress', he will find 'the subterranean remnants of a world he will think he had forgotten: piles of gold teeth, rings and spectacles, thousands and thousands of clothes in heaps, dusty card indexes, and stocks of poor-quality soap' (160–1).

As the truth about the camps emerges as if from the unconscious of this text, it thus demonstrates what Shoshana Felman describes as the psychoanalytic recognition that one does not have to *possess* or *own* the truth, in order to effectively *bear witness* to it; that speech as such is unwittingly testimonial; and that the speaking subject constantly bears witness to a truth that nonetheless continues to escape him, a truth that is, essentially, *not available* to its own speaker. (Felman and Laub 1992: 15)

It also demonstrates that that which 'he will think he had forgotten' will return, will not remain hidden, reconstructing for the reader the process of coming to knowledge of a shocking reality which we somehow realise we have always already known. The development of the fantasy also reproduces the way in which knowledge of the truth of the extermination was concealed or avoided not only within Nazi Germany but also in Allied Europe. It demonstrates the paradoxical exaltation and degradation of humanity which characterised the regime, and raises the question of whether such brutality always underlies the veneer of 'civilisation', in particular behind ideologies of utopia, or whether Nazi Germany was a unique aberration.

By the time that Perec rewrote his childhood fantasy of W, of course, the history of the camps was known and available to him: what he is attempting to represent in this rewriting is the unconscious or semi-conscious knowledge of the adolescent self. Towards the end of the 'autobiographical' part of the text, Perec describes how, some time after their return to Paris at the end of the war, his aunt took him to an exhibition about the camps. This is described quite dispassionately, almost as if the full meaning or horror of what he saw was not fully registered: 'I remember the photographs of the walls of the gas chambers showing scratchmarks made by the victims' fingernails, and a set of chessmen made from bits of bread' (158). The emotion we might expect is displaced on to the 'W' section which just precedes it, by which time the language of the camps – 'Raus! Schnell!' (155) – has completely broken through. We are not told whether the young Perec knew by this time how his mother died, nor whether he invented the fantasy of W before or after seeing the exhibition. Perec deliberately avoids constructing narratives which supply sequences of cause and effect, leaving the reader to speculate whether his adolescent fantasy might have been an unconscious or displaced representation of the horrors to which he was not quite a witness. What his drawings did attest to was a sense of profound dislocation, a dislocation which also characterised his memories of that time: 'mechanical vehicles with disconnected nozzles, discontinuous cordage, disengaged wheels rotating in the void . . . the legs of the athletes were separated from their trunks, their arms were out of their torsos, their hands gave them no grasp' (68). The reader also becomes aware of the way in which the memory of the concentration-camp exhibition has supplied a detail of the 'adventure-story': the 'deep scratches on the oak door' of the ship's cabin made by the 'bleeding fingernails' (58) of the child Gaspard's mother in her attempt to escape from the wrecked ship reinforces the oblique connection between Perec the child who lost his mother, and Gaspard who was lost at sea and never found.

In *Je suis né* Perec tells the story of how he ran away from home at the age of eleven or twelve, while he was living in Paris with the aunt and uncle who subsequently adopted him: he spent a lonely and pointless day, and when he was found, according to David Bellos, he 'sank into a defensive, almost autistic silence: he spoke to nobody, did not answer those who spoke to him'. At around the same time his psychotherapist Françoise Dolto said: 'But he's lost himself, absolutely!' (Bellos 1993: 99–100). This is one of the 'fragile overlappings' between the two stories which Perec refers to in his preface, and which 'make apparent what is never quite said in one, never quite said in the other'. What is 'never quite said' is, of course, the double displacement of Perec on to his adventure-story narrator, the second Gaspard Winckler, and on to the traumatised eight-year-old child whose body is never found. Otto Apfelstahl, who tells the story of the first Gaspard to the second, offers two possible interpretations of the loss of the child: from the evidence of the ship's log and its position when it was wrecked it was on its way back, either to find the child who had *escaped*, or because he had been *abandoned* by his mother, who had then changed her mind. Another 'fragile overlapping': a six-year-old child sent away by his mother as a means of *escape* would also have experienced this separation as *abandonment*, and possibly, as Bellos suggests, as a reason for guilt – the child was unable to protect his mother.

Perec had at one time intended to include a third section in *W*, to be called 'Critique ou Intertexte: (histoire du fantasme, du projet d'écriture, metadiscours)' (Lejeune 1990: 70). According to the three-fold structure of autobiographical writing which I examined in Chapter 2, the event, the memory of the event, the writing of (the memory of) the event, this would presumably have expanded what already exists in the text as a *fourth* layer, the writer's analysis of the writing of his memory. As suggested earlier, this missing 'metadiscours' tantalises the reader with the possibility of locating the 'real' Perec in the process of composing his text. But although he does 'decipher' the text of his memories in footnotes, there is, as David Bellos points out, a residue of 'uncorrected' details and false clues which function as defences or as signals to the reader that memory is always provisional, that 'the surest engagement with memory lies in its perpetual irresolution' (Young 1992: 269). The text is evidence of a residual refusal to be 'found': Perec uses 'dream and memory' (and fantasy) 'to reveal himself up to a determined point, then avails himself of their possibilities to conceal that which is consequent to the revelation' (Motte 1984: 98). What is 'found' instead is the island of W, which is 'really' the concentration camp, which can also 'never quite' be 'said'. The lost child – Perec himself when there was 'no mooring', an 'absence of landmarks', 'no sequence in time' (68), later claiming to have 'no childhood memories' – is thus finally identified with the 'History' which, he said, excused him from having a 'history' of his own.

MEMORY AS TEXT

Throughout the text, Perec evokes the *materiality* of writing in its relationship with memory in terms that recall Derrida's reading of Freud's 'Notes on the Mystic Writing Pad': 'The unconscious text is already a weave of pure traces, differences in which meaning and forces are united – a text nowhere present, consisting of archives which are *always already* transcriptions' (Derrida 1978: 211). Perec says: 'The idea of writing the story of my past arose almost at the same time as the idea of writing' (26), suggesting the identification between memory and writing made by David Farrell Krell – 'and so it seems that writing is of memory and memory of writing before there is writing in the usual sense – since time immemorial, as it were' (1990: 49). So, in spite of the fact that Perec knows that 'what I say is blank, is neutral, is a sign, once and for all, of a once-and-for-all annihilation', writing is still necessary: 'I write because we lived together . . . I write because they' (his parents) 'left in me their indelible mark, whose trace is writing. Their memory is dead in writing; writing is the memory of their death and the assertion of my life' (42). To write is

essayer méticuleusement de retenir quelque chose, de faire survivre quelque chose: arracher quelques bribes au vide qui se creuse, laisser, quelque part, un sillon, une trace, une marque ou quelques signes.
(to try meticulously to retain something, to make something survive, to tear some scraps out of the emptiness that opens up, to leave, somewhere, a furrow, a trace, a mark or some signs.)[5]

This need to leave behind a physical mark or 'trace' of one's existence or experience is close to James E. Young's account of the demand of some survivors 'that words not just signify experiences but that they become – like the writers themselves – *traces* of their experiences' (1988: 23). Despite his recognition that writing cannot create or re-create presence – 'their memory is dead in writing' – Perec also affirms that 'the unsayable is not buried inside writing, it is what prompted it in the first place' (42), thus asserting the existence of a reality outside of discourse; the camps did exist, his mother was killed there.

'All of this autobiographical work', writes Perec, 'was organised around a single memory which, for me, was profoundly obscured, deeply buried, and, in a sense, denied' (quoted in Bellos 1993: 549). His only surviving memory of his mother, of his parting from her at the age of six, demonstrates both the textuality of memory – 'the *points of suspension* on which the broken threads of childhood and the web of writing are caught' – and the continual process of retranscription to which it is subject. The memory is briefly recounted in section 8: 'the day she took me to the Gare de Lyon, which is where I left for Villard-de-Lans in a Red Cross convoy: though I have no broken bones, I wear my arm in a sling. My mother buys me a comic entitled *Charlie and the Parachute*: on the illustrated cover, the parachute's rigging lines are nothing other than Charlie's trousers' braces' (26). A slightly more fully developed version of this memory is given later, in Section 10, in a subsection entitled 'THE DEPARTURE': here Perec says that his aunt told him some time after the formation of the memory that he did not have his arm in a sling, that there would have been no need for him to pretend to be wounded (part of the child's fantasy) as he was leaving legally as a 'war orphan'. In fact, as he tells us in a footnote, he was wearing a truss, a 'suspensory bandage' for a hernia that was later operated upon in Grenoble (55). Perec does not reflect upon this 'retranscription' or subsequent alteration of the memory of a possibly embarrassing truss to that of a slightly more heroic sling – possibly the child fantasised at the time of the formation of the memory that he was wearing a sling, so that this is the 'reality' which is subsequently 'remembered'. Nor does he 'correct' what David Bellos has identified as another 'mistake' in this early memory: Bellos claims that it would have been impossible to buy a Charlie Chaplin comic in Paris in 1941, as Chaplin had been banned following his impersonation of Hitler in *The Great Dictator*.

Perec goes on to comment:

A triple theme runs through this memory: parachute, sling, truss: it suggests suspension, support, almost artificial limbs. To be, I need a prop. Sixteen years later, in 1958, when, by chance, military service briefly made a parachutist

of me, I suddenly saw, in the very instant of jumping, one way of deciphering the text of this memory: I was plunged into nothingness; all the threads
were broken; I fell, on my own, without any support. The parachute opened.
The canopy unfurled, a fragile and firm suspense before the controlled
descent. (55)

The fact that his early memory still incorporates the 'mistake' of
Chaplin's image is an acknowledgement of the fact that early memories are often reconstructed at least in part out of later events and
images, demonstrating Freud's claim about the nature of childhood
memories in the essay on Leonardo da Vinci: they 'show us our earliest years not as they were but as they appeared at the later periods
when the memories were aroused. In these periods of arousal, the
childhood memories did not ... emerge; they were formed at that
time. And a number of motives, with no concern for historical accuracy, had part in forming them' (1910a: 137). The parachute that
supported Perec's fall in 1957 has been superimposed upon a (different) comic his mother may actually have bought him: the memory
thus functions as a retrospective reconstruction of his first fall, his
separation from his mother.[6]

The meaning of this memory is reinterpreted again in the light of
another, similar 'false' memory. In section 15 Perec describes being
knocked over by a sledge while he was skating at Villard-de-Lans,
where he lived during his 'exile': his scapula was broken and his arm
had to be tightly strapped behind his back 'in a whole contraption of
bandages' which made any movement impossible. In his memory,
this accident evoked tremendous sympathy from others. On going
back to Villard in 1970 and talking with an old school friend, he
discovers that the accident – described identically in all its details –
happened not to him but to another classmate, Philippe. Perec was
thus 'not a heroic victim but just a witness' (80). These false memories
of physical, vaguely heroic, sympathy-evoking and relatively easily
mended 'breaks' have come to stand in for the real trauma, 'which
was mentioned only in an undertone', although 'today it seems to me
that the metaphor will not serve as a way of describing what had
been broken – and what it was surely pointless hoping to contain
within the guise of an imaginary limb' (80–1). These memories thus
represent a (not entirely successful) displacement of the diffused and
only-partly understood trauma of the loss of his mother on to more
specific and comprehensible injuries.

Another of Perec's early memories is 'not the memory of a scene,
but a memory of the word, only a memory of the letter that has
turned into a word' (77). This is the word/letter 'x' – 'a saw-horse'

(used by an old man in Villard) 'made of a pair of upended parallel crosses, each in the shape of an x . . . connected by a perpendicular crossbar, the whole device being called, quite simply, an x' (76). Derrida explains that Freud, 'in order to suggest the strangeness of the logico-temporal relations in dreams, constantly adduces writing, and the spatial synopses of pictograms, rebuses, hieroglyphics and non-phonetic writing in general' (1978: 217). The Hebrew alphabet is closely derived from the Phoenician, which was hieroglyphic, the letters developing from symbols which originally represented the objects themselves, then coming to denote the initial sound of the word for that object. 'X' is a letter which is still also the name of an object, and the representation of the shape of the object: such signs assert the materiality of language. Perec goes on to trace the changing referents and uses of the sign 'x', from sign of deletion, of words turned into blanks, to the 'geometrical fantasy, whose basic figure is the double V' (the sound of 'W' in French) 'and whose complex con-volutions trace out the major symbols of the story of my childhood' (77) – the W of his fantasy, the swastika and the star of David. This memory thus fits the pattern of those elicited at a later date and 'put into the service of later trends': one can even imagine that the 'x' of the saw-horse was remembered instead of the swastika the child may have seen on the uniforms of the German soldiers who visited his school (the headteachers were members of the Resistance). The hieroglyph also suggests Perec's description of his handwriting up to the age of seventeen or eighteen: 'that unjoined-up writing, made of separate letters unable to forge themselves into a word' (68), which he compares to the disconnectedness of his memories from his time in Villard, and which he also links to the disconnected figures he drew at the time of the invention of the island of W. Through the material sign of written language the child Perec represents not only the disconnectedness of his own life but also, perhaps, at some unconscious level, the sense of disconnection experienced by the inmates of the camps, and the degeneration and distortion of human bodies nevertheless compelled to 'work'.

Perec refers to the 'high wall of prefabricated memories' that had to be broken down during his psychoanalysis. Levi describes the way that memories 'evoked too often' become 'crystallised, perfect, adorned', taking the place of 'raw memory and grow[ing] at its expense' (1988: 11–12). Perec's account of his two earliest memories, and the way in which he footnotes and 'corrects' them, shows this process exactly, although here there is an insistence upon the impossibility of uncovering 'raw memory'. These memories, he says, 'are not entirely implausible, even though, obviously, the many

variations and imaginary details I have added in the telling of them
– in speech or in writing – have altered them greatly, if not completely distorted them' (13). In the first of these he sees himself as a
three-year-old sitting on the floor surrounded by Yiddish newspapers
and a warm, loving, complete family group, admiring the new-born
child – '(but didn't I say a moment ago that I was three?)' – who has
just deciphered his first Hebrew character, a letter which he calls the
'gammeth or gammel', which he reproduces in the text. A footnote
comments: 'Excess detail such as this is all that is needed to ruin the
memory or in any case to burden it with a letter it did not possess.
There is in fact a letter called 'Gimmel' which I like to think could be
the initial of my first name; it looks absolutely nothing like the sign
I have drawn which could just about masquerade as a "mem" or "M"'
(13). Bellos explains that the Hebrew 'letter' which Perec reproduces
in the text is a 'manifestly non-existent, Hebrew-seeming squiggle
that is in reality nothing other than a regularised mirror-image of
Perec's own handwritten first initial, G. Perec's first memory is thus
nothing of the sort; it is rather a (re)construction of his origin in
writing' (552). Perec goes on to explain that his aunt has recently told
him that one of his favourite games as a three-year-old when he
visited her was deciphering the letters in French, not Yiddish newspapers. Perec does not read the text of this memory any further, but
it is possible to do so in terms of Freud's analysis of screen-memories
– memories of apparently trivial events which have come to mask, or
stand in for, more significant or painful ones. Freud explains that
screen-memories can work retroactively: later events cause particular
aspects of earlier memory-traces to 're-surface' to consciousness, and
to acquire meaning that they did not have at the time. In the footnote
Perec claims that the letter he has drawn is closer to the first letter of
the word 'mother/mère/mama' – the mother who Perec lost at the age
of six. The referent of the sign thus slides between Perec (G, the
gammel) and his mother, suggesting both a displacement *and* wish-
fulfillment – the child is surrounded by 'the entirety, the totality of
the family', the family that was destroyed by 1941. The identification
of the sign which means 'mem' with the letter 'gimmel' suggests the
dyad of mother and child which is broken by the entry of the child
into the symbolic order, the reading and writing which Perec will
later state is 'the assertion of my life'.

In *The Psychopathology of Everyday Life*, Freud describes a
memory of a 25-year-old man which is similarly focused on a letter:
he remembers being taught the alphabet by his aunt, and having
difficulties over the difference between 'n' and 'm'. Freud suggests
that this memory acquired its meaning at a later date, when the boy

became anxious about another difference, that between men and women, represented retrospectively by the 'third stroke' of the letter 'm' (1975: 89). This difference is here elided with the 'difference' of Jewishness. The footnote tells us that 'really' the child Perec began to decipher letters in French, not Hebrew: here the memory (or its subsequent retranscription) reveals a truth that had to be concealed, the family's Jewish identity, the reason, of course, for the loss of his mother. In footnote 8 to section 8, Perec accounts for the origin, meaning, differing spellings and versions of his surname: 'This explanation signals but by no means exhausts the complex fantasies, connected to the concealment of my Jewish background through my patronym, which I elaborated around the name I bear' (36). Perec's 'inaccurate' early memory thus reveals a greater historical 'accuracy' – the fact of the family's Jewishness – than a 'true' memory of the event, if indeed such an event did take place.

One further memory that Perec retranslates suggests both that the body acts as a mediator or container of memory, but also that this mediation may be indirect, functioning as a screen for another, more deeply buried trace. Perec says that he has three memories of his time at school before he left Paris: the third is of being awarded a medal for good work, but then losing it when he accidentally pushed a little girl over on the stairs in a crush. The medal was torn off his chest, and he writes:

I can still physically *feel* that shove in the back, that flagrant proof of injustice; and the sensation in my whole body of a loss of balance imposed by others, coming from above and falling on to me, remains so deeply imprinted that I wonder if this memory does not in fact conceal its precise opposite: not the memory of a medal torn off, but of a star pinned on. (54)

The 'loss of balance imposed by others' recalls his parachute descent and the 'points of suspension' connected with his parting from his mother, not to speak of the dislocation caused by the war itself. The medal/star recalls the medals awarded to the victorious athletes on W, and the arbitrary ways in which they are subsequently lost. This memory 'of the body' could thus be seen as having come to stand in for other, more painful and significant injustices and losses.

Perec thus foregrounds the materiality of language and the written sign as a mark of absence. The child Gaspard is deaf and dumb, and apart from the story of the first Gaspard which is narrated to the second by Otto Apfelstahl, there is very little direct speech in the text. Primo Levi describes how, in the camps, 'use of the word to communicate thought, this necessary and sufficient mechanism for man to be man, had fallen into disuse' (1986: 70–1). He describes the language of the camps as 'orts-und-zeitgebunden' (tied to time and place): prisoners who could not pick up very quickly the debased German of the camps – the 'Raus! Schnell!' of the Olympian island of W – had very little chance of survival. It is on this question of language that a false note is struck in Begnini's film *Life is Beautiful*: the hero (not actually understanding any German) offers to 'translate' the guard's instructions to newly arrived camp inmates and turns them into instructions for the game he wants his child to believe they are playing. Levi also describes the paralysed child Hurbinek, born in Auschwitz, struggling to speak as he is dying: 'his eyes . . . flashed terribly alive, full of demand, assertion, of the will to break loose, to shatter the tomb of his dumbness . . . he fought like a man, to the last breath, to gain his entry into the world of men' (1987: 197–8). Speech, language and writing become essential means of restoring a sense of humanity as well as of bearing witness, in spite of Levi's recognition that 'our language lacks words to express this offence' (32). For Perec, also, writing is 'the assertion of my life' and making the Holocaust an 'extreme limit case' of the impossibility of writing would thus deny the claim to life and humanity here being made. To speak at all is to express the desire to be recognised and heard, whether as a trauma- tised child or as the inhabitant of a world in which there is no 'other' to address. *W* constitutes 'un appel: le lecteur est sommé de prendre la place de l'Autre' ('an appeal: the reader is summoned to take the place of the Other') (Leak 1990: 81, my translation), as well as also being *put in the place of* the subject coming to knowledge.

David Bellos suggests that the enforced but 'vitally necessary act of forgetting' his Jewishness caused Perec to grow up into a man 'always puzzled by memory and sometimes obsessed with the fear of forget- ting' (68). But in spite of Perec's obsessive documentation elsewhere in his work of memories – of dreams, places, meals eaten, objects in a room – almost in the process of their formation,[7] *W* demonstrates that 'remembering is not contrary to forgetting. "True memory" is found at the *intersection* of remembrance and oblivion, at the instant where the memory returns which was both forgotten and preserved by our forgetting' (Merleau-Ponty, quoted in Krell 1990: 101). *W* represents a refusal to 'inscribe in memory', which, using Lyotard's terms, 'might seem a good defence against forgetting', but which 'can be just the opposite' (1988: 26). It is a 'writing of the ruins' (43) – literally so in the case of the ruins of W – and a text which 'remem- bers that it has forgotten the Forgotten' – the 'forgotten' of childhood memories as such, and of the event which destroyed that childhood. A biographer might be concerned to establish which of Perec's memories are 'genuinely' false and which have been consciously reconstructed, but *W* is a text, not a slice of memory, and one which demonstrates the impossibility of a complete and accurate reconstruction of the past in a way which renders the question of the degree of consciousness of memory's retranscriptions irrelevant. Afterwardsness is built into the structure of the text not only because of Perec's constant retranslations of memory, but because the central event around which it is structured, his parting from his mother, is one characterised by unpreparedness and belatedness. One of his early memories represents a moment – very like Ronald Fraser's final vision of a family gathering and a sense of 'indestructible love . . . an unsurpassable assurance' (186) – of imaginary wholeness with 'the entirety, the totality of the family' (13), but it is a memory which is immediately acknowledged as at least in part constructed out of the fantasy which it represents. The text represents in material form – the 'points of suspension' – the gap between an initial, unassimilated and unrepresented shock – the loss of his mother – and its later manifestation, the fantasy of W and its subsequent retranscriptions. It is also a text which represents the 'silence' demanded of those who did not directly experience the Holocaust, but for whom it has become the material of fantasy, and, literally and of necessity, of words.

FUGITIVE PIECES: WITNESSING AND IDENTITY

'This writing of survival is itself gripped by the shame of not having succumbed, by the shame of still being able to bear witness and by the sadness engendered by being able to speak' (Lyotard 1990: 44). Jakob Beer, the protagonist of Michaels' novel, who as a seven-year-old survives the massacre of his parents by the Nazis in Poland, wonders as an adult: 'To survive is to escape fate. But if you escape your fate, whose life do you then step into?' (48). Both Perec and Michaels foreground the relationship between writing and survival. Perec explicitly acknowledges that writing is the mark of absence – in the case of his parents, of a 'once-and-for-all-annihilation' – but also, paradoxically, an 'indelible mark, whose trace is writing' and 'the assertion of my life' (42).

Jakob grows up to become a poet – and a translator of rediscovered diaries and memoirs of those murdered in the Holocaust, invoked by Michaels in her preface – for whom language is a mode of salvation: 'Write to save yourself', he is told by Athos, the Greek archaeologist who finds him in the mud of Poland, 'and someday you'll write because you've been saved' (165). Through Jakob, Michaels, herself a poet, uses a mode of language best described as metaphysical: metaphor is used to convey otherwise intangible meaning and language reaches beyond the material in an attempt to re-presence what is absent. Michaels does not re-create the perception or mode of expression of the traumatised seven-year-old: Jakob's memoir, which comprises the first section of the narrative, begins: 'Time is a blind guide. Bog-boy, I surfaced into the miry streets of the drowned city' (5). Jakob reconstructs and reflects upon his memories from the perspective of middle age when he has rediscovered the power of language and developed an identity quite different from the one he would have had growing up with his family in Poland: 'here, on Idhra, in the summer of 1992, I try to set down the past in the cramped space of a prayer' (191). As an adolescent he searches for a way of writing 'in code, every letter askew, so that loss would wreck the language, become the language' (111): this suggests rather the technique of Perec in *La Disparition* (1969), a novel written without the letter 'e', pronounced in French as 'eux', meaning 'them' – those whose disappearance during the war, like that of Perec's mother, was announced by an *Acte de Disparition*. Perec's word play and his fascination with the materiality of language finds an echo in *Fugitive Pieces* in Jakob's first wife Alex, who loves palindromes, a mode of language that refers only to itself, in contrast to Jakob, who 'invents' meaning through metaphor: 'The closest we come to knowing the location of what's unknown is when it melts through the map like a watermark... On the map of history, perhaps the water stain is memory' (137).

The structure of the novel reflects how 'time catches together what we know and do not know' (Steedman 1986: 141): we are told on the first page of the novel that Jakob 'was struck and killed by a car in Athens in the spring of 1993, at age sixty', his wife surviving him by a few days. This knowledge, of Jakob's random death, haunts the first part of the narrative, which tells the story of his survival and rescue by Athos and his subsequent life in Greece and Canada. His life in the present is shadowed by the memory of his sister and his ignorance of her fate, his memories of her seeming to resurface involuntarily – 'images rising in me like bruises' (19) and forming one of the most moving elements of the novel. Ben, the novel's second narrator, is the child of concentration-camp survivors, haunted by his parents' untransmitted memories and the loss of their first children, whose existence was never communicated to him. He finds a photograph which reveals the secret, and reflects: 'The past is desperate energy, live, an electric field. It chooses a single moment, a chance so domestic we don't know we've missed it, a moment that crashes into us from behind and changes all that follows' (253). After Jakob's death Ben searches for the notebooks he left behind, quotations from which echo Jakob's narrative and reinforce his absence. Before Ben finds the notebooks, in Jakob's house on Idhra, Ben finds a note pinned by his wife Michaela to his pillow:

> If she's a girl: Bella
> If he's a boy: Bela.

Jakob died before he knew that Michaela was expecting their child. The experience of Michaels' characters is thus marked by their knowledge or ignorance of key facts or moments in their past or present lives, as Perec's childhood was marked by his ignorance of his mother's fate.

Throughout Jakob's narrative the image of double exposure recurs: the present exists as an echo of the past, the past is always a shadow behind the present moment. Watching the candles of the Easter procession on Zakynthos,

I watched and was in my own village, winter evenings, my teacher lighting the wicks of our lanterns and releasing us into the street like toy boats bobbing down a flooded gutter . . . I . . . placed this parallel image, like other ghostly double exposures, carefully into orbit . . . Even now, half a century later, writing this on a different Greek island, I look down to the remote lights of the town and feel the heat of a flame spreading up my sleeve. (18)

Here the structure of memory is threefold: writing in the present, Jakob remembers a moment from the past which was haunted by the memory of an earlier moment, of an innocent time before the catastrophe, and is reminded of the first moment yet more intensely in the present. Memory is layered, like the strata of rock which hold the memory of the earth. Events, stories, images in the present are shadowed by the defining moments of his past, by what might have been, or what was, although he knew nothing of it: '[t]he shadow past is shaped by everything that never happened. This is how one becomes undone by a smell, a word, a place, the photo of a mountain of shoes' (17). His realisation that 'every moment is two moments' becomes especially acute during his first marriage to Alex, whose vitality saves him whilst also robbing him of his past: 'each time a memory or a story slinks away, it takes more of me with it'. Details of his present life are shadowed by images of his past: 'Alex's hairbrush propped on the sink: Bella's brush. Alex's bobby pins: Bella's hairclips turning up in strange places, as bookmarks' (140). Earlier, Jakob evokes the doubleness of time in a passage juxtaposing details of his life in hiding on Zakynthos with the fate of the Jews elsewhere in Europe, 'the events we lived through without knowing' (110): 'While Athos taught me about . . . Arctic smoke, and the Spectre of the Bröcken, I didn't know that Jews were being hanged by their thumbs in public squares' (46). 'History and memory . . . terra cognita and terra incognita inhabit exactly the same coordinates of time and space' (137); so Jakob's narrative 'catches together' past and present, memory (his own experience) and history (that of countless others). In Perec's *W*, 'history' (the reality of the camps) emerges as if from the unconscious of the text, from a fantasy constructed by the child: Jakob here inserts the reality he later discovered into the story of the life he lived in ignorance of it.

Jakob's 'failure' as a witness of his sister's fate – he sees his parents' bodies when he emerges from hiding, but does not realise until later that Bella had simply disappeared – leads to an obsession after the war with reports and histories of the concentration camps. His concern is not with the identity of those who suffered and died (although his listing of the places they might have come from and the possible manner of their deaths does evoke their individuality), but with the question of whether they witnessed their own deaths: 'were they silent or did they speak? Were their eyes open or closed? . . . I was focused on that historical split second: the tableau of the haunting trinity – perpetrator, victim, witness' (140). Perec claims that his mother died 'without understanding' (33) suggesting either the impossibility of 'witnessing' her death or (for anyone) of understanding its reason. Michaels seems here to be acknowledging that language and narrative must inevitably fail in the attempt to speak for the dead now that that 'historical split second' is past, echoing Primo Levi's recognition that 'we, the survivors, are not the true witnesses' (1988: 63).

Through Jakob Michaels raises the question of witnessing discussed earlier in this chapter in terms that at times are made to bear the weight of an excess of abstraction: 'The event is meaningful only if the coordination of time and place is witnessed', suggests Jakob, following a meditation which links the painted clock on the station at Treblinka and Einstein on the notion of simultaneity. For some, he suggests, to be a witness, or even a survivor, implied complicity: 'Witnessed by those who lived near the incinerators, within the radius of smell. By those who lived outside a camp fence, or stood outside the chamber doors. By those who stepped a few feet to the right on the station platform. By those who were born a generation after' (162). Here he invokes the position not only of children of survivors, like Ben, but of those who can only 'recover the past by inventing it', and the ethical questions involved in so doing. When Jakob realises what was happening to the Jews of Europe whilst he was in hiding on Zakynthos, he imagines the experience of those who were forced to dig up mass graves and burn the bodies: 'Their arms were into death up to the elbows, but not only into death – into music, into a memory of the way a husband or son leaned over his dinner, a wife's expression as she watched her child in the bath ... How can one man take on the memories of even one man, let alone five or ten or a thousand; how can they be sanctified each?' (52). The answer for the prisoner is 'to stop thinking', but Jakob, and through him Michaels, acknowledges that the survivor, or the writer of 'a generation after', whilst unable to speak for the dead, or forgive on their behalf, can acknowledge their loss. 'And even if an act could be forgiven, no one could bear the responsibility of forgiveness on behalf of the dead ... When the one who can forgive can no longer speak, there is only silence' (160–1). *Fugitive Pieces* embodies the paradoxical position of the writer who acknowledges that she cannot speak for the dead whilst also staking a claim for the restorative power of language.

The controlling metaphor of Michaels' novel – one she claims is not in fact metaphorical – is geological:

It's no metaphor to feel the influence of the dead in the world, just as it's no metaphor to hear the radiocarbon chronometer, the Geiger counter amplifying the faint breathing of rock, fifty thousand years old ... It is no metaphor to witness the astonishing fidelity of minerals magnetized ... We long for place; but place itself longs. Human memory is encoded in air currents and river sediment. (53)

Here natural processes are anthropomorphised and human memory given material form. It is through Athos that Jakob learns about the long history of the earth and the ways in which 'nature remembers'. Recognising the impossibility of an answer to the question 'Why?' in his researches on Nazi archaeology, Athos 'often applied the geologic to the human, analyzing social change as he would a landscape; slow persuasion and catastrophe'. It is Athos's stories of exploration and discovery, of rocks and weather, of bog-people and buried cities, of 'the earth itself' which rescue Jakob from the immediate weight of the past: 'Because of Athos, I spent hours in other worlds ... [H]e gave me another world to inhabit, big as the globe and expansive as time'. Rocks give material form to the passing of time, and Jakob is 'transfixed by the way time buckled, met itself in pleats and folds ... To go back a year or two was impossible, absurd. To go back millennia – ah! that was ... nothing' (30). The 'deep stratum' invoked by

Habermas here becomes the consolation of the persistence of the earth itself. Michaels gives more concrete form to Freud's archaeological model of memory: if archaeology can uncover and reconstruct buried cities, then perhaps the dead can be brought back to life, preserved intact like bodies in peat-bogs. Later, looking at the photographs of piles of possessions of those murdered in the camps, Jakob 'fantasised the power of reversal . . . I imagined that if each owner of each pair of shoes could be named, then they would be brought back to life' (50). Athos's 'backward glance' provides him with a 'backward hope. Redemption through cataclysm; what had been transformed might be transformed again' (101).

The older Jakob knows that language does not have the magical power of bringing the dead back to life, but continues to use it as a form of consolation – a 'prayer' – and as a way of making human suffering a part of some larger, 'natural' process. Athos's notion of history as 'the evolution of longing' makes Jakob realise that grief requires time, and he imagines the stars '[a]ching towards us for millennia though we are blind to their signals until it's too late, starlight only the white breath of an old cry' (53–4). In this sustained parallel between human grief and longing and the movements of the earth and stars, the novel often elides the human with the geological or biological. The migration of birds is compared to 'the black seam of that wailing migration from life to death' on the railways through Europe to the camps, with the suggestion that the dead, like migrating birds, might return: '[t]hough they were taken blind, though their senses were confused by stench and prayer and screams, by terror and memories, these passengers found their way home. Through the rivers, through the air' (52). Then follows the passage already quoted from, where prisoners dig up the bodies of the murdered, and 'the dead entered them through their pores and were carried through their bloodstreams to their brains and hearts'. Berel Lang suggests that the Nazi genocide against the Jews might be one of those circumstances 'when the occasion for writing makes its own mark, when the facts "speak for themselves"'. Then 'artifice tends to become conceit, and the writer's intervention . . . draws attention away from the subject itself' (1990: xi–xii). Here the metaphor, which we are invited to take literally, does draw attention away from the subject; the elision of natural, instinctive processes with politically motivated murder seems a mystification, and the kind of immortality here suggested a false consolation. The course and ending of a human life do not obey the same laws as those of the physical universe: when Jakob suggests that '[h]uman memory is encoded in air currents and river sediment. Eskers of ash wait to be scooped up, lives reconstituted' he (or

Michaels) seem to be claiming that memory, or the remains of the dead, exist in some material form available for reconstruction outside or beyond language. Michaels' use of metaphor here produces the effect of 'memorialisation' which Lyotard warns against, whilst her double narrative – of past and present, Jakob and Ben, history and memory – preserves the 'achronology' of traumatic time. Perec, on the other hand, allows the tenor of his 'metaphor' – the concentration camp – to emerge gradually and powerfully from its vehicle, the Olympian island of W: both, clearly are situated firmly within the realm of human and social activity.

The problem with Michaels' use of metaphor – and with her metaphysical approach to her subject matter – is especially acute at the moment when she allows Jakob's imagination – and through him, her own – to enter the gas chamber in the attempt to realise more fully the probable fate of his sister Bella. She frames this moment with Jakob's own reservations: 'I blaspheme by imagining . . . Forgive this blasphemy, of choosing philosophy over the brutalism of fact' (167–8). The image and the faith it momentarily inspires is quickly admitted to be a 'fabrication' – '[e]ven as I fall apart I know I will never again feel this pure belief' (169) – but the passage remains, provoking the kind of discomfort felt when Spielberg – for different reasons – takes the viewer into what *could* be the gas chamber in his film of *Schindler's List*. Jakob invokes '[t]he terrifying hope of human cells. The bare autonomic faith of the body' (168) as the dying attempt to reach the last remaining pockets of trapped air, and goes on to speculate on the meaning of their cries:

At that moment of utmost degradation, in that twisted reef, is the most obscene testament of grace. For can anyone tell with absolute certainty the difference between the sounds of those who are in despair and the sounds of those who want desperately to believe? The moment when our faith in man is forced to change, anatomically – mercilessly – into faith. (168)

This comes some six pages after Jakob's claim that 'when the one who can forgive can no longer speak, there is only silence'. Here Jakob – and through him, Michaels – does seem to be attempting to speak for the dead and to 'stage the obscene' by finding some 'grace' in their deaths. Jakob speaks of '*our* faith in man' (168, my italics): it is not clear here whether he is speaking as one of the dying – the most 'obscene' possibility – or as one who can only imagine their state of mind, surely presumptuous in any case. The use of 'anatomically' suggests a reduction to the body at this moment, eliding the biological with the spiritual, rational or social – or with whatever it is we consider makes us human. This is a moment where the attempt to find meaning in the deaths of millions (or, for Jakob, fuller knowledge of what happened to his sister) gives way to metaphor and abstraction instead of leaving the unsayable unsaid, as Perec chooses to do and Lyotard advises: 'What art can do is bear witness not to the sublime, but to this aporia of art and its pain. It does not say the unsayable, but says that it cannot say it' (1990: 47).

Fugitive Pieces tells the story of a man who has worked his way out of silence into language. Lyotard acknowledges that 'writing . . . is always of some restorative value to the soul because of its unpreparedness, which leaves it an infant ' (1990: 33). Unprepared for the sudden deaths of his parents and sister, Jakob later tried 'to bury images, to cover them over with Greek and English words' and later with 'train schedules, camp records, statistics, methods of execution'. Language is here admitted to be a defence against memory, '[b]ut at night, my mother, my father, Bella . . . simply rose, shook the earth from their clothes, and waited' (93). It is only with his second wife Michaela, who seems able to share the memory of Bella and whose love is presented as redemptive, that Jakob is able to let go of the dead and to realise that when Bella whispered to him it was 'not for me to join her, but so that, when I'm close enough, she can push me back into the world' (170). Rather like the ghostly return of the murdered Beloved in Morrison's novel, the presence of Bella is actualised through the mediation of Michaela and her loss acknowledged so that Jakob can finally release her. Michaels creates a fictional character for whom, like Georges Perec, 'writing is the memory of their [his parents' – and here his sister's] death and the assertion of my life' (*W*: 42), and another, Ben, for whom Jakob's life and writing enable an acceptance of his parents' choices and silences and a possible reunion with his wife Naomi, because, like Jakob and Michaela, they share their memories. 'On Idhra', writes Jakob, 'I finally began to feel my English strong enough to carry experience . . . The moment when language at last surrenders to what it's describing'. This suggests a fusion of word and image, but in the novel 'language', as I have suggested, is often foregrounded at the expense of 'what it's describing'. Jakob longs to 'honour every inch of flesh in words, and so suspend time' (162–3), suggesting a desire for language to embody absence and to overcome the belatedness of traumatic knowledge. He expresses a more certain faith in 'the power of language to restore' than does Perec, for whom memory is a text to be deciphered, full of holes and gaps that he acknowledges his sparse and meticulous language cannot fill. Jakob's early memories are so painful that Athos at first encourages him to forget so that his 'blood-past drained from' him; under the influence of Alex he feels that 'each time a memory or a story slinks away, it takes more of me with it' (144). But by the time he comes to write his memories, in the last year or so of his life, they are apparently fully available to consciousness although still marked by the gap of ignorance of Bella's fate. Lyotard acknowledges the restorative power of language whilst warning of the danger of forgetting that 'once again there is no salvation, no health, and that time, even the time of work, does not heal anything' (1990: 34). In *Fugitive Pieces* Michaels claims salvatory and healing powers for language, love and the sharing of memory. Although she acknowledges the necessity of letting go of the dead, Michaels uses language, and more specifically metaphor, to 'suspend time' rather than acknowledging the impossibility of fully restoring the past, and the dead, through language.

Notes

1. Georges Perec and Robert Bober (1981), *Récits d'Ellis Island: Histoires d'errance et d'espoir*, Paris: Sorbier, quoted by Warren F. Motte, Jr (1984), *The Poetics of Experiment: A Study of the Work of Georges Perec*, p. 112, my translation.
2. I use 'Holocaust' as the term most commonly used to refer to the Nazi murder of the Jews and others during the Second World War, whilst acknowledging that many find it unsatisfactory because of its connotations of sacrifice (it means, literally, 'whole burning'). Claude Lanzmann's choice, 'Shoah' or 'destruction', also has biblical precedents; the metonymical 'Auschwitz' seems to negate the experience of those who died by other means; 'the Event' mystifies; the euphemistic 'Final Solution' replicates Nazi ideology.
3. Lyotard has clarified his use of the term "the jews": 'the expression "the jews" refers to all those who, wherever they are, seek to remember and bear witness to something constitutively *forgotten*, not only in each individual mind, but in the very thought of the West. And it refers to all those who assume this anamnesis and this witnessing as an obligation, a responsibility, or a debt, not only towards thought, but towards justice' (1993: 141).
4. Wilkomirski's *Fragments: Memories of a Childhood, 1939–1948*, first published in 1995, won the *Jewish Quarterly* Award for Non-Fiction. Doubts have since arisen over the authenticity of his memories of Majdanek and Auschwitz, recovered during therapy. Elena Lappin (1999) explores the question in *Granta* 66, suggesting not that Wilkomirski deliberately fabricated his childhood in the camps and his Jewish identity, but that he came to believe in them as an explanation of his nightmares and fragmented memories of his early life in an orphanage and with unsympathetic foster-parents. The case throws a fascinating light on the relationship between identity, memory and trauma.

5. Perec, *Espèces d'espaces* (1974), quoted by Motte (1984), p. 106, my translation.
6. This memory is discussed by Eleanor Kaufman (1999) in 'Falling from the Sky: Trauma in Perec's *W* and Caruth's *Unclaimed Experience*' (*diacritics* 28.4: 44–53).
7. See Lejeune (1990) for a discussion of Perec's autobiographical projects, which included *Les Lieux*, a project involving the description of twelve places in Paris of significance to him, once from observation and once from memory. This project is also mentioned on pp. 47–9 of *W*.

Rememory and Reconstruction:
Toni Morrison's *Beloved*

INTRODUCTION

'Rememory' is a concept central to the structure and meaning of Toni Morrison's *Beloved*: as the narrative unfolds it develops into a sign of the complex and sometimes contradictory processes which it articulates. My analyses of the meanings of 'rememory', and of the associated term 'reconstruction', provide a framework for my reading of this novel, which has, over the past ten years, become a key text for the representation of memory and of the recovery of African-American history. Peter Nicholls has suggested *Beloved* as a text which articulates – in the form of the ghost of Beloved – the idea of 'a forgotten history [which] has the power to shake the social and metaphysical forms against which it breaks . . . the idea of history as a violent intrusion from somewhere else' (1996: 52). The 're' of rememory suggests the belatedness of traumatic memory: I shall argue that on the one hand the term confirms the view of memory as a process of 'retranscription' and 'retranslation', whilst on the other, the reliving of the pre-Oedipal mother–infant dyad in the relationship of Sethe and Beloved enacts the trope of memory as nostalgia for the 'pure' past, seen in this instance as both necessary but ultimately destructive. 'Rememory' also indicates a point of intersection between individual memory of personal experience and cultural or collective memory in *Beloved* a murdered child returns to exact due recognition of the pain and loss of the personal past, and is also made to bear the symbolic weight of the repressed or forgotten histories of her people.

Beloved, albeit based on a historical event, the killing of her child by the escaped slave Margaret Garner, is a novel. Like Anne Michaels, its author thus stands in a different relationship to her material than the authors of the autobiographical texts discussed in this book, both in terms of time and narrative voice. The novel comes 'afterwards' in a triple sense: published in 1987, the present time of the narrative is the year 1873, during the period of Reconstruction just after the Civil War. The central events, half-remembered and half-told during the first section of the novel, take place some sixteen years earlier, when Sethe, the central character, escaped from slavery in Kentucky, gave birth to her younger daughter Denver on the banks of the Ohio River, and murdered her older daughter to prevent her being taken back into slavery. Rememory – remembering again – thus refers to the events which Sethe at first tries *not* to remember, and to a period of American history whose remembering and representation is a necessary and political act. The term 'reconstruction' can be used to refer to specific psychoanalytic processes and to the work of the historian or archaeologist: Morrison has also spoken of her writing as the attempt to 'reconstruct a world' (1987b: 112). The 're' of reconstruction, like the 're' of rememory, signals something that takes place 'again', 'afterwards', 'for a second time': it suggests both repetition and the reinterpretation to which time inevitably subjects our knowledge of the past. The tension between differing psychoanalytic meanings of reconstruction – the complete and accurate re-creation of the past, and the continuous process of reconstructing previous constructions – is refigured here in the conflicting meanings and purposes of the term in a particular historical case. Reconstruction aimed to restore the Union and reunite a society shattered by civil war: it was also the time when ex-slaves struggled to reconstruct lives, families and identities in the wake of 'certain kinds of dissolution' which Morrison sees as having been experienced by blacks as 'the first truly modern people'; she speaks of 'the loss of and the need to reconstruct certain kinds of stability' (1988: 11). When Paul D attempts to reconstruct that stability for Sethe after the disappearance of Beloved, he remembers Sixo describing how he felt about his Thirty-Mile Woman: 'The pieces I am, she gather them and give them back to me in all the right order' (1987: 272–3). For Sethe, this process of reordering or reconstructing takes place through rememory – remembering again in a context of trust after a period of attempting to forget – but also through a later, and necessary, forgetting.

The language of the text also evokes the disintegration and reconstruction of shattered and fragmented *bodies*, bodies reduced to 'seared, divided, ripped-apart' (Spillers 1987: 67), *flesh* on the slave ships and under torture, divided and measured by Schoolteacher, and also the pre-Oedipal 'fragmented body imperfectly effaced by our illusions of coherence' (Abel 1990: 188). Sethe and Beloved reconstruct the imaginary unity of the mother–infant dyad of which they were deprived, both in terms of their own violent separation and the depleted possibilities of mothering under slavery, represented in the text by Sethe's absent relation with her own mother. Carole Boyce Davies suggests that 'reconstructions of mothering have been continuous' in black culture in response to the over-determination of the black woman slave as 'Mammy' and to the fact that, 'under slavery, the offspring of the female does not "belong" to the mother' (1994: 136). According to Jean Wyatt, Morrison 'reconstructs the acts of maternal heroism' in the narratives of Harriet Jacobs and Lucy Delaney 'as the reproductive feats of the maternal body' (1993: 475). Morrison explores what Sally Keenan describes as 'the power and the danger of the maternal inscription for black women' (1992: 278): the reconstruction which the novel enacts is both a powerful reaffirmation and a repetition which is ultimately destructive.

Defining slavery as a form of pathology, Morrison suggested in her 1988 *City Limits* interview that in order to construct and maintain it as a system, white people 'have had to reconstruct everything in order to make that system appear true', a process which continued after abolition in order to maintain supremacy. Reconstruction here means a radical revision of reality in order to justify slavery or racist ideology. But used in the sense of reconstructing a fuller and more accurate view of the historical past, a more positive process of reconstruction has demonstrated that slavery played a central role in the development of American culture and history: according to Morrison its previous dismissal as a 'tragic' or 'peculiar' aberration was part of the construction of America as an 'innocent future' in which 'the past is absent or . . . romanticised'.[1] *Beloved* is clearly part of a recent rediscovery and re-representation of the trauma and impact of slavery on American culture. Sally Keenan has suggested that Morrison's 'exploration of that liminal condition, between the then of slavery and the future of freedom, acts as an analogue to the relationship of contemporary African Americans to their past; the need, that is, to recover and recall their history, and the need to escape the cycle of oppression and violence it tells, and in which many remain entrapped' (1992: 240). It embodies a recognition of the uncomfortable fact that the legacy of slavery might be the tendency to inflict violence on the self, and of the need to acknowledge the traumas of the past in order to leave them behind.

Beloved is an imaginative reconstruction of the experience of slavery in that Morrison is representing something she did not directly experience. It is also an attempt to represent, or reconstruct, what has been only partially represented – the enslaved Africans' experience of the Middle Passage. In *Playing in the Dark*, Morrison describes how, '[o]ver and over, the writers [of slave narratives] pull the narrative up short with a phrase such as "but let us draw a veil over these proceedings too terrible to relate" . . . most importantly . . . there was no mention of their interior life' (1992: 33). More specifically, she refers to 'a silence of four hundred years . . . the void of historical discourse on slave parent/child relationships and pain' (22). Gina Wisker has suggested that *Beloved* 'articulates and embodies a history and experience which has been ostensibly, literally and "safely" recuperated but is actually still "raw"' (1993: 118). In Paul D's painful, hesitant account of Halle's traumatised witnessing of Sethe's rape the text recognises that some experiences cannot be fully articulated, that they might remain 'raw'. In the *South Bank Show* of 11 October 1987 devoted to *Beloved*, Morrison suggests the inadequacy of 'historical discourse' in the claim she makes for art: 'There is so much more to remember and describe, for purposes of exorcism and salvatory rites of passage . . . things must be made . . . some fixing ceremony . . . some memorial, something, some altar, somewhere . . . where these things can be released, thought, and felt . . . but the consequences of slavery only artists can deal with.' The tentativeness of this formulation suggests that Morrison is searching for a way to articulate the relationship between art and historical suffering; Leo Bersani (1990) has criticised the assumption that art can 'redeem' suffering, which might be suggested by Morrison's idea that the novel can provide 'salvatory rites of passage'. But in *Beloved* she uses the form of the novel to respect and represent the gaps, silences and dislocations which are the marks of such suffering; the novel attests to the impossibility of fully representing or recuperating such experiences as Halle's traumatised witnessing or the Middle Passage itself, except through the fragmented collective memory of Beloved herself. 'There is so much more to remember' not only as a counter to the mainstream myth of American 'innocence', but also because of the 'deliberate, calculated, survivalist intention to forget' which, according to Morrison, characterised African-American responses to slavery. *Beloved* testifies to the impossibility of forgetting without adequate remembering, whilst recognising that remembering – or finding form and expression for one's memories – may never be complete. As Asnaf Rushdy puts it: '*Beloved* is the story that stops haunting when told, and stops being when disremembered, but must be remembered to be told, and must be told to be disremembered' (1990: 317).

NARRATIVE VOICE: INTERPERSONAL ANAMNESIS

Although Morrison sees her task as one of restoring an interior life to people who were either presumed not to have one, or whose subjectivity had never been fully represented, *Beloved* is not written in the first person. Its often indeterminate narrative voice represents the communal or collective process of remembering, described by Satya P. Mohanty as a 'braiding of consciousnesses' (1993: 58). Morrison herself has spoken of her desire to 'have the reader *feel* the narrator without *identifying* that narrator' (Greene 1991b: 318). But this technique also raises the question of how far Sethe's subjectivity and memories are being directly represented – to what extent she is represented as reconstructing her own history, or having it reconstructed for her by the narrator. There are many passages in which it is unclear whether Sethe is 'speaking' or being 'spoken for' by the narrator: the power of the text is such that most readers ignore the fact that Sethe is a narrative construction, not a real person who speaks through the text. This indeterminate narrative voice gives rise to radically different readings of the text. Mae G. Henderson (1991) reads the novel as a representation of Sethe's successfully completed 'task' of becoming the narrator or historian of her own life; she 'reads' the sections of the text which deal with Sethe's experience as narrated entirely by her, ignoring any distinction between character and narrator.[2] Jean Wyatt also sees Sethe's dilemma in terms of an inability to represent her loss and trauma in language; she reads Sethe as spoken *for* by the narrator, the full story of the loss of Beloved still untold by Sethe herself: 'The hope at the end of the novel is that Sethe, having recognized herself as subject, *will* narrate the mother-daughter story and invent a language that can encompass the desperation of the slave mother who killed her daughter. Or will she?' (1993: 484, my italics). These readings, however interesting and suggestive, tend to treat Sethe as a client in therapy rather than seeing her as a narrative construction through whom a powerful story is told. Many such readings of the novel focus on the moment when, soon after the arrival of Paul D, Sethe begins to feel that '[h]er story was bearable because it was his as well – to tell, to refine and tell again. The things neither knew about the other – the things neither had word-shapes for – well, it would come in time: where they led him off to sucking iron; the perfect death of her crawling-already? baby' (99).

In fact, these episodes from the painful past are narrated for the reader by a voice which articulates the inner language of memory of the characters, not by the characters directly to each other. Asnaf Rushdy's description of this technique is 'interpersonal anamnesis' (1990: 321), suggesting that 'rememory' takes place outside, or independently of, any one individual consciousness. The reader is also forced to witness the killing of the baby through the alienated eyes of schoolteacher and the slavecatcher before approaching it more closely through Baby Suggs and Stamp Paid: even here, the reader is told what the character cannot bring himself to say. 'So Stamp Paid did not tell him [Paul D] how she flew, snatching up her children like a hawk on the wing . . .' (157). When Sethe is 'spinning' around Paul D in the kitchen, circling around him and the core of the story she is trying to tell, '[h]e knew exactly what she meant: to get to a place where you could love anything you chose – not to need permission for desire – well now, *that* was freedom'. But Sethe knows 'that the circle she was making round the room, him, the subject, would remain one. That she could never close in, pin it down for any body who had to ask' (162–3). According to Jean Wyatt, 'the omniscient narrator subsequently fills in' this 'gap . . . at the heart of her story' (1993: 476):

Because the truth was simple . . . Simple: she was squatting in the garden and when she saw them coming and recognized schoolteacher's hat, she heard wings. Little hummingbirds stuck their needle beaks right through her headcloth into her hair and beat their wings. And if she thought anything, it was No . . . She just flew. Collected every bit of life she had made, all the parts of her that were precious and fine and beautiful, and carried, pushed, dragged them through the veil, out, away, over there where no one could hurt them. (163)

The narrative voice here articulates not Sethe's *words*, but her internal representation of the event, the only 'word-shapes' (99) she can find to embody the 'outrageous claim' she made on the life of her child, a claim she hopes to be able to justify to Beloved before she leaves. The fact that the same image – the 'little hummingbirds' which stick their 'needle beaks' into her head – is used to represent Sethe's state of mind when she attempts to kill Mr Bodwin, mistaking him for the slavecatcher, suggests that it is Sethe's own internal consciousness which is being 'voiced' here by the narrator. All she is able to *say* to Paul D here is: 'I stopped him . . . I took and put my babies where they'd be safe' (164). When she recognises Beloved as the incarnation of the spirit of her baby daughter, she feels at first that she will not have to remember now that what is lost has been restored: repetition here functions, as Freud suggested, as a remedy for the failure of memory. Within the text, and for the reader, the re-enactment of the unspeakable drama of the past in the form of the symbiosis of mother and infant stands in for the full therapeutic narration of the traumatic event. The novel is the place where 'unspeakable thoughts' (199) – the internal monologues of the three women, articulating the ambivalences and intimacies of their relationships and memories – can be 'spoken' in a language that seems to come from a time *before* the constitution of the individual subject who might narrate a coherent or consistent story.

Like the Holocaust survivors interviewed by Dori Laub, Sethe has not forgotten the traumas of her past, but has not fully 'witnessed' or 'taken cognisance' of them. The novel enacts the process of her 'remembering something she had forgotten she knew', Bollas' 'unthought known'. If Beloved represents 'the return of the repressed', the 'repressed' is here not the completely forgotten, but the sign of an unassimilated, isolated event. Abraham and Torok's concept of 'preservative repression' is useful here: it 'seals off access to part of one's own life in order to shelter from view the traumatic monument of an obliterated event' (Rand 1994: 18). Such events are preserved in what they call an 'intrapsychic tomb': 'the tomb's content is unique in that it cannot appear in the light of day as speech. And yet, it is precisely a matter of words. Without question, in the depths of the crypt unspeakable words buried alive are held fast, like owls in ceaseless vigil' (1994: 159–60). As Jean Wyatt makes clear, Sethe's inability to substitute the sign of language for the presence of her daughter indicates her own refusal to acknowledge her loss. Beloved is the 'phantom' which, according to Abraham and Torok, 'represents the interpersonal and trans-generational consequences of silence' (1994: 130). The novel does find ways of breaking this silence, of speaking these 'unspeakable words': initially, however, the narrative reproduces the half-sensed knowledge of an untransmitted secret by placing the *reader* in this position. On the third page of the text we are told that Sethe's baby is haunting 124 because it is furious 'at having its throat cut' (5): the shocking incongruity of this statement remains unassimilated by the reader, who is not in a position to understand what exactly she is being told, or the possible reason or context for such a death. Morrison has described how, at the opening of the novel, '[t]he reader is snatched, yanked, thrown into an environment completely foreign . . . Snatched just as the slaves were from one place to another, from any place to another, without preparation and without defense' (1989: 32). This assimilation of reader to traumatised slave is problematic, but Morrison is indicating her attempt to position the reader in the place of the subject who has not yet fully 'given birth to' the event. The reader gradually realises that Sethe murdered her own baby daughter. This is made clear when we are told the reason for Denver's years of deafness and isolation – Nelson Lord's question 'Didn't your mother get locked away for murder?' (104). The reader is required to 'work *with* the author in the construction of the book', to participate in the reconstruction of the story (Greene 1991b: 318). As suggested above, this reconstruction is a textual event rather than one which occurs entirely within the minds of the characters. This collaborative process – a 're-membering' or putting together the fragments of the story – puts the reader in a better position to understand Sethe's 'perfect dilemma' when the killing of the child is finally narrated. Even here the position of the reader is further destabilised when the event is narrated first through the eyes of the slavecatcher, for whom the act was confirmation of 'the cannibal life they preferred' (151).

To the extent that Paul D stands in the position of witness to Sethe's story, the event remains incompletely asssimilated by the reader through *his* inability to accept it at this stage. Beloved's role as mediator of the 'unspeakable' experience of the Middle Passage further contextualises and historicises the event, and the re-enactment of the mother–infant dyad reworks it in terms of the psychic consequences of such a rupture. Using Cathy Caruth's formulation of the structure of trauma, the re-representing or re-remembering which the narrative of *Beloved* offers finally resituates the event 'in our immediate understanding', permitting 'history to arise where *immediate understanding* may not' (Caruth 1991: 182). In terms of Lyotard's account of *Nachträglichkeit*, the narrative presents the 'symptom' – the spiteful house, the baby ghost – before the event, the 'first blow', the theft of milk from Sethe's breast, the murder of the child: in its avoidance of diachronic time, the narrative refuses to 'neutralize violence', to 'reappropriate the improper, achronological affect' (1990: 16). Peter Nicholls suggests that 'anachronism' is the principal feature of the kind of postmodern historicity articulated here by Morrison: '"History" is no longer a sort of container in which events are serially disposed, but a collision of two temporalities . . . the past which seems now not to have been directly experienced . . . suddenly surges back into the self' – and into the text (1996: 56). The constant deferral of the narration of the trauma – manifest in the baby ghost and in the person of Beloved – represents Lyotard's 'immemorial' as 'always "present" but never' – or at least only very gradually and tentatively – 'here-now' (1990: 20).

REMEMORY: THE PERSISTENCE OF THE REPEATED?

The coinage of the term 'rememory' suggests that some part of the remembering process is left unacknowledged by the term 'memory'. When first encountered by the reader it suggests a vernacular form which blends 'remember' and 'memory': at one point Sethe refers to 'my rememory' as if it is synonymous with 'memory' and she uses 'to memory' as a verb interchangeably with 'to remember' (202). It stresses the afterwardsness of memory, the *an* in Lyotard's *an*amnesis, the fact that memory is always a *re*presentation. It suggests 're-remembering', a remembering *after* a forgetting, the psychic insistence of the traumatic event and the cyclical structure of the narrative. It acknowledges the rediscovery of the role of memory in culture as well as the recollection of specific events. Orlando Patterson has suggested that part of the 'social death' of the slave was the loss of social or cultural memory. 'Slaves differed from other human beings in that they were not allowed freely to integrate the experience of [their] ancestors into their lives, to inform their understanding of social reality with the inherited meanings of their natural forbears, or to anchor the living present in any conscious community of memory' (in Goodheart et al. 1993: 9). According to Spillers, even if the facts of the history of slavery have become familiar, 'the familiarity of this narrative does nothing to appease the hunger of recorded memory, nor does the persistence of the repeated rob these well-known, oft-told events of their power, even now, to startle. In a very real sense, every writing as revision makes the "discovery" all over again' (1987: 68–9). The disorientation of the reader and the startling embodiment of history as a ghost enacts this rediscovery within the text .

When Sethe begins to remember what Nan told her of her ancestry, it is like 'picking meaning out of a code she no longer understood'. Nan's insistence that Sethe should listen to and understand what she is being told about her mother's history – 'Telling you. I am telling you, small girl Sethe . . . She threw them all away but you' (62) – is part of her resistance to the idea of the slave as what Patterson called a 'genealogical isolate' (1993: 8). The recovery of ancestral memory which the text represents also historicises and gives specific meaning to Freud's idea that individuals are bound to 'the memory-traces of the experiences of former generations' (1934–8: 345). Denver's insistence on hearing again and again, and then reconstructing with her newly rediscovered sister Beloved, the story of her own birth also functions as a confirmation of ancestry and of memory as a communal act. Remembering again, in new and more enabling contexts, is the positive process which the novel enacts, yet Sethe's problem is also the question of how to give due weight to the past without allowing it to consume the present – to overcome, to adapt Spillers' phrase, the 'persistence of the repeated'.

Jane Miller defines 'rememory' as 'something like a willed remembering which includes its own strenuous reluctance to return to the past' (1987: 7–8), although it seems to me that memory in *Beloved* is more often *un*willed, involuntary, as in the early episode when Sethe is returning to 124 across the chamomile fields: 'The plash of water, the sight of her shoes and stockings awry on the path where she had flung them; or Here Boy lapping in the puddle near her feet, and suddenly there was Sweet Home rolling, rolling out before her eyes' (6). Mae G. Henderson suggests that 'rememory' 'is something which possesses (or haunts) one, rather than something which one possesses' (1991: 67): Beloved herself is, in part, an embodiment of this kind of 'rememory'. Sethe defines 'rememory' as the sense of being haunted or possessed by the past early on in the novel as a warning to Denver:

Some things go. Pass on. Some things just stay. I used to think it was my rememory. You know. Some things you forget. Other things you never do. But it's not. Places, places are still there. If a house burns down, it's gone, but the place – the picture of it – stays, and not just in my rememory, but out there, in the world. What I remember is a picture floating around out there outside my head. I mean, even if I don't think it, even if I die, the picture of what I did, or knew, or saw, is still out there. Right in the place where it happened . . . Someday you be walking down the road and you hear something or see something going on. And you think it's you thinking it up. A thought picture. But no. It's when you bump into a rememory that belongs to someone else. (35–6)

Rememory here expands to become shared, but still involuntary memory: it is defined by Asnaf Rushdy as 'signifying a magical anamnesis available to one not involved in the originary act' (1990: 304). Gina Wisker suggests that this kind of rememory indicates that 'history is a tangible, visible existent that a community can experience, bump into' (1993: 85). Toni Morrison describes her own process of 'literary archaeology' in similar terms:

[U]n the basis of some information and a litlc bit of guesswork you journey to a site to see what remains were left behind and to reconstruct the world that these remains imply. What makes it fiction is the nature of the imaginative act: my reliance on the image – on the remains – in addition to recollection, to yield up a kind of truth. By 'image' . . . I simply mean 'picture' and the feelings that accompany that picture . . . The approach that's most productive and most trustworthy for me is the recollection that moves from the image to the text. Not from the text to the image . . . The image comes first and tells me what the 'memory' is about. (Morrison 1987b: 112)

Morrison is not here specifically referring to her 'reconstruction' of the world of slavery: she has explained that she did not set out to write a novel about slavery, but was drawn into it, almost reluctantly, through her discovery of the story of Margaret Garner.[3] On the *South*

Bank Show Morrison talks about listening to the stories of her grandfather, who had been a slave: it is memory of this kind that she is
possibly referring to when she talks about 'images' and 'pictures' – as
well as contemporary drawings of the slave ships and slaves in irons.
But she here also evokes the kind of shared 'rememory' described by
Sethe: given that she is not talking about strictly autobiographical
reconstruction, and that in the case of slavery she is dealing with a
world no longer within living memory, her stress on visual images
and pictures suggests that collective memory is somehow available to
the individual, that memory can be held by places and objects (the
notion developed by Michaels in *Fugitive Pieces*) as well as within
human consciousness. 'Journeying to the site' suggests a replacement
of temporality by spatiality; that, as Sethe puts it, some things 'pass
on' whilst others 'just stay'. As with Abraham and Torok's idea of
'preservative repression', memory is here 'entombed in a fast and
secure place, awaiting resurrection'. Morrison's metaphor also evokes
Freud's analogy between the psychoanalyst and the archaeologist:
where Freud claims that he acknowledges where his 'constructions
begin', Morrison acknowledges the nature of the 'imaginative act'.
The possibility of knowing and sharing forgotten and painful history
is clearly vital, but the existence of pictures 'floating around there
outside my head' which other people can 'bump into' invokes random
and painful collisions with bits of the past rather than the possibility
of shared knowledge and understanding. And for Sethe the idea of
pictures of the events of the past still existing in the places where
they occurred involves a belief in the inevitability of repetition:

Where I was before I came here, that place is real. It's never going away. Even
if the whole farm – every tree and grass blade of it dies. The picture is still
there and what's more, if you go there – you who never was there – if you go
there and stand in the place where it was, it will happen again; it will be
there for you, waiting for you. (36)

When Denver asks whether that means that 'nothing ever dies',
Sethe confirms that '[n]othing ever does'. '[H]ow can I say things that
are pictures?' asks Beloved, when she becomes the medium of the
'unspeakable thoughts' or memories of those who experienced the
Middle Passage, for whom 'all of it is now it is always now' (210).
Freud's early work with hysterical patients suggested that it was
painful memories in the form of pictures or snapshots which gave
rise to the symptoms, pictures which faded when put into words.
Jean Wyatt sees this aspect of rememory in a similar way: 'Through
Sethe's reluctance to substitute words for things, not just Beloved but

all the painful events of the past that Sethe has not transformed into narrative are left there, where those events first occurred' (1993: 477). Rememory is here formulated as the imprinting of painful events on the mind and on the world: whilst these imprints might function as material evidence of the atrocities of the past – as some Holocaust survivors have expressed the desire for their writing to function as material trace of their experience – they also threaten repetition. This version of 'rememory' recognises the fact that there are some events that tear the fabric of social space or shatter our sense of time as normally experienced. Sethe's account gives imaginative form to the compulsive and involuntary reliving of the past in flashbacks or nightmares by the survivors of accidents and other traumas. That it is a model of memory eventually to be rejected is made clear by Denver's movement out of the 'crypt' of 124, and by the final 'passing' of Beloved. When Denver is hesitating on the threshold of the house, afraid to step out into the world 'where there were places in which things so bad had happened that when you went near them it would happen again', the voice of Baby Suggs asking her 'You don't remember nothing about how come I walk the way I do and about your mother's feet, not to speak of her back? I never told you all that?' (243–4) suggests that it is possible to use the memory of a painful past not as an avoidance of the future for fear of the past recurring, but as a way of refusing repetition. Jean Wyatt has also suggested that here the past is put into its proper place by the voice of Baby Suggs, that it becomes 'oral history'; situating her in a family with its own historical memory enables her to see herself as moving forward into the future. Rememory thus functions both as the necessary acknowledgement of the past and as the danger of its persistence or repetition.

PSYCHOANALYSIS AND SLAVERY

Morrison has suggested that '[t]he narrative into which life seems to cast itself surfaces most forcefully in certain kinds of psychoanalysis' (1992: v). Her account of the impulse which led to the writing of the novel – 'I had to deal with this nurturing instinct that expressed itself in murder' – also suggests that she is dealing with conflicts and relationships that have found their fullest expression and mode of analysis within psychoanalysis. Critics such as Hortense Spillers and Barbara Christian have questioned the application of psychoanalytic theory to 'social and historical situations that do not replicate moments of its own historic origins and involvements' (Spillers 1990: 128–9), although Spillers also suggests that Harriet Jacobs'

account of her relationship with her owners 'uncover[s] slavery in
the United States as one of the richest displays of the psychoanalytic
dimensions of culture before the science of European psychoanalysis
takes hold' (1987: 77). As Jacqueline Rose suggests in the case of
fascism, the institution of slavery, characterised by relationships of
power and oppression and the construction of a racial 'other' which
is also the object of fear, projection and desire, is one of the historical
moments which need 'psychoanalytic concepts of desire and identification in order for it to be [more] fully understood' (1991: 7). It is
also the site of the conditions which lead to the possible conjunction
of mothering and murder, of love and death.

However, Spillers has also warned against 'search[ing] vainly for a
point of absolute and undisputable origin' of slavery itself, 'for a
moment of plenitude that would restore us to the real, rich "thing"
itself'. Even a past as painful as that of slavery, she suggests, evokes
the desire to find a moment of pure identity or origin. To homogenise
or reduce it to an 'essence' is only to collude with the stereotypes
which slavery produced: 'the collective and individual reinvention of
the discourse of "slavery" is, therefore, nothing other than an attempt
to restore to a spatio-temporal object its eminent historicity, to evoke
person/persona in the place of a "shady" ideal' (1989: 28). Morrison
has also said that '[u]sually slavery is an abstract concept. The purpose of making the ghost real is making history possible, making
memory real' (quoted in Wyatt 1993: 475), although of course she
also exposes the dangers of the desire for 'a moment of pure identity
and origin' in the reconstructed pre-Oedipal relation of Sethe and
Beloved. Stuart Hall, in his insistence that our relationship with the
past, like that with the mother, 'is always already after the break', warns
against the homogenisation of 'Africa' as the lost organic community
or imaginary space of plenitude (1990: 224, 230). In her critique of
'The Moynihan Report' Spillers warns against the essentialising and
universalising tendency in which 'ethnicity' 'freezes in meaning, takes
on constancy, assumes the look and the affects of the Eternal' and
'embodies nothing more than a mode of memorial time' (1987: 66). If
psychoanalysis runs the risk of de-historicising and universalising
the human subject, the appeal to slavery as 'the "thing" itself' in a
critique of the applicability of psychoanalysis runs the corresponding
risk of essentialising 'race' and universalising a complex and shifting
set of social and familial relations. Whilst slavery clearly distorted family relationships, which in themselves originated in the very different
social arrangements of West Africa, it did so in complex and differing
ways. Spillers analyses the contradictory meaning of motherhood
under slavery, by which '"motherhood" as female blood-rite/right is

denied', whilst women still give birth to children in the *flesh*' (1987: 75). Jacqueline Jones stresses motherhood as a site of resistance, but also the dangers of maternal sacrifice: 'The gender kinship between mother and daughter provides the mother with a fundamental motive for resistance, that is, to prevent the daughter from being subjected to her own fate, the commodification of the female body . . . However, that very act of resistance seems inevitably to involve a sacrifice that may . . . bind them to a past they were trying to escape' (1985: 250), a process we see clearly at work in *Beloved*. Spillers, who dismisses object relations and the 'reproduction of mothering' 'as an account of female gender transmission entirely irrelevant to the brutally disrupted kinship bonds of persons in captivity', nevertheless uses the theory when she suggests that '[i]f the child's humanity is mirrored initially in the eyes of its mother, or the maternal function, then we might be able to guess that the social subject grasps the whole dynamic of resemblance and kinship by way of the same source' (1987: 75). Winnicott's concept of the mutual mirroring of mother and child as an essential part of the constitution of identity is here framed as deprivation or absence: she quotes Frederick Douglass on his relationship with his siblings – 'The early separation of us from our mother had well nigh blotted the fact of our relationship from our memories' – to suggest that 'the feeling of kinship is *not* inevitable. That it describes a relationship that appears "natural", but must be "cultivated" under actual material conditions' (1987: 75–6).

Morrison recognises this within the novel by representing a range of possible family arrangements. Baby Suggs knows that she would no longer be able to recognise her 'sold away' children. Sethe herself has little or no relationship with her own mother, 'who must of nursed me two or three weeks' and who then left her to be fed by another woman 'whose job it was' (60) while she went back to work in the fields. In this Sethe represents an exception: historians of slavery such as Deborah Gray White suggest that most slave children had more than this minimal contact with their mothers, and more opportunity to 'cultivate' 'the feeling of kinship' (1985: 27). Sethe had 'the amazing luck of six whole years of marriage to that "somebody" son who fathered every one of her children' (23), whose 'care suggested a family relationship rather than a man's laying claim' (25): her husband is Halle, the only one of Baby Suggs' children who was not 'sold away' and who 'rented himself out all over the county to buy her away from there'. Whilst the other Sweet Home men wait for Sethe to choose her partner, they resort to 'fucking cows' (11); none of them have sexual partners or children except for Sixo, who walks thirty miles in one day to see his woman, and dies crying 'Seven-O!' (226)

because she is pregnant. Whatever the *actual* role of the father, however, under slavery 'dual fatherhood is set in motion, comprised of
the African father's' actually or potentially '*banished* name and body
and the captor father's mocking presence' (Spillers 1987: 80). This is
one of the immutable premises upon which American slavery was
based, whatever the local variation: all slaves were owned as material
possessions; their marriages and parenthood were not legally recognised, so that their children or spouses could be 'sold away'; and the
first generation of slaves also experienced an abrupt and radical separation from their homeland, the trauma of the Middle Passage. The
fact that both psychoanalysis and the history of slavery recognise
the centrality of a radical separation – from the mother's body or
presence and from Africa – leads several critics to describe one in
terms of the other. Barbara Christian speaks of the 'monumental
psychic rupture' of the Middle Passage, 'that wrenched tens of millions of Africans from their Mother, their biological mothers as well
as their Motherland' (1993: 7). The fact that separation from the
mother in birth, and as part of the process of maturation, is inevitable
and necessary, whilst the radical rupture of enslavement was not, is
the root of one of the difficulties in using one to represent the other
which Morrison's novel does not entirely escape. Hortense Spillers
uses the discourse of the pre-Oedipal (or pre-natal) mother–child
relation to evoke the disorientation of the sea-crossing: 'Those African
persons in "Middle Passage" were literally suspended in the "oceanic",
if we think of the latter in its Freudian orientation as an analogy for
undifferentiated identity' (1987: 60). Morrison clearly employs this
conjunction of discourses in her use of Beloved as pre-Oedipal child
longing to re-merge with its mother and as mediator of the fragmentation and confusion of identities on the slave ships.

The 'oceanic' in Spillers' account is clearly terrifying and equated
with a kind of death. In much recent feminist psychoanalytic discourse
it is used positively to invoke the lost imaginary unity of mother and
child, the semiotic space before the separation of language, the Father
and the Law. When Paul D remembers his sexual encounter with
Beloved, he is 'thankful . . . for having been escorted to some ocean-
deep place he once belonged to' – the memory of his own early
relationship with his mother, who is never mentioned, and the place
of 'the dead female ancestors to whom he once "belonged"' (264). But
his desire for her is described as a kind of drowning which 'forced
him to struggle up, up into that girl like she was the clear air at the
top of the sea' (264). Although Mohanty and others have described
this encounter as 'profoundly renewing' and 'an emotional acknowledgement of his historical indebtedness' (1993: 66), it is also deeply

ambivalent. The 'ocean-deep place' is, paradoxically, also a place to struggle out of, as it eventually must be for Sethe and Beloved.

Paul D is one of the black men in Morrison's novels whose ability to 'keep moving', to 'do the other thing' she admits to finding attractive: 'the fact that they would split in a minute just delights me . . . it's part of that whole business of breaking ground' (Stepto 1980: 174, 180). For Paul D, 'walking off when he got ready was the only way he could convince himself that he would no longer have to sleep, pee, eat or swing a sledge hammer in chains' (40). The reader is put in a position to understand this desire by the reconstruction of his appalling experience of the Georgia chain-gang, where he was also sexually abused and humiliated by the parody of 'nursing' enforced by the guards. This humiliation is re-figured in Halle's compulsive smearing of 'the butter as well as its clabber all over his face because the milk they took is on his mind' (70). But Paul D's autonomy and humanity survive the chain-gang, his years of wandering, and the fact that he has shut all memory, and its attendant emotion, away in a 'tobacco tin'. When he arrives at 124 he has become 'the kind of man who could walk into a house and make the women cry. Because with him, in his presence, they could. There was something blessed in his manner' (17), as though 'all you had to do was get his attention and right away he produced the feeling you were feeling' (7–8). In spite of his need to 'walk off when he felt ready' Morrison constructs him almost in the role of a therapist, who can create Winnicott's 'holding environment' and the transference to enable trust and rememory in its positive sense. With him, Sethe feels that she might be able to trust enough to 'feel the hurt her back ought to' (18); he tells her 'Go as far inside as you need to, I'll hold your ankles. Make sure you get back out' (46).

Paul D is thus used to undermine the split between culturally 'masculine' and 'feminine' roles, formulated by Jessica Benjamin as that between the 'mother of attachment' and the 'father of separation' (1988: 141). Morrison has claimed that black women 'seem able to combine the nest and the adventure . . . They are both safe harbour and ship; they are both inn and trail' (Tate 1983: 122), but in fact none of the women in her novels, with the possible exception of Pilate in *Song of Solomon*, embody this ideal, and *Beloved* is the first of her novels to acknowledge the positive nature of a masculine presence. On her way to freedom, and during the few weeks she had with her children before the arrival of the slavecatchers, Sethe saw herself as exclusive and all-providing protector of her children – she had 'milk enough for all' (100). But when Paul D arrives Sethe has not left 124 since her time in prison except for brief daily journeys to work as a cook, and Denver has been unable to leave the yard since she heard Nelson Lord ask whether she was in prison with her mother. In Sethe Morrison represents a woman who, partly through necessity and partly through isolation from other members of the black community born of mutual distrust, has ended up as 'the ultimate single person', who represents not progression but 'a form of narcissism', locked into a relationship with her children which, as Morrison has described it, is like 'a love relationship in which one surrenders oneself to the lover' (1988b: 33).

THE OCEAN-DEEP PLACE: RELIVING THE PRE-OEDIPAL

It is in the relationship of Sethe and Beloved that the 'narcissism' of the love relationship is fully played out. In an interview with Gloria Naylor, Morrison explains the concept of the self which she was exploring during the gestation of the novel: 'as though the self were really a *twin* or a thirst or a friend or something that sits right next to you and watches you, which is what I was talking about when I said "the dead girl"' (quoted in Nicholls 1996: 62). This suggests that the self is fundamentally divided, needing an 'other' to reflect or complete it, as Elaine and Cordelia play the role of 'other' to each other in *Cat's Eye*. Morrison also says that she wanted to explore 'what it is that really compels a good woman to displace the self, her self' into another that she thereby believes she has the right to destroy: Paul D enables her to feel, for the first time, that 'you your best thing, Sethe. You are' (273). The return of Beloved represents the vital recognition of the buried past, satisfying Denver's 'thirst' for a friend and Sethe's for her lost daughter, but also the parasitic and destructive nature of the child who will not grow up and the past which overwhelms the present.

Peter Brooks has described the process of transference as 'actual-iz[ing] the past in its symbolic form so that it can be repeated, replayed, worked through to another outcome. The result is, in the ideal case, to bring us back to actuality, that is, to a revised version of our stories'; 'the transference succeeds in making the past and its scenarios of desire relive through *signs* with such vivid reality that the reconstructions it proposes achieve the *effect* of the real' (1984: 12–13). As Freud claimed in 'The Dynamics of the Transference', 'it is impossible to destroy anyone *in absentia* or *in effigie*' (1912: 108). Only the physical manifestation of Beloved as the nineteen-year-old she would have been, still embodying characteristics of the 'crawling-already' baby she was at the point of her death, enables the necessary confrontation with, and working through of the past. What Freud believed to occur in the transference – the reincarnation of the patient's mother, father or 'significant other' in the person of the analyst – occurs here in the form of a ghost or re-embodied spirit. Although Paul D breaks into and rearranges the feminine household of 124, Morrison avoids what Jessica Benjamin has described as 'the idea of the father as the protector, or even savior, from a mother who would pull us back to what Freud called the "limitless narcissism" of infancy' (1988: 135). In Paul D's absence, it is Denver who steps off the threshold of 124 to seek help from the community of women who decide that, whatever Sethe's crime and pride, 'the past [was] something to leave behind. And if it didn't stay behind, well, you might have to stomp it out', that 'the children can't just up and kill the mama' (256).

Even before Sethe has recognised the girl who 'walked out of the water' (50) as her lost baby daughter, Beloved behaves like the one-year-old she was when she died: incontinent, constantly thirsty and greedy for sweet things, and totally dependent on her mother's gaze for a sense of recognition: 'Sethe was licked, tasted, eaten by Beloved's eyes. Like a familiar, she hovered . . . It was as though every afternoon she doubted anew the older woman's return' (57). Later she asserts 'she is the one. She is the one I need.' Taken literally, their sudden and violent separation has meant that the child has been unable to come to terms with its mother's comings and goings, either in reality or through symbolic play as in Freud's grandson's *fort-da* game.[4] Abraham and Torok suggest that '[t]he passage from food to language in the mouth presupposes the successful replacement of the object's presence with the self's cognizance of its absence' (1994: 126). As Jean Wyatt points out, Sethe's refusal to allow her child to be fed by anyone else in her absence – she has to suck on a sugar-soaked rag until Sethe escapes and joins her – indicates a reluctance to substitute any other object for the maternal breast. According to Abraham and Torok, '[l]earning to fill the emptiness of the mouth with words is the initial model for introjection', or the successful internalisation of the object, but 'without the constant assistance of a mother endowed with language, introjection could not take place . . . the mother's constancy is the guarantor of the meaning of words' (1994: 128–9). In Abraham and Torok's formulation the counterpart to introjection is incorporation, 'which perpetuates the existence of the lost object as something alive and foreign within the self' (Nicholls 1996: 60). The manifestation of Beloved is a materialisation of the 'lost object' which then attempts to 'incorporate' or consume Sethe and has to be expelled once more.

Beloved 'died' before she became a speaking subject, and like a slightly older child, she is also hungry for stories: Sethe 'learned the profound satisfaction Beloved got from storytelling', and also the 'unexpected pleasure' of telling stories about the past which she had previously consigned to 'short replies or rambling incomplete reveries' (58). When Beloved seduces Paul D and insists that he 'touch me on the inside part' and 'call me my name' (116–17) she is looking for confirmation of absent or insecure identity; after Paul D has moved back into the house and into Sethe's bed, her tooth falls out and she fears the total disintegration of her body. Here she symbolically rehearses the manner of her own death, her experience of sexual abuse during her previous 'incarnation' – 'I am going to be in pieces he hurts where I sleep' (212) – and the fragmentation experienced by the bodies of tortured slaves: she also represents the child who has not yet reached the imaginary wholeness of the mirror stage or who realises just how precarious that unity is.[5] 'Pieces of her would drop maybe one at a time, maybe all at once. Or . . . she would fly apart. It is difficult keeping her head on her neck, her legs attached to her hips when she is by herself . . . She has two dreams: exploding and being swallowed' (133). Here she articulates the fear of the 'engulfing' mother (the mother of the psychoanalytic theories criticised by Jessica Benjamin) 'who didn't know where the world stopped and she began' (166), whose 'goodness' or 'too-thick love' (167) becomes a seductive threat to autonomy. Beloved retaliates by draining the life from her mother.

Beloved and Sethe collude in the reconstruction of a relationship in which the boundaries between self and other become increasingly blurred. Beloved's monologue expresses the desire to 're-join' with the mother from whom she was separated; as Rebecca Ferguson observes, her 'very existence is merged in the face and responding smile of her mother, corresponding closely to what Winnicott has described as "the mother's role of giving back to the baby the baby's own self"' (1991: 118).[6] Because this desire functions in part as a compensation for what was lost (as well as representing the spirit of the baby trying to find another body to inhabit, and Beloved as mediator of the experience of the Middle Passage), its representation is profoundly ambivalent. Their joint monologue ends: 'You are mine' (217) thrice repeated: this assertion of belonging recalls Sethe's explanation to Paul D earlier in the novel that she 'couldn't love em proper in Kentucky because they wasn't mine to love' (162). Here it is suggested that it was the fact of previously denied *ownership* that led to 'too-thick love', the love that led to murder in order to prevent re-enslavement. Denver's monologue expresses her fear, rehearsed in her dreams, that her mother will cut off her head too. She wants to warn Beloved not to love Sethe too much: 'Maybe it's still in her the thing that makes it all right to kill her children' (206). When the three women are alone once again in 124, Denver observes how her mother and sister become almost indistinguishable, and how gradually it is her mother who needs protection. 'Beloved made demands. Anything she wanted she got, and when Sethe ran out of things to give her, Beloved invented desire' (240). She is like the child at the stage defined by Margaret Mahler as 'rapprochement', when, as Jessica Benjamin explains, it appears to the child 'that his freedom consists in absolute control over his mother... He is ready, in his innocence, to go for complete control, to insist on his omnipotence... He will tyrannically assert [his] demands if he can, in order to assert – and have mother affirm – his will' (1988: 34).

Benjamin goes on to suggest that the child 'is ready to be the master in Hegel's account, to be party to a relationship in which the mutuality breaks down into two opposing elements, the one who is recognised and the one whose identity is negated' (34). Hegel's account of the relationship of master and slave, the self's paradoxical demand for recognition from the other which it also needs to dominate and control, has been recently developed within postcolonial theory as a model of the relationship between colonial power and racial 'other'. Benjamin sees the roots of this relationship, and the inability to tolerate difference, in a model of child rearing as 'dual unity' by which the mother is seen only as the 'other' of the child's demand: 'The other is represented as the answer, and the self as the need; the other is the breast, and the self is the hunger' (33). So Beloved articulates her sense of relationship with her mother/other: 'she is the laugh I am the laugher... she is my face smiling at me' (212–13). Benjamin questions the psychoanalytic model that sees the child's development in terms of 'a gradual separation and individuation from an initial symbiotic unity with the mother', because it 'contains the implicit assumption that we grow *out of* relationships rather than becoming more active and sovereign *within* them, that we start in a state of dual oneness and wind up in a state of singular oneness' (1988: 18). There is an implicit critique of this in Morrison's account also, in spite of her evocation of the bliss of the imaginary unity of mother and child: before the arrival of Paul D Sethe was living in a state of fierce and isolated autonomy; the step Denver takes into the world outside 124 in order to seek for help is a step into a new world of social relations; and it is the local community of black women who rescue Sethe from the succubus Beloved has become. It is as if Morrison is herself using and exploring different psychoanalytic models, or stages, of the relationship between mother and child, ultimately discarding that which would blur all boundaries and dissolve separate identities, the 'ocean-deep place' before individuation. In her analysis of the situation of Frederick Douglass, Spillers suggests that the *absence* of the mother's gaze prevents the child's internalisation of a feeling of kinship; here the *exclusivity* of the mutual gaze of mother and child as reconstructed by Sethe and Beloved precludes any awareness of difference and the ability to establish other social relationships.

Eric L. Santner describes the process of individuation as the emergence of the self from the 'primitive auratic symbiosis' with the mother, suggesting that this separation must be 'empathetically witnessed' and adequately 'mourned'. Otherwise

the thereby dangerously depleted and unstable self will permanently hunger not for the gaze that bears witness to one's grief over the necessary local spoilings of the auratic gaze but for the archaic aura of prelapsarian eyes, eyes that offered themselves before the need to mourn and become a self became necessary . . . A hunger of this kind is the beginning of secondary or pathological narcissism. (1990: 126)

It is narcissism of this kind, based upon an inability to mourn our primary losses by means of the entry into the symbolic order which can be used to represent them, which, Santner suggests, leads to the 'collective narcissism' of fascism, 'the return to the purity of a self-identity unmediated by any passage through alterity'. Fascist Germany, Santner suggests, was 'a world where the mournful labor that opens up the space between "I" and "Thou", "here" and "there", "now" and "then", could be banished as degenerate . . . A "respecularization" of identity, that is, the simulation of a pure, specular reciprocity between self and other, was achieved by finding those one could blame for having disturbed this utopian exchange of gazes' (5). Fascism attempts to create a world without difference by constructing an 'other' who is absolutely different and must therefore be excluded or destroyed; slavery was based on, or justified by, a theory of absolute racial difference and inferiority. Morrison has suggested that 'the trauma of racism is, for the racist and the victim, the severe fragmentation of the self, and has always seemed to me a cause (not a symptom) of psychosis' (1989: 16). Fragmentation might suggest the opposite of the imaginary unity of mother and child which the novel reconstructs: but as Santner and Benjamin make clear, it is the over-investment in this idea of unity, or the refusal to leave it behind, which causes an inability to tolerate separation or difference which in its turn leads to the psychosis. For Helene Moglen, 'the "ocean-deep" place of [Sethe's] relation to Beloved [is] the place of abjection which is both the cause, and, for the "others", the result of the cultural psychosis of racism' (1993: 34).

Santner suggests that the desire for the gaze of the other need not be seen as automatically regressive or narcissistic: 'What the self needs in order to mourn and assume its selfhood . . . is not the perfect, auratic gaze at all . . . but, to paraphrase Winnicott, the *good-enough gaze*', which requires the 'solidarity of the empathetic witness. Under the good-enough gaze of the empathetic witness the self may take leave of its more archaic hankerings for the full hallucinatory gaze that sees nothing because there are, in a sense, not yet any separate objects to be seen' (1990: 126). It is the 'good-enough gaze' which Beloved provides for Denver: 'to be looked at in turn was beyond appetite'. When Beloved looks at her 'with attention . . . [i]t was lovely. Not to be stared at, not seen, but being pulled into view by the interested, uncritical eyes of the other' (118). As Benjamin puts it in the context of infant development: 'To experience recognition in the fullest, most joyful way, entails the paradox that "you" who are "mine" are also different, new, outside of me' (1988: 15). It is a paradox that Beloved and Sethe cannot sustain, and their obsessive reconstruction of their lost or imaginary unity replaces the healing power of memory and recognition that Beloved initially provides.

Although the voice of Beloved 'speaks' the 'unspeakable thoughts' of lost and traumatic memory, it is a voice which seems to come from the realm of the semiotic or of an unconscious pool of collective memory. The text represents it for the reader, but by the end of the novel people 'realized they couldn't remember or repeat a single thing she said, and began to believe that, other than what they themselves were thinking, she hadn't said anything at all' (274). Dying as an infant, it is as if she has never become a 'speaking subject' whose 'fundamental vocation' according to Eric Santner is 'as a survivor of the painful losses – the structural catastrophes – that accompany one's entrance into the symbolic order' (1990: 9). In spite of the untransmitted secret which caused Denver's two-year silence, she *has* discovered the power of language: her 'original hunger' is for words, not for her mother's body. She delights in 'the capital w, the little i, the beauty of the letters in her name' (102), the sentences 'rolling out like pie dough' (121). As Jean Wyatt makes clear, the conflation of learning language with eating, and Denver's re-entry into the social by means of food and language – the pies and dishes left for her family, and the written messages which identify their owners – 'rewrites the entry into the symbolic in terms that retain the oral and maternal, challenging the orthodox psychoanalytic opposition between a maternal order of nurturing and a paternal order of abstract signification' (483) – although it was her father who 'loved . . . the alphabet' and was the only slave on Sweet Home who could 'count on paper' (208). Denver has always been able to 'step into the told story' (28) of her birth, but it is in the presence of Beloved that she is able to articulate and share it, 'to feel . . . how it must have felt to her mother . . . Denver spoke, Beloved listened, and the two did the best they could to create what really happened, how it really was, something only Sethe knew because she alone had the mind for it' (78). Denver's continual retelling to herself of the story of her birth might also be seen as the imaginative substitution of language and narrative for the imaginary unity with the mother, her birth marking the first moment of that process of separation.

CONCLUSION: 'NOT A STORY TO PASS ON'

'It was not a story to pass on' (274–5). The phrase that echoes through the last section of the novel, like the term 'rememory', suggests several contradictory meanings and possible relationships with the past. 'This is not a story to pass on' because the novel has demonstrated that the past is not doomed to repetition: the cycle of violence which began when the first slaves were taken from Africa, and which culminates in the murder of a child by its mother, can be broken. It is broken when Sethe turns her ability to kill in order to protect outside: as Mae G. Henderson puts it, she 'directs her response to the threatening Other rather than to "her best thing"' in her attack on Mr Bodwin, whom she believes to be the slavecatcher returning for her children. Henderson sees this event as 'a scene of re-enactment in which Sethe rethinks and revises her previous (re)action', comparing her to a historian who consciously reinterprets the events of the past (1991: 80). But this ascribes a much higher degree of conscious awareness to Sethe than the text and situation suggest. Although she *has* reworked elements of the past, at this stage she is so depleted through giving and attending to Beloved that she is hardly capable of being, and is certainly not represented as, a freely acting agent. The recurrence of the image of the 'little hummingbirds stick[ing] needle beaks right through her headcloth' and of the exact words of her resistance to the recapture of her children – 'And if she thinks anything, it is no no no. Nonono' (262) – inscribe the event as an unconscious and compulsive repetition: that is exactly how she experiences it, being unable to see that time has moved on and that Mr Bodwin is *not* the slavecatcher. It is Denver, and the women who have come to prevent Beloved from destroying her mother, who also prevent a second murder, and it is not until Paul D returns that Sethe begins to accept that she is her 'best thing' (273), not her children. It is this compulsive and ultimately destructive over-identification, the nurturing instinct that also leads to murder, that must not be 'passed on'.

But the story of Beloved has been 'passed on', as both warning and commemoration. It is not a story to *pass* on, not a story that one can, or, should, choose to ignore: it is ignorance, or inadequate recognition of the claims of the past, which, Morrison suggests, leads to the danger of repetition. Although Beloved herself 'erupts into her separate parts' and into the natural forces of the 'wind in the eaves, or spring ice thawing too quickly', hers is not a story to 'pass on', or die, in that it lives as long as the text which represents it is read. For a while, after her disappearance, 'her footprints come and go . . . [d]own by the stream in back of 124'. 'Should a child, an adult place his feet in them, they will fit. Take them out and they disappear again as though nobody ever walked there' (275). Like the novel itself, Beloved's footprints represent a history which is available for temporary reinhabitation or reconstruction, not a past which still exists 'elsewhere', waiting to recur: like the 'ocean-deep place' of her reunion with Sethe or her union with Paul D, they do not represent a permanent resting place.

Notes

1. See also Morrison, *Playing in the Dark: Whiteness and the Literary Imagination* (1992).
2. For example, Henderson states: 'Sethe's task is to transform the residual images . . . of her past into a historical discourse shaped by narrativity' (1991: 66).
3. Accounts of the case of Margaret Garner from the *Cincinnati Commercial* newspaper and by Levi Coffin (1876) are included in Gerda Lerner's anthology *Black Women in White America* (1973). What most critics who have gone back to these sources have missed is the account of what later happened to Garner: she was shipped to Louisville, but the ship had an accident, and she was thrown into the river with one of her surviving children. She was rescued, but 'displayed frantic joy when told that her child was drowned', and attempted to drown herself too. Another report said that 'she threw her child into the river and jumped after it. It is only certain that she was in the river with her child, and that it was drowned, while she was saved by the prompt energy of the cook' (pp. 62–3). These details give greater historical

   specificity to Beloved's account of trying to 'join' with the woman who
   threw herself off the slave ship.
4. In *Beyond the Pleasure Principle* (1910b: 283–7) Freud describes an eighteen-
   month-old child playing a game of his own invention which involved
   throwing a wooden reel with a piece of string attached out of his cot,
   saying a word which sounded like *fort* (gone), and pulling it back whilst
   saying *da* (there). Freud suggests that this may have been the child's unconscious way of mastering the alternating absence and presence of his
   mother.
5. See Jacques Lacan (1977), 'The Mirror Stage as Formative of the Function
   of the I' in *Écrits* trans. Alan Sheridan.
6. See D. W. Winnicott (1971), *Playing and Reality*. Jessica Benjamin modifies
   Winnicott's idea of mirroring: 'The mother cannot (and should not) be a
   mirror; she must not merely reflect back what the child asserts; she must
   embody something of the not-me; she must be an independent other who
   responds in her different way' (1988: 24).

Afterword

Reading the texts of memory shows that 'remembering the self' is not a case of restoring an original identity, but a continuous process of '*re*-membering', of putting together moment by moment, of provisional and partial reconstruction. As Linda Grant suggests (quoting Steven Rose):

The self isn't a little person inside the brain, it's a work-in-progress, 'a perpetually re-created neurobiological state, so continuously and consistently reconstructed that the owner never knows its being remade'. Memory . . . is a fabrication, a new reconstruction of the original. And yet out of these unstable foundations we still construct an identity. It's a miracle. (1998: 294–5)

In the case of traumatic memory, this may be a process of repetition with a difference, as we revisit painful or otherwise significant moments of the past with changed and changing emotion and understanding, as in Morrison's notion of rememory in *Beloved*. Memories – initially perhaps unbidden, visual, sensory, immediate – become texts as soon as we begin to describe them to ourselves and others, to put them into sequence or turn them into stories. These memories – often embodied in what Christopher Bollas terms 'mnemic objects' – seem to preserve or provide access to earlier states of being which we fleetingly inhabit when these memories are suddenly evoked. Michael Sheringham suggests that 'once they have been textualized, memories lose their potential: there is no way back to an original memory when writing has done its work' (1993: 301). Annie Dillard warns that the emotional charge which illuminates 'original memory' may be lost in writing:

Don't hope in a memoir to preserve your memories. If you prize your memories as they are, by all means avoid – eschew – writing a memoir.

Because it is a certain way to lose them ... The work battens on your memories. And it replaces them ... After you've written, you can no longer remember anything but the writing ... After I've written about any experience, my memories – those elusive, fragmentary patches of colour and feeling are gone; they've been replaced by the work. (Morrison 1987b: 35)

But this 'work' is inevitable, whether we are involved in the business of turning our memories into writing, or just the everyday process of constructing the story of our lives. As Walter Benjamin points out, 'Autobiography is to do with time, with sequence and what makes up the continuous flow of life', although in his autobiographical sketch 'A Berlin Chronicle' he is 'talking of a space, of moments and discontinuities' (1979: 316). Here he attempts to preserve in writing the sense of his original memories, or rather the form and feeling they assumed in the remembering moment: 'even if months and years appear here, it is in the form they have at the moment of recollection', taking 'strange form' which 'may be called fleeting or eternal' (316), but this form is represented here, of course, in language.

I grew up in a big Victorian house in south London which was owned by my grandmother, and where my mother and her brother and sisters also lived as children. '254', as the family always called it, had a garden which was magical to us as children, with an extra L-shaped piece at the end which we called 'the paddock', and where my uncle sporadically grew vegetables. It had a frog pond, old apple trees, walls to climb over into a mysterious back alley, and a tumble-down shed, where we made 'perfume' out of rose petals and where my father kept his tools and the fireworks for Guy Fawkes night. It was where we lit bonfires, dug for buried treasure, picked blackberries and collected grasshoppers in matchboxes. It is where my love of gardens was formed, and the place where I locate something central about my sense of self. And as I write this I can 'remember' the scent of lilac, the hot smell of marigolds and the sweetness of rose-petal perfume. Because I lived in that house until I was sixteen, and continued to visit it, and help in the garden, for the next ten years until my grandmother died, my memories have a continuity which would make it impossible to say when any of them were first recalled. One of the most vivid is of a moment which itself problematised memory. I remember walking on a warm summer's day along one of the narrow paths between flower beds and apple trees towards the swing which hung from an apple bough; somewhere near, or beside the swing, was an especially vivid red or pink flower, which must have been a rose but which, in the mental picture I now hold of that moment, looks like a lotus or camelia, flowers which did not grow in that garden. As

I walked towards the swing I had an acute sense of *déjà vu*, of having experienced that moment, seen that flower and swing in just that way before, a feeling that I somehow re-experience when I bring this memory to mind.

I also know that my memory of that garden has been formed, at least in part, out of a sense of loss and nostalgia and out of other texts. When I was in my teens I found and read part of a novel – or memoir? – that one of my aunts began to write when she had left London and was living with her new husband in Spain. It described that house and garden with a precision and nostalgia – she was also exiled from it when she was evacuated to Wales with her sisters during the war – that have become part of my memory of that place. Over the years it has also gathered the resonance of countless other representations of hidden, lost or secret gardens, the gardens at least in part created out of nostalgia for our lost and 'perfect' childhoods. I don't remember when I first read Frances Hodgson Burnett's *The Secret Garden*; I can't read it now without seeing the garden of 254 and I know that my memory of my garden has been blended some-how with the garden Mary finds and brings back to life in Burnett's story, and with the garden of the past found by Tom in Philippa Pearce's *Tom's Midnight Garden*. New houses have now been built where the paddock of 254 was, in spite of local protests that it was home to a colony of frogs, but in one corner is a newly constructed frog pond, the smallest nature reserve in London.

My cousin Sally Gutierrez, daughter of the aunt who wrote about the garden of 254, is now an artist living and working in Berlin and New York. She recently came back to London – where she lived for some months as a young child – to work on a project involving family history and the sense of place. Later she wrote to me: 'Since I got back to Berlin I have a feeling which I try to ignore that I shouldn't have gone back to . . . Nanny's house at Barry Road [254]. Not because of superstitious or even nostalgic reasons but because it seems that I have lost strong memories in exchange for something that I do not really understand. Like when you see a child who has changed a lot, grown into somebody else, and you ask yourself, when I used to know him he was real, I could touch him and he was solid, a being in itself, now it's the same person, the same object, but has changed completely, so where is the one I knew? Was it not real or is it still somewhere else? Is there one Barry Road or as many as the memories?' Sally here raises the questions with which we all struggle and with which I have been dealing in this book: the continuity of the self through time; the 'location' of the past; the truth or falsity of our memories; the centrality of memory to our sense of self..Linda Grant seeks to understand the nature of her mother's memory-loss with the help of a social worker, John Bridgewater, who tells her: 'When a member of the family starts to lose their memory it turns everything up because not only are they losing their recall of you, your recall of them is challenged. It's almost a challenge to your own existence. If you live in the memory of someone else and their memory starts to fade, where are you?' (1998: 268). And when a close relative dies, we want to hold them in memory as long and as clearly as we can, feeling that they do still somehow exist whilst we remember them. Losing our memory of them is almost as painful as losing their presence.

I may try to describe the garden of my childhood in words, but my memory of it is insistently pictorial – and sensual – the *déjà vu* scene of flower and swing having the quality of a photograph. It is this visual quality which represents one version of the 'remainder', that which cannot be fully reconstructed in writing. The relationship between the reconstruction of memory in writing and in the visual arts is one which I have not been able to explore fully in this book, but it has clear connections with the contrasting models of memory as a visual image and as text or narrative discussed in the first chapter. It might seem that painting or film offer the possibility of the most faithful representation of visual memory, but such attempts must also involve a process of reworking and reconstruction, employing the 'language' of paint and brush, shape and colour. The photograph is the medium which seems closest to the 'original' image which forms the content of memory, but the use of the photograph in the texts of Carolyn Steedman and Georges Perec show that it cannot be trusted as a representation of the past 'as it really was', that it functions rather as an unstable mediator of the relationship between past and present lives and selves. Steedman describes a photograph of herself as 'evidence' that 'the world went wrong that afternoon, soon after her father's humiliation in the bluebell wood'. When she describes this photograph it is clear that she has used it in order to reconstruct a memory which includes elements not actually represented in the photograph. 'My father said "Smile, Kay", and I smiled . . . I am irritated and depressed because she [her baby sister] has come to stay . . . Somewhere on the grass, beyond the photograph, is an apple that I've been given to cheer me up, but that I refuse to eat' (51). This photograph has become the marker of her 'first dislocation' and 'first deception', but it has clearly been subject to a long and complex process of interpretation, incorporating elements which she 'didn't know then', when the photograph was taken.

In *W or The Memory of Childhood* Perec reproduces two passages written 'fifteen years ago', attempts to describe and reconstruct the fates of the parents he can barely remember. The first begins with a description of a photograph of his father in a greatcoat, military boots and puttees, 'on leave in Paris . . . in the Bois de Vincennes'. The details make it sound as if the writer had the photograph before him as he wrote: but fifteen years later Perec corrects his description, even down to the length of the greatcoat. His missing memory of his father was filled up with fantasies connected with this photograph, which was itself elaborated in memory in accordance with the fantasy. Perec 'thought up various glorious deaths' for his father, and for some years had 'a passionate craze' for collecting and playing with toy soldiers (27–9). There is no basis, he now says, for the idea that the photograph was taken in the Bois de Vincennes: one of the five photographs he possesses of his *mother* was taken there. He later describes the photos he has of her in meticulous detail: her clothes, the setting, her posture are all recorded as if to recapture precisely a non-existent memory. In one, he writes: 'I have fair hair with a very pretty forelock (of all my missing memories, that is perhaps the one I most dearly wish I had: my mother doing my hair, and making that cunning curl)' (49).

Although newly-discovered photographs may provide the occasion for the recall of 'new' memories – or reveal previously hidden secrets, such as that of Steedman's father's first wife and child, or the first children of Ben's parents in Anne Michaels' *Fugitive Pieces* – the memory will never be identical to the precise moment or image represented by the photograph. As Annette Kuhn suggests in her memory-text, *Family Secrets*:

[M]emories evoked by a photo do not simply spring out of the image itself, but are generated in a network, an intertext, of discourses that shift between past and present, spectator and image, and between all these and cultural contexts, historical moments. In this network, the image itself figures largely as a trace, a clue: necessary, but not sufficient, to the activity of meaning making; always pointing somewhere else. (1995: 12)[1]

It is impossible to remember everything, to preserve a precise record of the ongoing experience of our lives. Christopher Bollas suggests that for this reason the passing of time itself is traumatic, involving as it does the 'loss of the self, its continuous destruction through consignment to oblivion' (1995: 119). 'When we refer to "the past" we agglomerate the fine details of lived experience under a word that signifies the eradication of the self' (134). But Bollas goes on to suggest that 'screen memories' – defined by him here as 'condensations of psychically intense experience in a simple object' (135), not necessarily 'screening' more painful or significant memories, as in Freud's use of the term – are ways of *preserving* the past:

Recollection of small details is a kind of screen function within the self, as the small memory evokes the self state that prevailed at the time ... the trauma of time passing is unconsciously managed by screen memories, which become underground wells in the deserts of time. Once tapped, these sources liberate private experiences and unconscious associations that prevailed in the past, and what was partially erased by the trauma of passing time is restored through free association to screen memory. (140–1)

The vocabulary used by Bollas here suggests the archaeological model with which I began, and Walter Benjamin's evocation of 'true' memory as 'treasures buried deep in the earth'. But this activity – undertaken by the historian and the analyst in similar ways, in Bollas' account – 'creates a new meaning that did not exist before, one that could not exist were it not based on past events and did it not transform them into a tapestry holding them in a new place. That new place ... is a psychic act: the work of the imaginary and symbolic *upon* the real' (143),[2] which Bollas also identifies as the action of *Nachträglichkeit* or 'afterwardsness'.

Historical construction collects in order to retrieve the self from its many meaningless deaths ... and then it generatively destroys those details and saturates them with new meaning created through the very act of retrieval, which has given them the imaginative and symbolic energy to make the past available for the self's future. (145)

Making 'the past available for the self's future' is the process we have seen at work – in very different ways – in the texts discussed in this book. I have argued that memory does not lie dormant in the past, awaiting resurrection, but holds the 'potential for creative collaboration' (Boyarin 1994: 22) between past and present. The work of 'memory' also involves a complex process of negotiation between remembering and forgetting, between the destruction and creation of the self. Individual memories of personal histories are constantly reworked and retranslated in the present; so traumatic historical events seem to demand re-representation and re-reading, to resist the memorialisation which is also a kind of forgetting, the forgetting that assumes that remembering is finished.

Notes

1. See also Jo Spence and Rosy Martin, *Double Exposure: The Minefield of Memory* (1987).
2. Bollas is using the terms developed by Jacques Lacan to signify three 'stages' of human development (although these are not to be thought of as merely chronological): the 'real' is inaccessible except through the imaginary and the symbolic; the 'imaginary' is the dimension of images, perceived or imagined; and the 'symbolic' is the realm of language. See Translator's Note to *Écrits* trans. Alan Sheridan (1977).

Bibliography

Abel, Elizabeth (1990), 'Race, Class and Psychoanalysis? Opening Questions', in Hirsch, Marianne and Keller, Evelyn Fox (eds), *Conflicts in Feminism*, New York: Routledge, pp. 184–204

Abraham, Nicolas and Torok, Maria (1994), *The Shell and the Kernel*, vol. 1, trans. and ed. Nicholas T. Rand, Chicago: University of Chicago Press

Adorno, Theodor (1973 [1949]), 'After Auschwitz', in *Negative Dialectics*, trans. E. B. Ashton, New York: Continuum

Adorno, Theodor (1982 [1962]), 'Commitment', in *The Essential Frankfurt School Reader*, ed. Andrew Arato and Eike Gebhardt, New York: Continuum

Amis, Martin (1991), *Time's Arrow*, Harmondsworth: Penguin

Anderson, Linda (1997), *Women and Autobiography in the Twentieth Century: Remembered Futures*, Prentice Hall

Appignanesi, Lisa (1999), *Losing the Dead*, London: Chatto and Windus

Atwood, Margaret (1988), *Cat's Eye*, London: Virago

Auster, Paul (1982), *The Invention of Solitude*, London: Faber and Faber

Azienda di Promozione Turistica di Trasimeno (1995), 'Discover the Hundred Faces of the Trasimeno'

Bass, Ellen and Davis, Laura (1988), *The Courage to Heal: A Guide for Women Survivors of Child Sexual Abuse*, New York: Harper and Row

Bauman, Zygmunt (1989), *Modernity and the Holocaust*, Cambridge: Polity Press

Bellos, David (1993), *Georges Perec: A Life in Words*, London: HarperCollins

Benigni, Roberto, dir. (1999), *Life is Beautiful*

Benjamin, Andrew (1992), 'The Unconscious: Structuring as a Translation', in Fletcher and Stanton (eds), *Jean Laplanche: Seduction, Translation, Drives*, pp. 137–57

Benjamin, Jessica (1988), *The Bonds of Love: Psychoanalysis, Feminism, and the Problem of Domination*, London: Virago Press

Benjamin, Walter (1979 [1932]), 'A Berlin Chronicle', in *One Way Street and Other Writings*, trans. Edmund Jephcott and Kingsley Shorter, London: New Left Books, pp. 293–346

Benstock, Shari (1988), *The Private Self: Theory and Practice of Women's Autobiographical Writings*, Chapel Hill: University of North Carolina Press

Berger, Alan L. (1985), *Crisis and Covenant in American Jewish Fiction*, Albany: State University of New York Press

Bersani, Leo (1990), *The Culture of Redemption*, Cambridge: Harvard University Press

Blanchot, Maurice (1986), *The Writing of the Disaster*, trans. Ann Smock, Lincoln: University of Nebraska Press

Blum, Harold P. (1994), *Reconstruction in Psychoanalysis: Childhood Revisited and Recreated*, Madeson, CN: International Universities Press Inc.

Bollas, Christopher (1987), *The Shadow of the Object: Psychoanalysis of the Unthought Known*, London: Free Association Books

Bollas, Christopher (1993), *Becoming a Character: Psychoanalysis and Self Experience*, London: Routledge

Bollas, Christopher (1995), *Cracking Up: The Work of Unconscious Experience*, London: Routledge

Borowski, Tadeusz (1976 [1959]), *This Way for the Gas, Ladies and Gentlemen*, trans. Barbara Vedder, Harmondsworth: Penguin

Boyarin, Jonathan (ed.) (1994), *Remapping Memory: The Politics of Time Space*, Minneapolis: University of Minnesota Press

Brennan, Teresa (1992), *The Interpretation of the Flesh: Freud and Femininity*, London: Routledge

Bristow, Joseph (1991), 'Life Stories: Carolyn Steedman's History Writing', *New Formations* 13, pp. 113–31

British False Memory Society (1994–5), *Newsletter* 2 and 3

Brooks, Peter (1984), *Reading for the Plot: Design and Intention in Narrative*, Oxford: Clarendon Press

Brooks Bouson, J. (1993), *Brutal Choreographies: Oppositional Strategies and Narrative Design in the Novels of Margaret Atwood*, Boston: University of Massachussetts Press

Brown, Laura S. (1995), 'Not Outside the Range: One Feminist Perspective on Psychic Trauma', in Caruth, Cathy (ed.), *Trauma: Explorations in Memory*, pp. 100–12

Cardinal, Marie (1983 [1975]), *The Words To Say It*, trans. Pat Goodheart, London: Pan

Carroll, David (1990), 'Foreword: The Memory of Devastation and the Responsibilities of Thought: "And let's not talk about that"', in Lyotard, Jean-François, *Heidegger and "the jews"*, pp. vii–xxix

Carruthers, Mary (1990), *The Book of Memory*, Cambridge: Cambridge University Press

Caruth, Cathy (1991), 'Unclaimed Experience: Trauma and the Possibility of History', *Yale French Studies* 79, pp. 181–92

Caruth, Cathy (ed.) (1995), *Trauma: Explorations in Memory*, Baltimore: Johns Hopkins University Press

Caruth, Cathy (1996), *Unclaimed Experience: Trauma, Narrative and History*, Baltimore: Johns Hopkins University Press

Casey, Edward S. (1987), *Remembering: A Phenomenological Study*, Bloomington: Indiana University Press

Christian, Barbara (1993), 'Fixing Methodologies: *Beloved*', *Cultural Critique* 24, pp. 5–15

Cohen, Sande (1992), 'Between Image and Phrase: Progressive History and the "Final Solution" as Dispossession', in Friedlander, Saul (ed.), *Probing the Limits of Representation*, pp. 171–84

Crews, Frederick (1995), *The Memory Wars: Freud's Legacy in Dispute*, New York: New York Review Imprints

Culbertson, Roberta (1995), 'Embodied Memory, Transcendence, and Telling: Recounting Trauma, Re-establishing the Self', *New Literary History* 26, 1, pp. 168–95

Davies, Carole Boyce (1994), *Black Women, Writing and Identity: Migrations of the Subject*, London: Routledge

Derrida, Jacques (1978), 'Freud and the Scene of Writing', in *Writing and Difference*, trans. Alan Bass, London: Routledge, pp. 196–231

des Pres, Terrence (1976), *The Survivor: An Anatomy of Life in the Death Camps*, Oxford: Oxford University Press

Donald, James (1991), *Psychoanalysis and Cultural Theory: Thresholds*, London: Macmillan/ICA

Elkins, Stanley M. (1968), *Slavery: A Problem in American Institutional and Intellectual Life*, Chicago: University of Chicago Press

Evans, Mari (ed.) (1985), *Black Women Writers: Arguments and Interviews*, London: Pluto Press

Felman, Shoshana and Laub, Dori (1992), *Testimony: Crises of Witnessing in Literature, Psychoanalysis and History*, London and New York: Routledge

Fentress, James and Wickham, Chris (1992), *Social Memory*, Oxford: Blackwell

Ferenczi, Sandor (1932), 'Confusion of Tongues between Adults and the Child', in Masson, Jeffery, *The Assault on Truth*, pp. 291–303

Ferguson, Rebecca (1991), 'History, Memory and Language in Toni Morrison's *Beloved*' in Sellers, Susan (ed.), *Feminist Criticism: Theory and Practice*, New York: Harvester Wheatsheaf, pp. 109–127

Fine, Ellen S. (1988), 'The Absent Memory', in Lang, Berel (ed.), *Writing and the Holocaust*, New York: Holmes and Meier

Fletcher, John and Stanton, Martin (eds) (1992), *Jean Laplanche: Seduction, Translation, Drives*, London: Institute of Contemporary Arts

Foley, Barbara (1982), 'Fact, Fiction, Facism: Testimony and Mimesis in Holocaust Narratives', *Comparative Literature* 34, pp. 331–60

Forrester, John (1990), *The Seductions of Psychoanalysis: Freud, Lacan and Derrida*, Cambridge: Cambridge University Press

Forster, Margaret (1995), *Hidden Lives: A Family Memoir*, London: Viking

Fraser, Ronald (1984), *In Search of a Past: The Manor House, Amnersfield, 1933–1945*, London: Verso

Fraser, Sylvia (1987), *My Father's House: A Memoir of Incest and Healing*, London: Virago

Freeman, Mark (1991), *Rewriting the Self: History, Memory, Narrative*, London: Routledge

Freud, Sigmund (1896), 'The Aetiology of Hysteria', in *The Standard Edition of the Complete Psychological Works of Sigmund Freud* (1953–74), vol. 3, trans. and ed. James Strachey, London: Hogarth Press, pp. 189–221

Freud, Sigmund (1899), 'Screen Memories', in *The Standard Edition of the Complete Psychological Works of Sigmund Freud* (1953–74), vol. 3, trans. and ed. James Strachey, London: Hogarth Press, pp. 301–22

Freud, Sigmund (1905a [1901]), 'Fragment of an Analysis of a Case of Hysteria' ('Dora'), in *The Pelican Freud Library* (1973–85), vol. 8, trans. and ed. James and Alix Strachey, London: Penguin, pp. 31–164

Freud, Sigmund (1905b), *Three Essays on the Theory of Sexuality*, in *The Pelican Freud Library* (1973–85), vol. 7, trans. and ed. James and Alix Strachey, London: Penguin, pp. 33–169

Freud, Sigmund (1907), 'Delusions and Dreams in Jensen's *Gravida*', in *The Pelican Freud Library* (1973–85), vol. 14, trans. and ed. James and Alix Strachey, London: Penguin, pp. 27–118

Freud, Sigmund (1909), 'Notes upon a Case of Obsessional Neurosis' ('The Rat Man'), in *The Pelican Freud Library* (1973–85), vol. 9, trans. and ed. James and Alix Strachey, London: Penguin, pp. 33–128

Freud, Sigmund (1910a), *Leonardo da Vinci and a Memory of his Childhood*, in *The Standard Edition of the Complete Psychological Works of Sigmund Freud* (1953–74), vol. 11, trans. and ed. James Strachey, London: Hogarth Press, pp. 57–137

Freud, Sigmund (1910b), *Beyond the Pleasure Principle*, in *The Pelican Freud Library* (1973–85), vol. 11, trans. and ed. James and Alix Strachey, London: Penguin, pp. 271–338

Freud, Sigmund (1912), 'The Dynamics of the Transference', in *The Standard Edition of the Complete Psychological Works of Sigmund Freud* (1953–74), vol. 12, trans. and ed. James Strachey, London: Hogarth Press, pp. 97–108

Freud, Sigmund (1914), 'Remembering, Repeating and Working Through', in *The Standard Edition of the Complete Psychological Works of Sigmund Freud* (1953–74), vol. 12, trans. and ed. James Strachey, London: Hogarth Press, pp. 145–56

Freud, Sigmund (1915), 'Repression', in *The Pelican Freud Library* (1973–85), vol. 11, trans. and ed. James and Alix Strachey, London: Penguin, pp. 141–58

Freud, Sigmund (1917 [1915]), *Mourning and Melancholia*, in *The Standard Edition of the Complete Psychological Works of Sigmund Freud* (1953–74), vol. 14, trans. and ed. James Strachey, London: Hogarth Press, pp. 237–58

Freud, Sigmund (1918), 'From the History of an Infantile Neurosis' ('The Wolf Man'), in *The Pelican Freud Library* (1973–85), vol. 9, trans. and ed. James and Alix Strachey, London: Penguin, pp. 227–366

Freud, Sigmund (1919), 'The Uncanny', in *The Pelican Freud Library* (1973–85), vol. 14, trans. and ed. James and Alix Strachey, London: Penguin, pp. 335–76

Freud, Sigmund (1925 [1924]), 'A Note Upon the "Mystic Writing Pad"', in *The Pelican Freud Library* (1973–85), vol. 11, trans. and ed. James and Alix Strachey, London: Penguin, pp. 428–34 Pelican Freud Vol. 11, 428–434

Freud, Sigmund (1934–8), *Moses and Monotheism*, in *The Pelican Freud Library* (1973–85), vol. 13, trans. and ed. James and Alix Strachey, London: Penguin, pp. 239–386

Freud, Sigmund (1936), 'A Disturbance of Memory on the Acropolis', in *The Standard Edition of the Complete Psychological Works of Sigmund Freud* (1953–74), vol. 22, trans. and ed. James Strachey, London: Hogarth Press, pp. 237–48

Freud, Sigmund (1937), 'Constructions in Analysis', in *The Standard Edition of the Complete Psychological Works of Sigmund Freud* (1953–74), vol. 1, trans. and ed. James Strachey, London: Hogarth Press, pp. 255–69

Freud, Sigmund (1950 [1895]), *Project for a Scientific Psychology*, in *The Standard Edition of the Complete Psychological Works of Sigmund Freud* (1953–74), vol. 23, trans. and ed. James Strachey, London: Hogarth Press, pp. 283–397

Freud, Sigmund (1975 [1901]), *The Psychopathology of Everyday Life*, Harmondsworth: Penguin

Freud, Sigmund and Breuer, Joseph (1893–5), *Studies on Hysteria*, in *The Pelican Freud Library* (1973–85), vol. 3, trans. and ed. James and Alix Strachey, London: Penguin, pp. 53–69

Friedlander, Saul (ed.) (1992), *Probing the Limits of Representation: Nazism and the 'Final Solution'*, Cambridge: Harvard University Press

Frye, Joanne S. (1986), *Living Stories, Telling Lives: Women and the Novel in Contemporary Experience*, Ann Arbor: University of Michigan Press

Funkenstein, Amos (1992), 'History, Counter-History and Narrative', in Friedlander, Saul (ed.), *Probing the Limits of Representation*, pp. 318–34

Gallop, Jane (1982), *Feminism and Psychoanalysis: The Daughter's Seduction*, London: Macmillan

Gardner, Sebastian (1990), 'Psychoanalysis and the Story of Time', in Wood, David (ed,.) *Writing the Future*, London: Routledge, pp. 81–97

Gates, Henry Louis (1987), *Figures in Black: Words, Signs, and the 'Racial' Self*, Oxford: Oxford University Press

Genette, Gerard (1980), *Narrative Discourse*, trans. J. E. Lewin, Oxford: Blackwell

Goodheart, Lawrence B., Brown, Richard D. and Rabe, Stephen G. (1993) *Slavery in American Society*, Lexington: D. C. Heath

Gorz, André (1989 [1958]), *The Traitor*, trans. Richard Howard, London: Verso

Grant, Linda (1998), *Remind Me Who I Am, Again*, London: Granta Books

Greene, Gayle (1991a), *Changing the Story: Feminist Fiction and the Tradition*, Bloomington: Indiana University Press

Greene, Gayle (1991b), 'Feminist Fiction and the Uses of Memory', *Signs*, 16, 2, pp. 290–321

Greer, Germaine (1989), *Daddy, We Hardly Knew You*, London: Penguin

Gunn, Daniel (1988), *Psychoanalysis and Fiction: An Exploration of Literary and Psychoanalytic Borders*, Cambridge: Cambridge University Press

Gutman, Herbert G. (1976), *The Black Family in Slavery and Freedom, 1750–1925*, New York: Random House

Habermas, Jürgen (1972), *Knowledge and Human Interests*, trans. Jeremy J. Shapiro, London: Heinemann

Habermas, Jürgen (1988), 'A Kind of Settlement of Damages (Apologetic Tendencies)', trans. Jeremy Leaman, *New German Critique* 44, pp. 25–33

Hacking, Ian (1995), *Rewriting the Soul: Multiple Personality and the Sciences of Memory*, Princeton: Princeton University Press

Halbwachs, Maurice (1992), *On Collective Memory*, trans. and ed. Lewis A. Coser, Chicago: University of Chicago Press

Hall, Stuart (1990), 'Cultural Identity and Diaspora', in Rutherford, Jonathan, (ed.), *Identity: Community, Culture, Difference*, London: Lawrence and Wishart, pp. 222–37

Hartman, Geoffrey H. (1992), 'The Book of the Destruction', in Friedlander, Saul (ed.), *Probing the Limits of Representation*, pp. 318–34

Hartman, Geoffrey H. (ed.) (1994), *Holocaust Remembrance: The Shapes of Memory*, Oxford: Basil Blackwell

Harvey, David (1989), *The Condition of Postmodernity: An Enquiry into the Origins of Social Change*, Oxford: Basil Blackwell

Hass, Aaron (1991), *In the Shadow of the Holocaust: The Second Generation*, London: I. B. Tauris

Hawking, Stephen W. (1988), *A Brief History of Time: From the Big Bang to Black Holes*, New York: Bantam Books

Henderson, Mae G. (1991), 'Toni Morrison's *Beloved*: Re-Membering the Body as Historical Text', in Spillers, Hortense J. (ed.), *Comparative American Identities: Race, Sex and Nationality in the Modern Text*, London: Routledge, pp. 62–86

Herman, Judith Lewis (1992), *Trauma and Recovery: From Domestic Abuse to Political Terror*, London: Pandora

Hirsch, Marianne (1989), *The Mother/Daughter Plot: Narrative, Psychoanalysis, Feminism*, Bloomington: Indiana University Press

History Workshop Journal (1985), 'Review Discussion: *In Search of a Past*: a dialogue with Ronald Fraser', *HWJ* 20, pp. 175–88

Homans, Peter (1989), *The Ability to Mourn*, Chicago: University of Chicago Press

hooks, bell (1982), *Ain't I A Woman: Black Women and Feminism*, London: Pluto Press

Howells, Coral Ann (1995), *Margaret Atwood*, Basingstoke: Macmillan

Huggins, Nathan Irvin (1990), *Black Odyssey: The African-American Ordeal in Slavery*, New York: Random House

Jacobus, Mary (1987), 'Freud's Mnemonic: Women, Screen Memories, and Feminist Nostalgia', *Michigan Quarterly Review* 26, 1, pp. 117–39

James, Liz (1994), 'This Is Me: Autobiography and the Construction of Identities', in Stanley, Liz (ed.), *Lives and Works: Auto/biographical Identities, Auto/biography* 3:1 and 3:2, pp. 1971–82

Jameson, Fredric (1983), *The Political Unconscious: Narrative as a Socially Symbolic Act*, London: Methuen

Jameson, Fredric (1984), 'Postmodernism, or the Cultural Logic of Late Capitalism', *New Left Review* 146

Jones, Jacqueline (1985), *Labour of Love, Labour of Sorrow: Black Women, Work and the Family from Slavery to the Present Day*, New York: Basic Books

Jordan, Elaine (1993), 'Not My People: Toni Morrison and Identity', in Wisker, Gina (ed.), *Black Women's Writing*, London: Macmillan, pp. 111–26

Kafka, Franz (1994 [1925]), *The Trial*, trans. Idris Parry, London: Penguin

Kaplan, Cora (1986), 'Pandora's Box', in *Sea Changes: Culture and Feminism*, London: Verso, pp. 147–76

Kaufman, Eleanor (1999), 'Falling from the Sky: Trauma in Perec's *W* and Caruth's *Unclaimed Experience*', *diacritics* 28.4, pp. 44–53

Keenan, Sally (1992), 'From Myth to Memory: The Revisionary Writing of Angela Carter, Maxine Hong Kingston and Toni Morrison' (unpublished PhD thesis, University of Essex)

Kermode, Frank (1966), *The Sense of an Ending*, Oxford: Oxford University Press

Klein, Melanie (1988), *Love, Guilt and Reparation and other works 1921–1945*, London, Virago

Krell, David Farrell (1990), *Of Memory, Reminiscence and Writing: On the Verge*, Bloomington: Indiana University Press

Kristeva, Julia (1979), 'Women's Time', trans. Alice Jardine and Harry Blake, in Moi, Toril (ed.), *The Kristeva Reader*, Oxford: Basil Blackwell, 1986, pp. 187–213

Kristeva, Julia (1982), *Powers of Horror: An Essay on Abjection*, trans. Leon S. Roudiez, New York: Columbia University Press

Kuhn, Annette (1995), *Family Secrets: Acts of Memory and Imagination*, London: Verso

Lacan, Jacques (1981 [1968]), *Speech and Language in Psychoanalysis*, trans. Anthony Wilden, Baltimore: Johns Hopkins University Press

Lacan, Jacques (1982 [1966]), *Écrits: A Selection*, trans. Alan Sheridan, London: Tavistock, [repr. 1982]

LaCapra, Dominick (1983), *Rethinking Intellectual History: Texts, Contexts, Language*, Ithaca: Cornell University Press

LaCapra, Dominick (1994), *Representing the Holocaust: History, Theory, Trauma*, Ithaca: Cornell University Press

Lang, Berel (1988), *Writing and the Holocaust*, New York: Holmes and Meier

Lang, Berel (1990), *Act and Idea in the Nazi Genocide*, Chicago: University of Chicago Press

Langer, Lawrence L. (1975), *The Holocaust and the Literary Imagination*, New Haven: Yale University Press

Langer, Lawrence L. (1991), *Holocaust Testimonies: The Ruins of Memory*, New Haven: Yale University Press

Lanzmann, Claude, dir. (1985), *Shoah*; text published by Pantheon Books: New York

Lapham, Lewis (1995), 'Reactionary Chic: The Right Thing for the 1990s', *Guardian*, 11 March, p. 29

Laplanche, Jean (1981 [1970]), *Life and Death in Psychoanalysis*, trans. Jeffrey Mehlman, Baltimore: Johns Hopkins University Press

Laplanche, Jean (1989 [1987]), *New Foundations for Psychoanalysis*, trans. David Macey, Oxford: Blackwell

Laplanche, Jean (1990), 'Psychoanalysis, Time and Translation', in Fletcher, John and Stanton, Martin (eds) (1992), *Seduction, Translation, Drives*, London: Institute of Contemporary Arts, pp. 161–77

Laplanche, Jean (1992), 'Notes on Afterwardsness', in Fletcher, John and Stanton, Martin (eds) (1992), *Seduction, Translation, Drives*, London: Institute of Contemporary Arts, pp. 217–23

Laplanche, Jean and Pontalis, J.-B. (1973 [1967]), *The Language of Psychoanalysis*, trans. Donald Nicholson-Smith, London: The Hogarth Press and the Institute of Psychoanalysis

Lappin, Elena (1999), 'The Man With Two Heads', *Granta* 66, pp. 9–65

Leak, Andy (1990), '*W/Dans un réseau de lignes entrecroisées: souvenir, souvenir-écran et construction en W ou le souvenir d'enfance*', in *Parcours Perec: Colloque de Londres, Mars 1988: Textes réunies par Mirielle Ribière*, Lyon: Presses Universitaires de Lyon, pp. 75–90

Lejeune, Philippe (1990) '*Les Projets autobiographiques de Georges Perec*' and '*Points de repère chronologiques et bibliographiques*', in *Parcours Perec*, pp. 59–74

Lerner, Gerda (ed.) (1973), *Black Women in White America: A Documentary History*, New York: Random House

Lessing, Doris (1986), *The Good Terrorist*, London: Grafton Books

Levi, Primo (1987), *If This is a Man/The Truce*, trans. Stuart Woolf, London: Sphere Books

Levi, Primo (1988), *The Drowned and the Saved*, trans. Raymond Rosenthal, London: Sphere Books

Lifton, Robert Jay (1986), *The Nazi Doctors: Medical Killing and the Psychology of Genocide*, London: Macmillan

Locke, John (1975 [1690]), *An Essay Concerning Human Understanding*, ed. Peter H. Midditch, Oxford: Clarendon Press

Lukacher, Ned (1986), *Primal Scenes: Literature, Philosophy, Psychoanalysis*, Ithaca: Cornell University Press

Lyotard, Jean-François (1984 [1979]), *The Postmodern Condition: A Report on Knowledge*, trans. Geoff Bennington and Brian Massumi, Minneapolis: University of Minnesota Press

Lyotard, Jean-François (1988 [1983]), *The Differend: Phrases in Dispute*, trans. Georges Van Den Abbeele, Manchester: Manchester University Press

Lyotard, Jean-François (1989), 'Defining the Postmodern', in Appignanesi, Lisa (ed.), *Postmodernism: ICA Documents*, London: Free Association Books, pp. 7–10

Lyotard, Jean-François (1990 [1988]), *Heidegger and "the jews"*, trans. Andreas Michel and Mark S. Roberts, Minneapolis: University of Minnesota Press

Lyotard, Jean-François (1993), *Political Writings*, trans. and ed. Bill Readings and Kevin Paul Geiman, London: UCL Press

McGwire, Scarlett (1989), 'Who Was Sylvia?' (interview with Sylvia Fraser), *Observer*, 23 February

Maier, Charles S. (1988), *The Unmasterable Past: History, Holocaust and German National Identity*, Harvard: Harvard University Press

Mannix, Daniel P., in collaboration with Malcolm Cowley (1962), *Black Cargoes: A History of the Atlantic Slave Trade 1518–1865*, New York: Viking Press

Marcus, Laura (1994), *Auto/biographical Discourses: Theory, Criticism, Practice*, Manchester: Manchester University Press

Marcus, Stephen (1976), 'Freud and Dora: Story, History, Case-History', in *Representations: Essays on Literature and Society*, New York: Random House, pp. 247–310

Marcus, Stephen (1984), *Freud and the Culture of Psychoanalysis: Studies in the Transition from Victorian Humanism to Modernity*, Boston: George Allen and Unwin

Marcuse, Herbert (1969) *Eros and Civilization*, London: Sphere Books

Masson, Jeffery (trans. and ed.) (1985), *The Complete Letters of Sigmund Freud to Wilhelm Fliess, 1887–1904*, Cambridge: Harvard University Press

Masson, Jeffrey (1992), *The Assault on Truth: Freud and Child Sexual Abuse*, London: Fontana

Michaels, Anne (1997), *Fugitive Pieces*, London: Bloomsbury

Miller, Jane (1987), 'Understanding Slavery': review of Toni Morrison, *Beloved*, *London Review of Books*, 12 November, pp. 7–8

Mitscherlich, Alexander and Mitscherlich, Margarete (1975), *The Inability to Mourn: Principles of Collective Behaviour*, trans. Beverley R. Placzek, New York: Grove Press

Moglen, Helene (1993), 'Redeeming History: Toni Morrison's *Beloved*', *Cultural Critique* 24, pp. 17–40

Mohanty, Satya P. (1993), 'The Epistemic Status of Cultural Identity: On *Beloved* and the Postcolonial Condition', *Cultural Critique* 24, pp. 41–80

Møller, Lis (1991), *The Freudian Reading: Analytical and Fictional Constructions*, Philadelphia: University of Pennsylvania Press

Morrison, Blake (1993), *And When Did You Last See Your Father?*, London: Granta Books

Morrison, Toni (1984), 'Rootedness: The Ancestor as Foundation', in Evans, Mari (ed.), *Black Women Writers 1950–1980: A Critical Evaluation*, Garden City, New York: Doubleday Anchor

Morrison, Toni (1987a), *Beloved*, London: Picador

Morrison, Toni (1987b), 'The Site of Memory' in Zinsser, William (ed.), *Inventing the Truth: The Art and Craft of Memoir*, Boston: Houghton-Mifflin, pp. 103–24

Morrison, Toni (1988a), 'Living Memory': interview in *City Limits*, 31 March–7 April, pp. 10–11

Morrison, Toni (1988b), 'Literary Excavation': Toni Morrison talks to Pratibha Parmar, *Marxism Today*, April, p. 33

Morrison, Toni (1989), 'Unspeakable Things Unspoken: the Afro-American Presence in American Literature', *Michigan Quarterly Review* 28, 1, pp. 1–34

Morrison, Toni (1992), *Playing in the Dark: Whiteness and the Literary Imagination*, London: Picador, 1993

Morse, Jonathan (1990), *Word by Word: The Language of Memory*, Ithaca: Cornell University Press

Motte, Warren F. Jr (1984), *The Poetics of Experiment: A Study of the Work of Georges Perec*, Lexington, Kentucky: French Forum

Motte, Warren (1995), 'Georges Perec and the Broken Book', in Kritzman, Lawrence D. (ed.), *Auschwitz and After: Race, Culture and 'the Jewish Question' in France*, New York: Routledge, pp. 235–49

Mulvey, Laura (1987), 'Changes: Thoughts on Myth, Narrative and Historical Experience', *History Workshop Journal* 23, pp. 1–19

Nicholls, Peter (1996), 'The Belated Postmodern: History, Phantoms, and Toni Morrison' in Sue Vice (ed.), *Psychoanalytic Criticism: A Reader*, London: Polity Press, pp. 50–67

Nora, Pierre (1989), 'Between Memory and History: *Les Lieux de Mémoire*', *Representations* 26, pp. 7–25

Patterson, Orlando (1982), *Slavery and Social Death: A Comparative Study*, Cambridge: Harvard University Press

Perec, Georges (1989 [1975]), *W or The Memory of Childhood*, trans. David Bellos, London: Collins Harvill

Ramadanovic, Petar (1999), 'When *"To Die in Freedom"* is Written in English', *diacritics* 28.4, pp 54–67

Rand, Nicholas T. (1994), 'Introduction: Renewals of Psychoanalysis' in Abraham and Torok, *The Shell and the Kernel*, vol. 1, pp. 1–22

Ricoeur, Paul (1984, 1985), *Time and Narrative*, vols 1–3, trans. Kathleen McLaughlin and David Pellauer, Chicago: Chicago University Press

Rigney, Barbara Hill (1987), *Margaret Atwood*, Basingstoke: Macmillan

Rigney, Barbara Hill (1991), *The Voices of Toni Morrison*, Columbus: Ohio State University Press

Rose, Gillian (1996), 'The Beginnings of the Day: Fascism and Representation' in *Mourning Becomes the Law*, Cambridge: Cambridge University Press

Rose, Jacqueline (1991), *The Haunting of Sylvia Plath*, London: Virago

Rose, Steven (1993), *The Making of Memory: From Molecules to Mind*, New York: Doubleday Anchor

Rushdy, Asnaf (1990), ' "Rememory": Primal Scenes and Constructions in Toni Morrison's Novels', *Contemporary Literature* 31, 1, pp. 300–23

Santner, Eric L. (1990), *Stranded Objects: Mourning, Memory and Film in Postwar Germany*, Ithaca: Cornell University Press

Santner, Eric L. (1992), 'History Beyond the Pleasure Principle: Some Thoughts on the Representation of Trauma', in Friedlander, Saul (ed.), *Probing the Limits of Representation*, pp. 143–54

Schapiro, Barbara (1991), 'The Bonds of Love and the Boundaries of Self in Toni Morrison's *Beloved*', *Contemporary Literature* 32, 1, pp. 194–210

Sheringham, Michael (1993), *French Autobiography, Devices and Desires: Rousseau to Perec*, Oxford: Clarendon Press

Smith, Sidonie (1987), *A Poetics of Women's Autobiography: Marginality and the Fictions of Self-Representation*, Bloomington: Indiana University Press

Snead, James A. (1984), 'Repetition as a Figure in Black Culture', in Gates, Henry Louis Jr (ed.), *Black Literature and Literary Theory*, New York: Methuen, pp. 59–79

The South Bank Show (1987), 'Toni Morrison', ITV, 11 October

Spence, Donald P. (1982), *Narrative Truth and Historical Truth: Meaning and Interpretation in Psychoanalysis*, New York: W. W. Norton and Co.

Spence, Jo and Martin, Rosy (1987), *Double Exposure: The Minefield of Memory*, London: Photographers Gallery

Spillers, Hortense J. (1987), 'Mama's Baby, Papa's Maybe: An American Grammar Book', *diacritics* 17, 2, pp. 65–81

Spillers, Hortense J. (1989), 'Changing the Letter: The Yokes, The Jokes of Discourse, or, Mrs Stowe, Mr Reed', in McDowell, Deborah E. and Rampersad, Arnold (eds), *Slavery and the Literary Imagination: Selected Papers from the English Institute*, Baltimore: Johns Hopkins University Press, pp. 25–61

Spillers, Hortense J. (1990), 'The Permanent Obliquity of the In(pha)llibly Straight: In the Time of the Daughters and the Fathers', in Wall, Cheryl (ed.), *Changing Our Own Words: Essays on Criticism, Theory and Writing by Black Women*, London: Routledge, pp. 127–49

Steedman, Carolyn (1982), *The Tidy House: Little Girls Writing*, London: Virago

Steedman, Carolyn (1986), *Landscape for a Good Woman: A Story of Two Lives*, London: Virago

Steedman, Carolyn (1992), *Past Tenses: Essays on Writing, Autobiography and History*, London: Rivers Oram Press

Stepto, Robert B. (1980), 'Intimate Things in Place: a Conversation with Toni Morrison', in Fisher, Dexter (ed.), *The Third Woman: Minority Women Writers of the United States*, Boston: Houghton-Mifflin, pp. 167–82

Tate, Claudia (ed.) (1983), *Black Women Writers at Work*, New York: Continuum

Tomiche, Anne (1994), 'Rephrasing the Freudian Unconscious: Lyotard's Affect-Phrase', *diacritics* 24, 1, pp. 43–62

Vine, Barbara (1986), *A Dark Adapted Eye*, Harmonsworth: Penguin

Vine, Barbara (1993), *Asta's Book*, London: Viking

Vine, Barbara (1998), *The Chimney Sweeper's Boy*, London: Viking

Warnock, Mary (1987), *Memory*, London: Faber and Faber

White, Deborah Gray (1985), *Ar'n't I A Woman? Female Slaves in the Plantation South*, New York: W. W. Norton

White, Hayden (1973), *Metahistory: The Historical Imagination in Nineteenth Century Europe*, Baltimore: Johns Hopkins University Press

Wiesel, Elie (1987), *The Fifth Son*, trans. Marion Wiesel, Harmondsworth: Penguin

Wilkomirski, Binjamin (1996), *Fragments: Memories of a Childhood, 1939–1948*, trans. Carol Brown Janeway, London: Picador

Williams, Linda Ruth (1995), *Critical Desire: Psychoanalysis and the Literary Subject*, London: Edward Arnold

Willis, Susan (1987), *Specifying: Black Women Writing the American Experience*, Madison: University of Wisconsin Press

Winnicott, D. W. (1964), *The Child, the Family, and the Outside World*, Harmondsworth: Penguin

Winnicott, D. W. (1971), *Playing and Reality*, London: Tavistock Publications

Wisker, Gina (ed.) (1993), *Black Women's Writing*, London: Macmillan

Wolf, Christa (1976), *A Model Childhood*, trans. Ursule Molinaro and Hedwig Rappolt, London: Virago

Woolf, Virginia (1976 [1939–40]), 'A Sketch of the Past', in Schulkind, Jeanne (ed.), *Moments of Being*, St Albans: Triad/Panther

Woolf, Virginia (1992 [1927]), *To the Lighthouse*, London: Vintage Books

Wright, Elizabeth (ed.) (1992), *Feminism and Psychoanalysis: A Critical Dictionary*, Oxford: Blackwell

Wyatt, Jean (1993), 'Giving Body to the Word: The Maternal Symbolic in Toni Morrison's *Beloved*', PMLA 108, 3, pp. 474–88

Yates, Frances (1966), *The Art of Memory*, London: Routledge and Kegan Paul

Young, James E. (1988), *Writing and Rewriting the Holocaust: Narrative and the Consequences of Interpretation*, Bloomington: Indiana University Press

Young, James E. (1992), 'The Counter-Monument: Memory Against Itself in Germany Today', *Critical Inquiry* 18, pp. 267–96

Index